Holy Sinners
Search of Kashmir

Attention Authors

'We Convert Fighters into Writers'. That's the motto of Manas Publications for more than four decades. Our message to the world is that India can win the battle not only by the bullet but also by the pen. There is no dearth of intellectuals in our country, but their knowledge is confined to them only. No sincere effort has been made by any other publisher to channelise their knowledge in national interest. That is why the talent of a large number of intellectuals remains latent. An author transforms his knowledge into a manuscript, and it is our job to spread his/her knowledge by converting it into a beautiful book. For over four decades, Manas has been motivating the intellectuals by publishing their manuscripts and would like to publish your manuscript too. If you or your colleagues have any manuscript ready for publication or are working on it, kindly contact us with detailed synopsis and list of contents. We will transform your work into a valuable publication. If you wish, we can also suggest you the suitable subjects for writing the books related to your area of expertise. Manas is known for its publishing quality and commitments. We take utmost care in production and give wide publicity to the book as well as its author through our national and international distribution network.

Holy Sinners
Search of Kashmir

Major Saras Tripathi

Manas Publications
(We Convert Fighters into Writers)
New Delhi-110002 (INDIA)

MANAS PUBLICATIONS

(Publishers for IAS, IPS, IFS, IRS, Defence, Press, Judges etc.)
(Publishers, Distributors, Importers & Exporters)

4402/5-A, Ansari Road (Opp. HDFC Bank)
Darya Ganj, New Delhi-110 002 (India)
Off. 23260783, 23265523, Res. 23842660
Fax: 011-23272766
E-mail: manaspublications@gmail.com
manaspublications@yahoo.com

Website: www.manaspublications.in

ISBN 978-81-7049-495-9

₹ 995/-

Designed at
Manas Publications

Printed in India at
Glorious Printers, Delhi and published by
Mrs Suman Lata for
Manas Publications, 4402/5-A, Ansari Road,
(Opp. HDFC Bank),
Darya Ganj, New Delhi-110 002 (INDIA)

****

The book is dedicated

To

"The people (Awaam) of
Jammu and Kashmir,

And

Brave soldiers of Indian Armed Forces;
Who have been contra-positioned,
To go through the muddle of Kashmir,
That none of them have created."

****

Contents

National flag at Lal Chowk of Srinagar

26 Jan 1992, BJP leader Dr Murli Manohar Joshi hoisted National Flag in Lal Chowk despite all warnings by terrorists. Our Unit (6 Maratha LI) was given the responsibility to ensure security of Lal Chowk, which it did with reasonable efficiency. Standing from left to right after flag hoisting (National Flag seen in the background): Major (Now Brigadier) S K Kurup, Lt Col (Now retd Maj Gen) C D Sawant (then Commanding Officer), Major (Now retd Lt Gen) Narendra Singh and (right most) Col Neeraj Jha.

Oct 1991:Abduction by terrorists and rescue by army of Wakhloo couple. Mrs Khemlata Wakhloo, Minister in Jammu and Kashmir government's council of ministers, with her husband immediately after rescue. Encircled by army the abductors released the couple and ran away before army could catch them.

From left to right; CO 3/4 GR, Mrs Wakhloo, then Brig later Maj Gen (Retd) Pandit, (Cdr 56 Mtn Bde), Mr Wakhloo, then Lt Col later Maj Gen (retd) C D Sawant (CO 6 MARATHA LI).

The rebellion of JKAP (Jammu Kashmir Armed Police) and subsequent siege of PCR headquarters was freed by our Unit in sync with other army units of different formations including Mechanised columns. 2 X BTR-16 (APC) were used to crash through the secured gate of PCR headquarters at Srinagar.

OP RAKSHAK
SRINAGAR 1991 - 94

Part of arms and ammunition seized from the terrorists after encounter and search: Captured flag of JKLF and other outlawed outfits are also displayed with self-explanatory writing (part in Urdu and English) on them.

Part of arms and ammunition seized from the terrorists after encounter and search: Display at Unit location at Haft Chinar. Seen in the photograph are:

The then CO, Col (Retired as Major General) Chandrashekhar D Sawant (tallest in the centre). On to his right are then Brig (Now Maj Gen (Retd) Naseeb Katoch, Sub Area Cdr; to his right the officer wearing para maroon beret is then Maj Gen (COS) of 15 Corps (Retd as Vice Chief of the Army, Lt Gen Chandrashekhar. All persons to his left are from 6 Maratha L I and to the right are from 10 GARH RIF.

Flag of Hizbul Mujahideen (L) reads thus: *"jab tak meri jaan mein jaan hai azaadi aur galba ke liye ladta rahunga (Hizbul Mujahideen)".*

Flag of JKLF (R) read thus: *"Shaheed Kashmir ka kya irshaad, Kashmir banega khud mukhtaar (on top green part of the flag)*

– JKLF

Prologue

Conflicts all over the world have taught us a very important lesson: **women and children are the worst sufferers in any conflict**. It is between two governments, between governments and civil societies or between any two warring entities. This is equally true about ethnic or sectarian conflicts or even sponsored/spontaneous insurgencies like one in Kashmir. The sufferings are both sides: the front side which basically comprises people living in and belonging to the conflict zone, and the hind side which comprises the people living but not necessarily belonging to the conflict zone. The former comprises the civilian population in the conflict zone and is visible. Whereas the latter comprises the soldiers and their families: an entity not so visible.

Unfortunately, one side, most of the time, fails to see the sufferings of the other side. When wars or conflicts erupt, mostly men fight, get maimed and killed. Mothers, wives, daughters, children and even elderly and sick are left behind: helpless, shattered, devastated, and most of the time left without financial and emotional support. **But there is a striking similarity between the two. Most (certainly not all) of those killed and maimed are from the lower strata of the society: average civilians and average foot soldiers.**

Such conflicts are rarely caused by those who bear the brunt: average civilians and low ranking members of the armed forces. Mostly it is caused by political, sectarian and ethnic leaders who are well secured from all angles. On the other hand, decision of deployment of the armed forces comes from the elite, powerful and well secured groups: the political leadership, bureaucracy and top ranking officers of the defence forces. The armed forces become the face of the government by virtue of implementing the orders, and are looked upon as villain or perpetrators.

The civilian population becomes the target of the forces since insurgents originate from amongst them and reside/hide there. Consequently majority of the population, the innocent citizenry; which may have no role to play either side, becomes helpless victim between the two entities and suffers collateral damage. On the other hand insurgent groups overlook the government and the bureaucracy, who have created the mess by omission or commission, and start targeting the 'face': the low ranking members of the armed forces. **The conflict in Kashmir has similar characteristic where innocent citizens and soldiers are paying the price for a mess which neither of them has created.**

The pain, paradox and dilemma of local Kashmiri masses were articulated very aptly by a vibrant and cheerful young man with whom I had a long conversation during one of the operations at village New (Nau)Theed: a suburb of Srinagar city. While sitting in an assembly of 'cordon and search' in April/May 1992, he described the state of Kashmiri people thus:

"We are like 'football' being played between two teams of military and militants: neither of them having any 'goal post' anywhere; near or far. The referees, siding with the military, are sitting in Delhi whereas coaches tutoring the militants are in Muzaffarabad and Islamabad. Its state of complete disconnect in a never ending game."

The book is written in the above said background **by a soldier, who has been there, seen it all and done it himself.** He has gone through the conflicts of emotions, where his empathies are with average Kashmiris' sufferings but his duties are with the army. He has gone through the conflict of morality and propriety, humanity and duty. Such conflicts are not limited to fights and emotions but stretch beyond: the dilemma and paradox of broader spectrum of human relations. The book is written from a humanitarian perspective to highlight the suffering and loss of both sides; the group in front side or the civilian population in the conflict zone, and the hind side or the soldiers and their families. The focus of the book is general populace or common people *(Aam Aadmi or Awaam)* and the soldiers who have no personal substantial stake in the 'win or lose' of the conflict.

Kashmir; the land, I fell in love at first sight. Kashmiris; the people, I fell in love at first interaction. Most of them, I found, extremely beautiful, and more beautiful from within; from their heart and emotion. Kashmir shows more shades of emotions than the rainbow. It has broader shade of grey than black and white have together. I was intrigued at the simplicity and complexity of the people, some of whom proved to be unbelievably simple and some immeasurably clever. That is what I have revealed through 14 stories based on real time military operations. No such book seems to have ever been written, at least on Kashmir, by anyone, certainly not by an army officer. Different stories bring out different spectrum of emotions and very naturally reveal the players behind the conflict: Pakistan, ISI, fundamentalists, religious leaders and the politicians. The devastation and the death of the hapless are result of a game played by well secured men having no sympathy either for sufferings of average Kashmiri or any value for the supreme sacrifice of the soldiers.

I found people of Kashmir most interesting of all I came across. In due course a few proved to be immeasurably sly, shrewd, slippery and deceitful, but many were unbelievably simple. However majority have been as good or as bad as a society in turmoil can be. Many old and motherly women, youth and average Kashmiri have touched my heart by displaying great human values even while interacting and treating a 'perceived enemy': a military man. Their humane side was not always result of 'reciprocation' but many times spontaneous; without want of any favour.

`Mozi' is a saga of heart touching human side of a pious hearted illiterate village woman, a mother beyond boundaries, who despite losing her son, presumably in the hands of armed forces, does not abandon humanity and bestows her affection on soldiers when she feels they are in need. **'The Prized Possession'** is a story of old and educated urban woman who bestows the officer best and most prestigious 'award' of entire Kashmir tenure, not in material form but only in words; a few words of appreciation. She dismantles the stereo type portrayal of a soldier as a perpetrator. **'Grand Mother's Questions'** touches the very nerve of sufferings of women and children which no outsider other than Kashmiris or soldiers can feel and tell since no one else has seen it and done it. It is a story of devastation, sufferings and misery of a grandmother who unknowingly poses several difficult questions when her terrorist son has been arrested by the army. Her plight throws several questions to the world including one as to who is responsible for her ruin.

'Encounter with Hardened Terrorists' is a chilling account of an encounter with a group of five hard core terrorists. It also reveals the mind-set of a religious-fanatic-terrorist completely blinded by Islamic fundamentalism and is submerged in deadly cocktail of politics and religion. On the other side it uncovers the bravery and dare devilry of the soldiers. It shows what havoc Pakistan and its ISI have brought to the people of Kashmir. **'Love, Loss and Illusion'** is a revelation of truths, during interrogation, by a Pak trained terrorist that very few have inkling about. It reveals designs of religious bigots to convert the whole of India into Jehad battle-field to spread **'Rule of Allah'** and probably in the entire world by persecuting 'non-believers.' It is also a 'tell-tale' of devastation of youth of Kashmir and their suffering, their irreparable losses through; missed opportunities of education, growth, achievements and all youthful endeavours including life of love and romance. Similarly, ***'Salafi Baba'*** is story of an immeasurably sly, shrewd, slippery and deceitful 'Maulvi' in the village of New Theed near Srinagar, who lives double life of two characters standing on opposite poles. Another story **'Death in a Cordon'** is a classical example of deceit, chicanery and use of women and children as shield to achieve their goal. It reveals the brilliant plan of deception of Syed Salahuddin; the HM chief to get out of the cordon of the army by exploiting the humane side and secular credentials of the Indian Army.

'Balaa' is an account of irreparable and immeasurable psychological damage done to the psyche of people of Kashmir, particularly to the women and children. It also reveals the innovative propaganda ISI has been devising to drive all kind of wedge between the army and the local people. On the lighter side it also shows locals' belief in supernatural, ghosts, spirits, etc. and consequent exploitation. **'The Protesting Women'** is an account of effective use of women as a shield by the terrorists and as a tool to discredit army in the eyes of the world by creating environment that leaves the forces nowhere but to use force and get damned and defamed. On the hind side it also highlights the impact of media on the decision making of the armed forces which severely affects the quality of military operation.

`Sep Bajirao Roundal, Shourya Chakra' is a saga of bravery, courage and going beyond call of duty by a soldier who sacrifices his life for his motherland, leaving a childless widow and sonless parents. His young wife becomes a widow within a year of marriage. Similarly **'CHM Shivaji Jagtap, Kirti Chakra'** is a story of a martyr's highest moral values displayed in face of imminent death. The story dispels the misconception that the military men are indifferent to the safety of the civilian population while carrying out military operations. The story also touches the sufferings of the family of a soldier who takes barrage of terrorist's bullet on his chest so that rest of his colleagues are not harmed and the countrymen can breathe easy in their lungs. **'When Silence Cried'** is story of a Pundit who poses tremendous faith in his neighbours and is determined not to leave place of his birth; Kashmir, where his forefathers had planted the seedlings of human civilization several thousand years back. It brings out the dilemma average Kashmiri Pundits have gone through before their mass exodus to become refugee in their own country. It brings out the peculiar love-hate relationship they have with their Muslim brethren; almost all of whom once were Pundits or Hindus.

Story **'The Gift of Shroud'** reveals the great qualities, traditionally, people of Kashmir possess; conventional wisdom, intelligence, respect, craving for knowledge, good education, hospitality, family values, etc. And most importantly 'Kashmiriyat': which include all said and much more un-said. The story also brings out the hidden true fears an average Kashmiri lives with: Custodial deaths and disappearances. **'Toys on LOC'** is a chilling revelation of games played by the ISI and Pakistanis to use the locals as tools to achieve their goals. It portrays the life of a spy and its logical conclusion; mysterious death or disappearance. It also reveals the obsessive side of Pak army which is so fanaticised that it does not believe a Muslim officer can serve with complete loyalty in Indian army.

'The Travelogue' is to quench the thirst of the reader to understand who the story teller is and how he reached Kashmir from campuses of University of Allahabad. It reveals the journey of a post graduate youth with a burning desire to become an army officer and serve his mother land, abandoning his plan of pursuing Ph.D. or joining the mad rush of a career in the civil services. 'The Travelogue' ushers the reader to walk through the process of Services Selection Board, life in a military academy and the ordeals; a youth has to go through to put on the Olive Green uniform with brass on the shoulders.

I am convinced that most of the people; the elderly, the women, the children, the youth of Kashmir are wonderful people. I found most of them, to be among the best in all aspects; intelligent, beautiful, civilised, extremely hospitable very loving and most sensible and sensitive. The youth of Kashmir have all the potential to be the best in any field.

The book is result of a strange mix of all; the unforgettable love bestowed on me and the unbearable and undeserved hate thrown on me. It is revelation of the pain. I saw of Kashmiris (mostly Muslims) living in the valley, the silent symbols of devastation of Kashmiri Pundits left by them in the shape of their houses, books on the shelves, plates on dining tables, their untended orchards, their disrespected temples, etc. It is a memoir of the shrieks of mothers, the cries of children, the fear floating in the air, the gun powder smelling in the surrounding. Many scenes, many incidents remained embedded in my heart and mind due to extreme good or extreme bad reasons, extremely galling or sweet experiences.

The insurgency in Kashmir conceived in eighties and bursting and hurting the entire nation in 1989-90 was mostly (but not exclusively) sponsored from the across; to inflict 'thousand cuts on the Indian State to bleed it to death.' To achieve this nefarious goal, Pakistan recruited, imported, trained and pushed Kashmiri youth into armed struggle to carry out selective killings of Hindus (Kashmiri Pundits) by portraying them as Indian agents but not limiting it to Pundits. They killed everyone, including Muslims, perceived to be pro India or anti-secessionist.

Murder of both types was devoid of any apparent reason or provocation. Beginning from H L Khera, to PN Bhatt, Lassa Kaul, Tikka Lal Taploo, Neel Kanth Ganjoo, among Hindus and Dr Mushirul Haq, the then vice chancellor of Kashmir University, are a few to mention from among the victims of sponsored terrorism. All were murdered sans mercy and reasoning. Practically there was no government in late 1989 and early 1990 as elaborated by Mr Jamil Qureshi adviser to the then Governor:

"The people, almost the whole lot of them, believed that Kashmir was going to be either independent or become part of Pakistan in January 1990 itself. In fact Jan 26 was promised by the militants to be a day of supposed deliverance, when new Peoples' Republic of Independent Kashmir was going to be declared and foreign correspondents invited to witness the birth of new independent state."- (From *"My Frozen Turbulence in Kashmir"- written by Mr Jagmohan, the then Governor of J & K State*).

There are historical, political and geographical reasons for Pakistani involvement but more galling for Pakistan is omnidirectional growth of Indian Muslims supported by overwhelming population of Hindus in all spheres of life, in secular India. There is no field where Indian Muslims have not excelled: education, science, technology, business, art, literature, music, cinema, politics, bureaucracy, policing and even armed forces. Air Chief Marshal I H Latif had been one of them. It's so hurting to Pakistan that Dr Kalam was elevated to the Presidency by a 'Hindu Party'. What can be more 'hurting' to Pakistan than seeing that top intelligence agency of India 'Intelligence Bureau' is headed by a Muslim, Mr Syed Asif Ibrahim? Except the post of Prime Minister, Muslims have served in almost all positions including the (three) Presidents of the Republic.

The entire idea and basis of 'two nation theory' have been defeated. Indian Muslims proving to be among the most Intelligent Muslims in the world, living among 'over whelming Hindus' in a 'secular India', creates severe 'acidity' and 'indigestion' in the stomach of Pakistani rulers. Hence they do what they know the best to do: destruction.

On the other hand the alleged rigging of assembly elections of 1987 led the fundamentalists, and to some extent the vulnerable and gullible populace of the state, into unprecedented frustration, anger and helplessness. This `pretention' resulted into uprising and looking for help even from the enemy: to connive, corroborate, cooperate, conspire and confederate to congeal the joint agenda of 'thousand cuts.' All this was in the name of Islamic confraternity, to conflagrate Kashmir; the crown of Indian secularism. The role of the two dynasties, both originating from Kashmiri roots and dominating Delhi and Srinagar political spectrum, in scuttling free democratic process in the state is also alleged to be one of the reasons for the disquiet.

All above and many unmentioned factors created so much of unrest in Kashmir that it became among most disturbed places in the world. Even a weak central government of 1990, possessed by imbecility of political will and manned by permanently laid back indifferent bureaucracy had to wake up to the anarchy which had engulfed the valley. The lawlessness and armed uprising crossed all limits, unprecedented in the history of independent India, forcing the government to impose Armed Forces Special Power Act; the AFSPA on 05 July 1990. The Act enables and empowers the armed forces with extra ordinary powers of arrest, search, seizure and detention.

My Experience in the valley; The Seedling of the Book

I served in the Kashmir valley in 6 Maratha LI as a newly commissioned army officer from 1992 to 1995 under Armed Forces Special Power Act and from 1997 to 1999 on the Line of Control. Based on my operational experience, interaction and observation, I have scripted this book consisting of fourteen stories, which portray different emotions, directions and aspects of Kashmir conflict. These are the incidents which touched my heart and remained entrenched deep within. These stories are based on true incidents, which reveal more than any analytical/academic book.

Writing a book which involves army actions is extremely

difficult proposition, particularly when the writer himself had been under oath to maintain secrecy under Official Secret Act. I cannot place several facts and photographs in public domain despite the temptation and apparent need. Another difficulty I faced is about use of terminology. Many words are peculiar to the army parlance and a civilian may face difficulty in correctly comprehending the meaning. I have tried to overcome this handicap by creating a 'Glossary' and placing it at the end of the book so that any one facing difficulty may refer to them.

Third but most intricate difficulty I faced was about mentioning the names of my colleagues who were part of all the actions mentioned in the book. Since many of them are still serving in various positions (most of them at very senior positions), it was imperative to take their consent to mentioning their names. It was an ordeal of wait and persuasion that never came through. If one agreed, some other disagreed. I did not want to make it look like a 'cock and bull story' by mentioning half the characters by their real names and half by assumed names or by the designation. I overcame that problem by giving all of them assumed names in all the stories. Now real names are mentioned only in two stories written about the Martyrs: 'Sepoy Bajirao Raundal, SC' and 'CHM Shivaji Jagtap, KC' that also only of the martyrs' since rest of the real characters did not consent to mention their names in the two stories too.

I deem it my earnest responsibility to inform the reader that liberties have been taken to elaborate and attribute statements/dialogues to various characters to reveal and explain the meaning of what they originally said. At places, literary freedom has also been exercised to moderate, contract or expand the impacts of an action or statement.

Today, when Kashmir is under unprecedented deluge, the citizenry is fighting for their life and for the life of their near-dears; it's the Indian Defence Forces, which have come to their rescue in most visible and most effective way. These saviours: the men of the Army/Air force/Navy have put their

hunger, thirst, pain and fatigue behind. They have even put their own life at risk, their own family at the back burner; just to save the life of their 'fellow citizens' from the peril. It only proves that they love Kashmiris to the core, minus the traitors; who have since gone in 'comatose'. Hiding in their secured burrows, these traitors are even now instigating the 'stray youth' to throw stone on the 'saviours'.

The book is an account of a bitter truth that makes me feel more sad than nostalgic. It is a memoir of the senseless devastations: deaths, encounters, killings, firing, cries, shrieks and detention of youth, many found to be innocent later. It is remembrance of the interrogations, the chest beating mothers, hair plucking fathers and missed opportunities of education and growth. It is a mirror of devastation of Kashmiri Hindus; their empty, and at places, burnt houses, their mass exodus, their pitiable conditions in the refugee camps. It is reminder of dead bodies of soldiers' being `embalmed' and airlifted in the aircrafts to their home towns or just cremated nearby. It is an account of my wonder as to what we have gained from these losses. This book is a wish that all above ends soon so that none of eyes is wet, while remembering Kashmir; including mine.

Acknowledgements

At New Delhi: Sri Syed Iftikhar Sultan Ahmed IPS (Retd); ex-DG CISF and CRPF for continual encouragement, pre-publication review and gratifying words, Col Rohini Pathak for unstinting enthusiasm about the book, Sqn Ldr Ajay Gairola, Deepak Bhardwaj, Aniruddha Kar, Nalin Srivastava, Fazru Khan, Saurabh Mishra, Vivek Khulbe, Utpal Barua, Lucky Bhaskar, Kapil Sabbarwal and Sourabh Jyoti Sharma for assuring me that my stories are worth telling, Tuhin Chakraborty for listening and reading the same stories so many times over and still finding them interesting, Sunil Raina for coding, decoding and correcting my broken and transliterated Kashmiri, and all my colleagues at IGI Airpot, New Delhi for encouragement and support.

At Pune: Major General CD Sawant (Retd) for teaching me most important lessons of humanity, as my first CO, for providing invaluable inputs & rare photographs and most importantly, for continual encouragement. Subedar Major (Honorary Capt) Laxam Bhore. At Aizawl Col Neeraj Jha, at Aurangabad Col Samir Chaudhary for consummate support and assistance in collecting the facts and figures. At Akhnoor: Col Mayur Shekatkar, Subedar Major Bhagwan Bholave, Subedar Major Prabhakar Nikam and all ranks of 6 Maratha LI. At Avantipur (Kashmir) Col Manish Chitnis, at Bengaluru Col PM Muthappa, at Siliguri Col Rakesh Yadav and Major Dheeraj Kumar, at Dirang Col Gulshan Chadha. My special thanks to all my course mates of SS-53 (Officers Training Academy Madras) spread all over the country protecting our motherland, for their support and encouragement.

At Noida: Sri Bhartendu Sharma and Smt Anjali Sharma for standing up beside me, holding me every time I stumbled, for doing everything to see my script is converted into a book and for creating my website. Sri Amit Singhal, for working unflinchingly and putting important part of the book on the web. At Australia, Sri Amarnath Sen for ironing out any crumps in balancing my view about Kashmir, Muslims, Jehad and all kind of fundamentalisms.

At Ghaziabad: Janab Ismail Sheikh and Mohtarma Razia Sheikh for all the support in assisting me to understand verses from the Holy Quran and the *Azaan*.

My perfect friend, life partner and sweet heart: Sheel, who gave me all the liberty to engage with words than with her, forsaking her right over my time. My two strongest critics: my son Kartikeya and daughter Shubhra for making me realise I am far from good enough leave apart being perfect. My brother Prabhat, for reading almost all the stories so many times but not feeling bored and for giving valuable inputs to present them better. My deepest gratitude is due to my parents: Smt Manraji and Sri Rajnath Tripathi for imbibing those human values and upbringing me so sensitively.

To Manas Publications for converting my script into book, for accepting cheerfully changes at inconvenient times and for shaping the book in present form. My thanks are due to the editors and staff for their tireless effort.

Travelogue: My Journey from Allahabad to Srinagar via Madras

Reflections: Feb/Mar 1992

In Chanakya auditorium of Officers Training Academy Madras, during the session organized for declaration of allotment of regiments for soon would be commissioned officers, when my name was announced and it was disclosed that I had been commissioned into 6 Maratha Light Infantry: I was overjoyed. Overjoyed because I got the regiment I had opted for and as far as battalion was concerned, I had no specific choice since there was no one from my family who had ever served in the army; leave apart any regiment. The only person whom I could relate was adjutant of the Academy, Major Kaushal Chaturvedi who had insisted that I opt for Maratha Light Infantry; the regiment he belonged to. His insistence had become intense since the time he had come to know that we were from same Alma Maters; university mate, and originated from the same city: Allahabad.

"Your Battalion is in Srinagar in Counter Insurgency operations"- informed one of my batch-mate who was from hard core army background and whose cousin was already a captain in the same battalion where I was going to be. He continued with a grudge and disgust: "These buggers gave me Marathas; the regiment I had opted, but did not give me the battalion of my choice. Instead of 9 Maratha LI, where my father has served, they have given me 7th".

From this moment onwards my fascination started that I will be fighting the insurgents to protect the unity and integrity of my beloved country: a dream cherished from my childhood that had forced me to choose army instead of civil services, defying trend at University of Allahabad. About the state of affairs in the Kashmir valley, I imagined extremes of good and bad; from winning highest gallantry award and becoming a hero to dying unsung, based on the discussion in the peer group, newspaper reports, and most importantly on the feedback or discussion with the officers who had already served in the valley and were now instructors in the Academy. I did serve in the valley and fought the insurgents, but my imagination of both the extremities remained unfulfilled; neither have I died fighting nor could I get the highest gallantry award, rather no award at all.

I left the army within nine years and changed, since then, a few professions, finally, anticipating quitting all jobs and dedicating my life to social, political and literary cause. Among my serving coursemates, many were side-lined after the time bound promotions saturated and selection grade promotions fell in others' plates. A few, who made it to selection grade and persisted, are still in the army fighting one or other type of 'enemy', hoping and waiting to become brigadier. Rest, either left the army to pursue different life styles in different parts of the world by pursuing other professions, or left altogether the world itself; mostly in their prime age fighting various insurgent groups or vagaries of nature. Very few died naturally. After all we are just in mid-forties and natural death is most 'un-natural'.

Now, the world has changed so much that Madras where our academy is situated, has become Chennai and I have travelled a long distance in my life from that moment; from a gentleman cadet to an army officer to a civilian. When I look back I remember those were days of extreme excitement. After ten months of excruciatingly tight schedule of training, when our orientation remained lost and when ten directions looked converted into a circle, last fifteen days were days of relaxation and internal administration. It was less of training and more of preparation for passing out parade (POP), filling of various forms, attending sessions on various topics relating to allotment of arms or services to gentleman cadets (we were called GCs in the academy), attending sessions of officers visiting from army HQ, talking to parents about their visit to attend POP, reservations and accommodations of their stay, etc. We were enjoying these busy schedules and re-inventing liberty of interaction with the outside world. It was contrary to the 'posh ghetto' which had cut us off so much from the world that we came to know about the assassination of ex-PM Rajiv Gandhi executed just 60 km away (at Sriperumbdur) from our Academy at Madras, only next day when the day's training was cancelled on 22 May 1992; the only day of cancellation of training during the entire period.

At Allahabad, Dec 1990: Before Joining Army

Today I remember some day of Dec 1990 at my room at Allahabad, when my younger brother came to me excited, holding a copy of *Employment News*. The magazine regularly carried details of vacancies of various posts in various department of the Government and occasionally carried results of competitive examinations conducted by UPSC (Union Public Service Commission). He wanted to show me the result of Combined Defence Services, where he had located my roll number also in the list of qualified candidates. I was not even ready to see the roll number, as I was no more interested to go for the third time; four days of torturous personality test conducted by Services Selection Board (SSB). As I used to perceive then, the SSB was a terrifying board dominated by large number of robotic mannered armed forces officers whose all moves were angular and never circular, and grim-faced secretive psychologists.

Before this I had qualified the same examination twice, had faced the SSB and was not selected. I had developed despise for the SSB and so were majority of the youth who were consistently rejected, renaming the SSB as SRB; Services Rejection Board, puzzled what they want in a potential army officer. Average rejection was 90 to 94 per cent from among those who had qualified the written examination of the UPSC. No other selection board rejects such overwhelming percentage of candidates after they have qualified the written test that also conducted by apex examining constitutional body of the country.

My junior sibling insisted that not only I see the result but get prepared to go for SSB, leave the philosophy, history and general knowledge books, stop visiting the libraries and start some physical exercise and training; which were very crucial to cross the hurdle of SSB standing between me and OTA or in stretched imagination, between me and the rank of a Lieutenant. I told him that it looks very demeaning, getting stamp of "rejected" or "failed". If they do not want me, I won't run behind them any more as I have several other options. I told him now I will either pursue civil services; like most of my class/batch mates are doing, as we all had already completed our post-graduation, or become a lecturer after completing my PhD which I had started contemplating.

He insisted and prevailed upon to convince me by reminding that how much I dreamt to become an army officer and that it is my last chance. He reminded that when I have gone through the "humiliation" of failing twice, "once more" will not rob me of anything more. "You lose your stamp of 'fresher' only once' and you have already lost after your first failure" he had taunted smilingly. 'After all you had appeared in the written examination with some motive'- he reminded.

This time I was expecting Allahabad, my own city, as centre for my personality test. At other two, out of three centres conducting personality test for the army; Bangalore and Bhopal, I had already been called. But it was not to be. When I received the call letter for personality test-cum-interview a few days later; last week of Dec 1990, it was Bhopal again. First February '91 was the reporting date and fourth February '91; last day of my stay and, naturally, date of declaration of result of SSB. It takes 3-4 days to complete personality test in SSB. By now I knew the process without their declaring or elaborating it.

At Bhopal: Going through the Services Selection Board

I reached Bhopal from Allahabad after overnight plus journey by train on the first day of February 1991. At the railway station the SSB representatives received us and after small formalities moved to the SSB centre in the Cantt in a military bus. Same neat and clean lanes, well-marked roads, clear signage, green and serene surroundings; the environment was alien for any citizen who lives in middle class localities of medium sized cities of India: crowdie, dirty, dusty, absence of signage, maddening traffic and all activities of homeless -poor on the road. I wished cities were also managed and maintained like cantonments. The aspirants, particularly from non-military background, joked "in cantonment everything static is painted red/white and everything moving salutes."

There were clearly two groups of aspirants: repeaters and freshers. The former was scorned by the latter; "bloody failures, rejects", - their eyes used to say it all. That is the way the freshers used to look at the 'repeaters'and used to keep a safe distance lest the contagion infect the 'freshers'. Individually, almost all freshers thought, they would get selected defying the trend of mass rejection. The only interaction with repeaters was interesting when the freshers wanted to know about the experience of going through different tests and when they had to go through.

I went through all tests with sufficient interest but without much of hope, with a bit of disdain, cynicism and indifference assuming result would be same; rejection. Like I, many had developed the misconception that only children of defence officers/personnel are selected in SSB. I was almost sure I would not be selected, hence never tried to pursue or prove a point beyond a limit with an attitude of "who cares"; leaving it to others to conclude whatever they wanted to. During group discussion, lectures, group tasks, etc. and even during interview with the Vice President of the board; a brigadier, the attitude was the same: due regard and respect to the assessing officers but no over-pursuance, overacting or overture to 'please or convince.'

On 04 February 1991, the fourth and last day of our stay at the SSB centre they declared the result in the conference hall after a small pep talk. We all were given chest number just after arrival and were supposed to put it on all the time, including during this conference. The robotic mannered, extremely agile and impressively smart Colonel in spotless crisp Olive Green uniform adorning medals and colours on his left chest, with impeccable manners, delivered his pep talk in flawless and effortless Victorian English with artificial Yankee twang, which I would summarise thus;

"Good Morning Gentlemen"—And after a pause continued;

"Look gentlemen, we are looking for youth with OLQs; officer like qualities, who have mental, psychological and physical make up of military leaders and who can lead men in war and peace. If you are not selected here it does not mean you have no substance or you are inferiors to those selected. It also does not mean that you are unfit for any other profession or there is something lacking in you. If you are not selected here it only indicates that we have not found you suitable for army officer. You may have read and heard many stories that several gentlemen who were not selected someday by SSB, later excelled individually in different arena of life at different point of time. They include film stars, scientists, educationists, economists, civil servants, diplomats, politicians, so on and so forth. So you should not be disheartened if you are not selected. We do not want to fit "a squire peg in a round hole" and spoil both. If you very strongly feel to become an army officer, try again."

He paused, looked around and opened the file which was brought in by equally smart junior level military man and kept on the table before his arrival, and declared thus;

"OK, gentlemen, you were a group of thirty two candidates and we have selected two. They are; chest number eight and twenty. Please get up these two."

Chest number eight, a candidate from Tamil Nadu; not-knowing a single sentence of Hindi properly and an object of butt of joke among dominating majority group of north Indian Hindi speaking candidates from Gangetic plains, Haryana, Rajasthan and the Punjab: got up. But chest number twenty was nowhere to be standing. For few seconds all including me, were puzzled and tried to figure out whether chest number twenty was present or not. Suddenly the Colonel, after scanning almost entire hall, fixed his eyes in disbelief on me. That was when I realised it's me; chest number twenty, who had to get up. I got up in a huff. The 'statue like'Colonel smiled, and said to all, while leaving; "Thank you gentlemen; I wish all the best to all of you for your future."

Suddenly several paradigms changed. All freshers; who were in highest number, became 'rejects'. I became a successful candidate and was surrounded by many, who wanted to enquire without delay about so many things; what answers I gave during interview, how I tackled a particular task, what

I wrote in psychological test or spoke in favour or against during group discussion about India going nuclear, etc. One candidate, who was rejected, started crying openly. Son of a serving colonel from Haryana, who had never imagined a life out of army, had attempted his last chance and failed to make it. He was heartbroken. He was consoled by many candidates, under the watch of military men from far; who had been seeing it all every week. I also consoled him saying life is like that; those who expect are rejected and those who stop expecting are selected and that God may have stored something better for him.

"You will prove a failure in army"- One rejected candidate hailing from Punjab passed an expert comment on me, based on what he had seen of me during those four days of stay together. He thought I was philosophical, idealist, impractical and sober more than needed with intellectual bent of mind, 'which is not needed in army.' I could manage only a smile on my face. I could not tell him, at least, two greatest warriors and strategists; Lord Krishna and Guru Gobind Singh ji were the greatest philosophers who ever came on the earth.

I was or rather never have been in hurry to inform or share; sorrow or celebration, happiness or sadness, pain or pleasure, even to the irritation of people close by. Unlike others, I did not ring at home immediately. In the evening I came to the main city; Bhopal, called from STD booth to inform my parents and siblings about my selection and about further stay back for SMB, roamed around and visited Bharat Bhawan; a cultural and convention centre with mesmerising architecture of Charles Chorea on the banks of a lake.

Except two of us, all were packed up and given sent off. We stayed for further SMB; Services Medical Board, another ordeal which was to test all parts of our body; internal and external, if they were in the best of the state and shape. Another new group of 'selected' candidates was formed amalgamating from previous selections, to go for medical check-up in the military hospital in several attempts stretching several days. We both were found 'fit' on all counts, a few were temporarily rejected.

Churning at OTA Madras

After a few days of my return from Bhopal I received a big registered packet from OTA; Officers Training Academy, Madras (Now Chennai) Tamil Nadu. It was containing, besides offer to join, detailed instructions about what all needed to be done before coming to the Academy; dresses, shoes, personal belongings, demand draft and dos and don'ts. It further stated that I had to report to the Academy on 03 May 1991, describing in detail how to reach the Academy if one was coming by rail or air, creating undue anxiety in my mind about a 'Madrasi city' known for its perpetual anti-Hindi instance and recent anti-Hindi agitation. I remembered the TV images wherein all the hoarding, signage, names or just anything written in Hindi was either destroyed or blackened. I felt relieved when at the end I read that Military transport would be provided and Academy representatives would come to receive the cadets at all the terminals; rail or air, if they intimated their date and time of arrival. I wondered why they did not write such important and 'all anxiety slaying' information at the beginning itself.

I had never experienced such heat mixed with humidity in my life as on my first arrival at Chennai railway station to join the Academy. Summers are hot in the Gangetic plains as well but not this hot and humid. I felt I would collapse and went to get a bottle of packaged cold water from the nearest shop while waiting for the Academy rep to receive us. I thought the female shopkeeper was deaf since she did not give me water despite I placing a high denomination currency note and repeatedly indicating and asking for '*Paani*'; water in Hindi.

I kept on standing mystified until another customer came and asked her the same thing saying 'Tanni; water in Tamil.' The 'deaf' lady immediately handed him over water bottle and rest of the money. I realised her 'deafness' was Hindi-specific and indifference only to Hindi speaking people. I was more amused than angry realizing we do not fight exclusively over our claim; that name of God, only in my language is correct and in any other language is not name of God. It is true for language also. People from many far flung parts of India like North East, Sikkim, Bengal, Odisha, Kashmir, Southern states etc complain that they are ridiculed and discriminated by north Indians. Here I was also feeling something like that. We love to ridicule each other; our incredible India.

The life in OTA was extremely tough; beyond imagination. I was already lean and thin, hence not much of change in my physique. But those with a lot of flab on their frame, melted within two months. From a sack weighing 80-90 kg, some even touching century, were now a stick of bone covered with skin and attached together with sufficient muscle, nothing else. No fat, no flab. It would be more appropriate to say that if` we were not sleeping, which we did minimally, we were running or sweating it out in one way or the other, at least in the first term. I learnt new terminologies like 'CC', 'sissy', and unofficial full form of GC; Gentleman Cadet, which no 'GC' would ever forget. I also learnt new 'acrobatics' like front roll, back roll, side roll and many simian type tricks. The 'style' of haircut was such that we were 'tonsured' from sides as deep as it was possible without using razors. Whenever we went on outing to Madras city, onlookers derived a lot of pleasure out of our style of haircut. The schedule was so demanding and punishments without reason so intense that it took a few weeks to literally understand which side was north in the Academy.

I was placed in 8th platoon (other being 7th) of Naushera Company under Shivaji Battalion. Shivaji Battalion had two Companies, the other being Mectila with only one platoon; Mectila-2. Those days' girls were not permitted to join army (they started coming to OTA three courses after mine from SS -56). There were only two battalions: Shivaji and Ranjit Singh with combined strength of six platoons of three each.

Out of 210 (if I remember correctly) who had joined the training, 12 left within a period of fifteen days to a month. They could not bear the physical, mental and psychological stress of the training. They were counselled several times, before being let off, by officers at various levels and advised not to leave. They were assisted in overcoming any kind of difficulty they were facing. A few of them were also taken to the Deputy Commandant/Senior officers of the Academy who did some 'fatherly sweet talks' but to no avail.

Before leaving some of them kept on instigating others as well to leave the Academy and commented frequently:

"This training is not for 'human beings', only animals can be put through it."

Their uncharitable comments somehow reached the senior officers. One of them, a colonel from Rajputana Rifles regiment (our battalion commander) deputed one of the Company Commanders to sort out the issue. The Company Commander, a Rajput regiment officer and a known maverick, came and counselled them in a 'fall in'. After a lot of sermon and inspirational talk to the rest, he aimed his lethal 'talk-gun' towards the 'leavers' summarising his talk thus;

"This training has been designed for 'men' with 'V' and not with 'C'; sissies. Only virtuous men full of valour, virility, vigour, vibrancy with victorious attitude can go through it. It is good that you unmasked yourself early and saved the environment from pollution. Now you all can go back home, sit on the lap of your moms and suck some more milk from their breast to become man and grow up. All those want to leave can come to the adjutants' office to complete the formalities of leaving."

All did not leave due to stress only. Some left due to humiliation and physical assault by a few senior batch GCs and a few instructors; Captain/Major ranking officers. Their behaviour was appalling and maddening. Most of them were 'gentlemen' but a few of them behaved erratically. They never hesitated in physically hitting the 'would be' commissioned officers (Group 'A' gazetted officers) in the name of being their well-wisher and doing it all for their good future. One of them; a Major from Rajput regiment, hailing from Bengal, was most abusive. Unfortunately, a few GCs of his 'types' considered him their role model. In one of the exercises I also had to face his short-fused unbearable anger and its disproportionate abuse of physical assault. Ultimately, out of 210 only 189 could get commission. Rest 21 left the Academy before completing the training.

A few were rendered partially disabled and unfit for further training, some among them disabled for life. They were sent back to their homes, that the army calls 'boarding out'. The training which is spanned in a period of 18 month in Indian Military Academy Dehradun is squeezed to be completed within nine months in OTA. Many believed it was second toughest military academy in the world, first being, as they perceived, Israel's military academy. Several times my skin on the back came off like scab due to heat, humidity and resultant sweating. Every time we took water we mixed it with table salt to maintain salt level in body. From instructors to cadets everyone cursed: "who damn fool has chosen this place for military academy where there are only three seasons; hot, hotter and hottest?"

Our orientation remained lost during entire training. During first half of the training, almost initial five months, I could not even see the headlines of newspaper; an unimaginable thing for a person who used to have breakfast only after reading at least one national daily. We did not know what was happening out there in the world. I came to know about disintegration of USSR, and formation of CIS by my brother's letter mentioning, just for some other reason, formation of several independent republics besides Estonia, Latvia and Lithuania which were already independent states from USSR. It was not because there were no newspapers but because there was no time. The time was utilised in either catching up sleep or enduring unofficial punishments meted out by senior batch GCs for no reason/fun or, as they used to say, 'for strengthening and toughening us'.

It was tiredness in eternity. We used to sleep while doing everything; in academic classes, in games, physical training, weapon training, long marches, route marches, walking, talking, and eating, near swimming pool and in the club. Some slept during club activities skirting; horse riding, music and drama, parasailing, driving etc. However the best place for catching up a good sleep was the auditorium-cum-movie hall showing during twice a week movies in Hindi and English. After end of the movie very few knew which movie was shown and what the cast was. At the end of the three hour movie, I meant sleep, almost every one said and rest agreed, 'Very short movie, I doubt it was even one hour's duration'.

Finally the moment of glory arrived on 07 March 1992, date of our POP; passing out parade. Symbolically and formally the President and ex-officio supreme commander of armed forces of India, issued gazette notification to commission us as 'commissioned officers'. Our parents were formally invited to be the part of the glorious moment. One of my fast friends and my younger brother also accompanied my parents from Allahabad to Madras to be part of the guests during POP. The POP was preceded by grand get together party on the eve.

Many parents were serving or retired defence officers. It was a gala time for many. My parents had come from civilian background and struggled to find some companion; a person who could talk something different from defence matters and who preferably was a non-drinker. They felt alienated and a bit surprised to see their mother tongue and so called 'Rashtra Bhasha'; Hindi, hiding somewhere fearfully in the submerged environs of high pitched shrill sounding words of a language which originated from a tiny island situated on the north eastern corner of the Atlantic Ocean, thousands of kilometre away from 'Bharat' (Madras).

On the day of POP when I could manage sometime in the tight schedule to reach my parents and seek their blessings after the grand parade, my mother hugged me, her eyes moist overwhelmed with joy; she was extremely emotional and impressed by the parade and more so that her son was a part of it. She had never seen so closely such co-ordinated, precise, synchronised and flawless movement of 200 'boys' or human endeavour of this nature. My father looked on and smiled. He never had allowed his emotions to come on the face; pain or pleasure, happiness or sorrow, birth or death, glory or gloom, he was the same or could manage to look the same: a typical 'emotionless, strong man' of 'his generation.'He believed good and bad both are transient.

From POP we immediately moved to Chanakya Auditorium where we were to be 'piped in' and where 'stars' were to decorate our shoulders. The military secretary, a Lieutenant General ranking officer from the army HQ was to read out the order from the President to 'commission' us in the army. Occasionally His Excellency him/herself graces the occasion by accepting the invitation as chief guest at OTA and IMA. Our batch was not among them. Our parents piped us as officers designated as 'Second Lieutenant' that marked the end of training, the POP programmes, and beginning of new life. Now I had joined a very special and elite group; not in terms of having tremendous power and facilities, but pledging their life in writing for the cause of their motherland. No other government servant or professional pledges in writing to give his/her life for the 'nation/state' when needed.

After the POP we were granted 21 days leave and out of that more than ten days I spent with my parents in south tour. We already had planned our trip to south and all bookings done in advance; Madras, Mahaballipuram, Madurai, Kanyakumari and Rameshwaram, touching the edge of Palk Strait between main mass-land of Indian subcontinent and tiny island of Sri Lanka; which looks like a 'drop' below Indian peninsula. We all were impressed by Southern architecture everywhere, particularly Gopurams of Madurai Temple; 170 feet tall; a splendour in stone. Serenity and 'virginity' of Kanyakumari beach was no less enchanting. It was pilgrimage, tour and togetherness of one week; unforgettable.

At Regimental Centre In Belgaum

After spending rest of the days out of 21 day's leave at my home town with parents, family, friends and relatives, I had to report to the Maratha Light Infantry Regimental Centre at Belgaum. We were four officers commissioned in the Maratha Light Infantry from our course one each in 5th, 6th, 7th, and 16th battalion. For fifteen days we had to learn and understand the origin, history, tradition and peculiarity of the regiment besides going for tour of the area from where bulk of our troops come. It was very enriching experience to see rural areas of southern Maharashtra and northern Karnataka. Our regimental centre was the 'launching pad' for 'liberation of Goa' from the Portuguese in 1961 and 1st Maratha LI had been prominent unit of the assault brigade under 17 Infantry Division and 50 Parachute Brigade. Among the toughest courses of Indian Army; the Commando Course is conducted at Belgaum. In Bollywood movie *Prahaar,*most of the scenes were shot in Belgaum, including some in our regimental centre and in our officers' mess.

I was to take one of the longest train journeys, after end of my visit at the regimental centre, from Belgaum to Jammu; the rail terminus to Jammu and Kashmir State. Jammu is almost 300 km south of Srinagar city where, somewhere on the periphery of the city my unit was located. After Pathankot entire area was more of intermittent garrison than civilian settlement until Jammu; which was stranger than the rest. In Jammu local civilian population, military men from all over Indian ethnicity and 'exiled' Kashmiri Pundits; 'refugee' in their own country, were presenting a very peculiar view. It looked a city 'just on the periphery of war zone', where everyone; the original residents, the 'refugees' and the soldiers were 'preparing' to cope up in the new environment.

Jammu To Srinagar; Grandeur of Himalayas

There were regular military buses/trucks for pick up and drop of officers and Jawans from the railway station to transit camps. The movements were so dense that, without requisition, pick up buses/trucks reached the railway station and were full, at times taking second or third round for the military men landed by single train. I reached the officers transit camp at about ten in the morning. There just after tea the first thing I was told, almost 18-20 hours in advance, that the officers' bus will leave early tomorrow morning for Srinagar. I was allotted a room on twin sharing basis with another officer. No officer was retained or allowed to stay more than 24 hours in the transit camps so that his services were utilised in the operations area. If national highway 1A, from Jammu to Srinagar (though it goes beyond; up to Muzaffarabad in POK), was closed due to snow or land slide, officers were air lifted by the air force transporter IL-76. The Russian origin transporter, among the biggest in contemporary aviation world and rechristened in Indian *Avatar* as *Gajraj*; king of Elephants, was used as alternative to closed highway.

Next day early morning I boarded the exclusive officers' bus carrying officers of various ranks below Colonel. Colonel and above, I was told, mostly travelled in light exclusive vehicles, which were positioned in the transit camps before their arrival. Hereafter everything was new to me; the terrain, the environment, the mountains, the ridges, the people, the attire and the whole surrounding. The bus had its first stop at Udhampur at transit officers' mess for breakfast. The bus moved through narrow road which has been carved by cutting the mountains on the edges of banks of river, rivulets, Nala gorge, etc. I kept my fingers crossed all the time thinking if the driver made minor mistake we all would go down and then immediately up, up and up in the company of the Almighty.

I was overwhelmed by the sheer beauty of the panorama astride the road I was travelling. Most of the officers discussed various things including the insurgency on one hand and cribs against the organization on the other hand, amid my lost conscious charmed by the splendour of the nature. We crossed several small and big towns and villages on the way including the hill resort of Patni Top and crossed extremely beautiful army transit camp of Ramban but did not stop because it was meant for officers coming from the valley. It is situated on the west bank of river Chenab. We were served lunch at Banihal which is a few kilometres before the Jawahar tunnel. From Banihal onwards our convoys were protected and led by heavily armed soldiers standing on moving vehicles mounted with light machine guns and assorted weapons including rockets launchers. It looked entry in a war zone. Here most of the soldiers had shed their ceremonial uniforms, in which I was used to seeing them till now, and were in war gears looking extremely ferocious.

Jawahar tunnel, the only link between Kashmir valley and rest of India, has been created by cutting, no, rather 'boring' mighty ranges of Himalayas known as Pir Panjal. Before partition of India all good routes to the valley were via Punjab, which were now in Pakistan. To overcome this handicap first Prime Minister of India on whose name the tunnel has been titled, engaged western engineers. Consequently the tunnel was constructed for round-the-year surface transport by Mr. Alfred Kunz and Mr C. Barsel (both Germans) between 1954 and 1960. The tunnel has saved several kilometres of detour to reach the Kashmir valley and torturous climbing of the Pir Panjal Mountains. The length of tunnel is around 2.5 km, and it is situated between Banihāl; the last town before the valley and Qazigund; the first town of the valley. When one comes out of the tunnel, one is in the valley. Suddenly the flora and fauna changes noticeably and one enters again in the plains after 250 km of adventurous mountainous journey.

There were a few things peculiar which I could have not missed. The military was omnipresent. Soldiers, who were part of the ROP or road opening parties, had been standing whole day astride road to secure the road until the last vehicle of the last military convoy passed. The attire of civilians was ethnic and unique and one thing common: Pheron; a loose long Kurta touching above ankle. Heap of semi-finished cricket bats were seen near Qazigund, as if being manufactured to meet the demand of entire world. Military vehicles were more visible than civilian transport or the latter hid and got aside to give way to the military convoy? - was a question I had to learn in detail later.

I noticed a very unique thing after entering the valley. When military convoys moved, roads were vacated or rather got almost vacated of civilians. I saw carefully there were soldiers in the front vehicle with long bamboo sticks called Dandamen, both side of the soldier manning the light machine gun in the centre. Both the 'flunkies' were getting the road cleared for smooth movement of military convoys. Whereas the LMG man was meant to engage far flung targets, if one popped up; the Dandamen were to clear the obstacles on the road. If someone did not get aside the Dandamen used their baton on whichever part of the 'obstructer' was closer. I was shocked and appalled to see this treatment to our fellow citizens. I expressed my doubt to the fellow travelling officers. One of them, a Major, smiled and enquired whether I was travelling this side of the Pir Panjals tunnel for the first time? On my affirmation he described the reasons for incorporation of 'Dandaman' in detail.

The Major tried to clear my doubt, joined by another officer a bit later. They gave me retrospection of the origin of the Dandaman. During initial days of start of military operations, after enforcement of AFSPA in the state; the forces lost several men since passage was not given to the moving military columns by the locals. The moving columns of the armed forces were obstructed by placing slow moving tongas, carts, trucks, etc. So that the military convoy is held up and the terrorists can take pot-shot on them from the roof tops or balconies of the close by buildings. When front moving vehicles were forced to slow down intentionally or otherwise, the militants used to throw grenades or fire on them inflicting heavy casualty on forces. Hence originated the Concept of Dandaman: 'when going gets tough, the tough gets going'-they reminded me of old mantra of the army.

By the time I heard the details, I reached Pantha Chok; Main roundel before entering Srinagar city. It was quite chaotic due to heavy military vehicular movement. My image of Srinagar as a beautiful city got shattered. Before entering Badami Bagh cantt, I saw several board displaying:

"Soldiers are not permitted to walk on foot in this area"- obviously due to security reasons.

The bus reached transit camp at about 5.00 pm and all had to stay put in the officers transit camp for the night since ROP; the road opening parties had been withdrawn and no movement of military vehicles was allowed without convoy protection or ROP. I reached my unit in Sharifabad at the outskirts of Srinagar city next morning and met unique set of people, who were to be my companions and team mates in the game of life and death.

After staying together for some time, I made a mental picture of every officer. Irrespective of my mental picture, there were already several nick names given to the CO and other officers: some known and some unknown to them by a group of close knit officers; the company commanders, the real power centres in an Infantry Unit in operation. Since I was new and had not yet won the confidence of the inner circle of these colleagues; or to be more precise senior officers, they all tried to hide the nick names from me, thinking I might 'spill the beans' resulting into their secrecy going for a six. Man despite growing in all sphere; age, experience, knowledge, position, authority, etc; retains some traits of a child within his own circle or within himself. So were my seniors, yep all were senior to me; with varied amount of child inside them.

When they got together, which they often did since all were staying single including the married, they talked and at times cribbed about 'cat', 'mongoose', 'meat chopper', 'Janbaaz', 'rhino', 'bandit', 'turtle' 'Panda', etc. and laughed to the heart, passing jokes on action, inaction and incidents of these 'code names. 'They also remembered 'Raja', 'Pome(ranian)', 'spidy', 'Harry', 'Shaky', etc. But most of the talks were about 'cat' and 'mongoose'. "They must be among the senior most in the unit, most likely the Commanding Officer and Second-In-Command (2IC), but not necessarily in that order"- I guessed and my seniors had air of my guess. To test I was called to confirm whether I had really 'breached and penetrated' into their secrecy codes, one of them asked me a straight question, with hidden cunningness: 'Trips, Tell us why we call him mongoose?'

'I think because he kills the poisonous snakes; the terrorists.'- I replied innocently. All broke in laughter because they realised I had not been able to pin point the 'quality' which had prompted the said code name. One of them commented:

"You are like a typical Pundit; not reading writing on the wall but searching meaning between the lines. Don't you observe his eyes and neck move like a mangoose".

Subsequently I learnt a lot from each of them. They taught me everlasting invaluable lessons for improvement and growth of my professional and personal life. All of them were men of sterling qualities, with of course, individual human weaknesses differentiating them from each other. Later in various operations they were my companions and hence integral part of my stories which are based on true incidents. Since they did not agree to my proposal of mentioning their real names, to avoid any controversy, I have given them nick names; as I viewed them in my mental image. By design it is not in order of seniority; else purpose would have been defeated.

'Major Stalin', who had physique and moustache like Joseph Stalin, in addition to Stalin like ideas of 'Communists', was the first officer I had met in 6 Maratha LI. I was aghast to know his views on militancy. During my maiden meeting, out of over enthusiasm, when I asserted that the terrorists should be dealt with ruthless iron hand, he retorted:

'Why? They have a right to fight for their freedom; if they are not comfortable under the 'suzerainty' of your country, they can demand it as their 'democratic right.' Later I came to know; in one of the operations he had let off a group of men out of empathy and compassion who were feigning to be sick but actually dreaded terrorists. He, at least overtly, was an 'atheist' and thought all religions are 'opium' to exploit and befool innocent masses.

'Major Kishor' (Ever Young) was big contrast to 'Major Stalin' in juxtaposition. He thought undue liberty destroys a nation. Most of the problems in India are due to limitless liberties of expression and action. He questioned why so called 'liberals' do not go and ask for equal rights for other religious groups in Pakistan, Iran or Saudi Arabia. All their demands of equality are only in India, where in the eyes of the law, all are equal. He opined why the 'liberals' or advocates of 'freedom' did not stand up when Kashmiri Pundits were being butchered, persecuted and forced to leave their motherland; Kashmir, which they had nurtured from the beginning of the human civilization. He was sure the so called 'leaders of freedom struggle' are frauds, crooks, religious zealots and double agents; minting money from both India and Pakistan, from the former by blackmail and from the latter in the name of fight for so called freedom. In his opinion all such traitors should be lined up and shot.

"Major Marathe" was a fashion icon of the unit with latest fashion gadgets flowing from his home city of Bollywood. He was youngest and all elder siblings were sisters. So all new cosmetics, bought by sisters were tried on him in his younger days, which 'habituated' him towards the cosmetics' world. His 'empire' of cosmetics and toiletries was all pervading; it overflew from his bedroom to bathroom and vice-versa and stretched up to kitchen, so much so that once a newly recruited fauji cook mistaking 'Park Avenue styling gel' for some ingredient had put it into Upama for breakfast.'

He was extremely temperamental and had fragile ego. He was blessed with extraordinary capabilities of; hurting and caressing, abusing and praising, cursing and cuddling, loathing and loving in the same breathe. His pet lines "Do not think bloody you are the wisest person this side of Suez Canal" and my mental retort within myself used to be - "Until your misconception is removed, no one can dream of being wise leave apart wisest." He was extremely affectionate to me and always gave very appropriate advice on professional and personal matters.

"Major Kamal" was master of minor SD; comma, full stop, hyphens, semi-colon, etc. have to be exactly where they are supposed to be. Same attitude was about life; minor details have to be correct, even at times, at the expense of major and main theme. His assistant was a harassed lot since he had to carry a big rucksack in operations carrying all possible things in imagination he might need; under wears, vests, socks, woollen scarfs, shoes, extra jackets, even a pair of civvies, in case….; all in double triple numbers. Bryle hair cream, sun screen lotion of assorted companies with different SPF, shampoo, after shave etc had to be carried irrespective of its likely use. His room used to be spic and span and envy of other officers.

I learnt a lot from him, at times he not teaching me in an instructive way. He treated me like his younger brother and ticked me off instantly if I went wrong. He improved everything in me; from English grammar to etiquette and manners. He was captivating story teller.

"Captain Anil" was like oil well; hundred times hidden than revealed, containing precious material within. He looked completely disorganised from outside but was most organised in the matters of professional and personal life. He was capable of confusing his seniors with same ease as his juniors. Most of the time he never meant what he said and rarely said what he meant. He was capable of handling multiple responsibilities at the same time since he individually did little and delegated most of the work to his colleagues; mostly to juniors but not exclusively. He would innocently tell the Commanding Officer that which senior officer had done a particular work last time so well, generating a natural temptation in the mind of the Commanding Officer to delegate the said task to the best performer in the known history.

"Captain Shaant Singh" was a thorough gentleman with an attitude of 'who cares'. A quotation on his table 'face the music, feel the difference' had multiple meaning which he never tried to find out. He had kept the quotation to literally remind him to keep on listening to music, in continuum, Jagjit and Chitra's Ghazals. Coming from the 'Jat land', though himself not a Jat, he was man of a few words; by nature or may be probably, due to bottlenecks of the Queen's language. An officer with extremes of personal honesty and integrity, he taught me a few lessons of maintaining human dignity even at the time of distress and extreme provocation in the charged environment of Kashmir; where, at times, one had to pay by his life while trying to treat the hostile and abusive crowd with dignity and civility.

"Major Nirbhay Singh" was among the first to reach and jump in the critical situations; voluntarily taking risk and exposing himself to avoidable dangers. He was a work horse and a war horse; darling of those who wanted to be cosy on other's cost. He was often recommended for gallantry awards and regularly got it; at times twice the same. He was a regimental officer with a lot of espirit-de-corps and was an excellent host. He would extend all kind of help to me even on hint and go extra mile to ensure I had got what I wanted.

Major Prasanna was an officer always smiling and frequently laughing. He cursed reading to the extent that it was herculean task for him to even study to prepare for mandatory promotional examination. But he was a decorated soldier and practically most successful. He was excellent in generating intelligence sources among locals by his shrewd public relations skills. He was very proud to be from a race which gave first Indian-origin Chief of the Army Staff after independence. He always prided that during British days, due to their unflinching loyalty, they were the only Indian race allowed to keep arms without licence.

I served under two Commanding Officers; Colonels, during valley tenure. Both were excellent professionals and both reached 'General' rank. But more than professionals they were great human beings.

One of them was code named, among ladies; 'rest half.' I could not decode the meaning of the phrase, until I learnt the true meaning of another word; 'better half.' Surprisingly it was not the 'rest half' but the 'better half' who was more discussed, among ladies, during get together and AWWA meets. I understood it was result of jealousy, the rest of the ladies felt due to extreme influence of the 'better half' on the 'rest half'. But in my eyes he was an excellent military man. I always thought of him as great human being so referred him in this book as 'Manav Singh.'

He always entrusted me a lot of responsibilities. He had a knack of planning successful operations. No one could say for sure that it was his luck or professional acumen that brought him unexpected positive results. Where we thought, the operation was a waste, we got results beyond expectations. His style was a bit casual and during briefing, he left a lot to be understood by the junior commanders by not elaborating. And it was with a purpose; if things went well he would take credit and if something went wrong he would blame it on the person who took initiative in absence of any clear instruction: so the gap in his briefing.

However, it was Colonel Gangadhar who was my ideal despite his unpredictable mood swings. His sharp wit always created more fear than fun.

I always thought of him a Maratha 'icon', an epitome of Maratha symbol; "Duty, Honour, Courage". He was dominating, towering and imposing. His personal integrity was frightening. Those days there were no mobile phones and we had a lot of difficulty getting in touch with our families through STD since there were limited lines from Srinagar to rest of the country. Once he refused to talk to his family, through a 'tapped' (parallel line from someone else's connection) line, arranged by other officers with the help of our signal men. Despite some distress at home he didnot talk through the line and chastised all to remain a 'gentlemen' and 'army men' by keeping away from small and big temptations.

Eventually, after serving for almost eight plus years, I decided to leave the army and look for second career, mostly due to personal and domestic reasons. Subsequently I served in central PSU and very closely worked with various ministries of central government at New Delhi. I had the opportunity to work in close co-ordination and in close vicinity of top bureaucrats. My perception about Indian army is, after living with other wings of the government, that it is 'the best' organization to serve. But unfortunately it is not, always, manned by best of the people. Rigidity, ego-centric work culture, adherence to the perceived great traditions of colonial era, sycophancy, huge gap between the status and privileges of officers and PBOR (personnel below officers' rank) are off late seen as 'dated' by gen 'Y'.

Governments' apparent and visible discrimination in treating the military men vis-à-vis their civilian counterparts has created noticeable disquiet in the ranks and file of the army. The nation and the government have to look after their soldiers to attract 'the best' men for 'the best' organization of the nation. Disdainful, narrow-minded and lacklustre attitude of civilian bureaucracy, known as IAS, is not doing any good to military men and in long run to the nation. I will end my Travelogue with words of Chanakya; among greatest political thinkers ever born:

"Take care of your soldier, O' King , the day should never arise when a soldier has to ask you for justice. He lays his life on border for the kingdom, so that you, me and our people can sleep peacefully."- Chanakya to King Chandragupta Maurya.

Chapter 1

Encounter with Hardened Terrorists

Gund Hassi Bhat Village, Dist. Badgam: 29 Dec 1992

Ahead of me were a few soldiers; my scouts and behind me the group of soldiers carrying medium machine gun; the MMG, followed by rest of the Company. We were cordoning most crucial part of the village; the bund, dividing the village from the lake of low lying wetland of Hokarsar. Suddenly my vanguard spotted five young civilians running from the village towards the lake, taking advantage of the gap between my Company and the neighbouring Company; with whom I was moving to marry up to complete the cordon. They were breathing like rhinoceros after a long tiring run; breathless and growling, their mouth wide open to suck in maximum oxygen possible. My vanguard challenged them to stop and ordered them to raise their hands to prove they are innocent but to no avail.

They kept on running toward the lake. My vanguard shouted, noticing assault rifles in their hands; to warn all of us that these are terrorists trying to run out of the cordon while simultaneously, cocking their weapons to fire on the escaping terrorists and in lieu were fired upon. I, my vanguard and all other soldiers in the vicinity did what they were trained to do; fire on the terrorists. We rained heavy volume of fire on the terrorists who had already fired on us and had left us in no doubt who they were and what they were carrying in their hand and heart. Some might have received our bullets but their act did not reveal any such sign. They crossed the bund with whirlwind speed and jumped into the lake surrounded by large area of marshland; later a part of which was going to turn red due to human blood.

This most 'deadly' encounter of my entire tenure in the valley; resulting into death of four hard core terrorists of Hizbul Momeen (said to be a Shia Sect Militant organization) after fierce encounter, was in the village Gund Hassi Bhat, 16-17 km from Haft Chinar; our Unit location which was situated in the heart of Srinagar city. The village is located on the Srinagar Baramulla highway; spread 2-3 km south-east of Srinagar -Baramulla-Gulmarg tri-junction, sandwiched between NH1A and Hokarsar wetland.

The previous night on 28 Dec 1992, the Commanding Officer had briefed us about the operation just after the dinner, spreading the military map of the area; marked in several colours on the talc sheet covering it, on a big table. He had moved his pointer while showing the route, boundaries of the village, company deployment and areas of responsibilities while giving verbal briefs-cum-commentary of relevant topics;

"Gentlemen, tomorrow we are going to cordon off village Gund Hassi Bhat on NH1A; near Srinagar-Baramulla-Gulmarg highway just short of village Narbal, on very specific input. As you can see on the map, the village is sandwiched between the Srinagar-Baramulla highway and bund of Lake Hokarsar.

All four companies will participate. As you can see there is a road going from centre of the village dividing the entire village roughly into two parts. We will take this road once we reach the village via Srinagar-Baramulla road. We have information that tomorrow morning at about 07.00 h area commander of Hizbul Momeen alongwith his group of hardcore cadre consisting of 5-6 terrorists is coming to celebrate birth day of his girlfriend.

By now, knowing pattern of military operations, they have decided to celebrate during day time and leave the place before dusk. It is learnt they have concluded that army generally lays cordon during early morning; before dawn, to trap them in the bed; so this change of timing of celebration. Hence we have decided to lay our cordon only after they are inside the village and in the mid of their celebration. Accordingly I plan to cordon off the village after 11.00h. So you all have to move after breakfast, keep your companies ready to move by 10.15 h; 45 minutes for travelling from our location to the village keeping in mind heavy traffic of morning. By now all of you are so conversant with all aspects of operation that I need not elaborate much. However a few salient points I would like to touch upon."

He paused, removed his sight from the map, lay back on the cushioned chair and elaborated plan in detail expounding areas of responsibility, administrative arrangement, order of move etc. I was to marry up with Charlie Company led by Major Kishor after crossing the village and we jointly were to block any exit towards the lake of Hokarsar.

He looked at me; the 'Bravo' Company Commander, and then at Charlie Company Commander who was 7-8 years senior to me to be sure that we were clear about our role. He gave some more routine instructions and then looked at all of us saying he had finished and we might ask questions if any.

'No sir'- all of us said,almost, simultaneously.

'OK then all the best for your hunt of "Majnoos". I am sure some of you will bring "Majnoos" in front of me; dead or alive.'- He indicated end of briefing by referring jokingly and figuratively to the legendary lover Majnoo and his lady love 'Laila' and compared them with the area commander and his gang of Hizbul Momeen cadre and their endeavour to celebrate his girlfriend's birth day.

'Any questions.'- he asked as a matter of procedure in the army to be sure that everybody was clear about every aspect.

'Yes sir, one doubt'- Major Kishor; the senior most Company Commander, who used to take a bit of liberties with the Commanding Officer (CO), spoke up.

'Yes, go ahead please'- The Commanding Officer took deep breath and prepared himself for some would be"difficult question".

'Sir what if we catch "Laila" also along with Majnoo or only 'Laila' without Majnoo.'- He said with a mischievous smile on his face. Everyone had hearty laugh.

"At least you will not be allowed to keep her since you are already married. If you do that, I will get you court martialled. Rest all can think but they have to cajole the girl and convince her family to agree. No force is allowed in the matter of love. Military might does not work in the matter of heart, be very clear"- he said smilingly.

"Great experience narrated so eloquently"- Major Kishor pricked with short and sweet comment outwitting the boss.

Col Manav Singh; the CO had smiled to cover up being outwitted by his junior. Colonel Manav Singh was very jovial and always carried the team together. Everyone had hearty laugh on superb 'mischief' of the Company Commander.

As per plan my company was to cross the village without getting down from the vehicles, reach the far end of the village, get down, turn right towards the lake of Hokarsar and seal half extent of the bund and marry up with the Charlie Company; who were to seal rest half of the bund under the command of Major Kishor. We reached the village as per our plan. In the order of march Alpha and my company; that were Bravo, were to cross the village, reach the far end of the village without stopping, then turn left and right respectively and cover half extent of the village.

But as soon as we touched the close end of the village boundary, something very strange and unusual happened. Seeing our convoy, several women; who looked under extreme duress, signalled us to stop. We thought it was their tactics to stop or delay us from cordoning off the village as already anticipated and briefed by the Commanding Officer, there was likely presence of area commander of Hizbul Momeen along with his cronies. The women signalled us frantically, shouted something with their folded hand to beg; which could not be heard due to roar of engines of the vehicles. They beat their chest, raised arms and some of them cried.

Somewhere in my gut feeling it came that I should stop and find out what the problem was, but abandoned the idea realising; behind me were two more Companies, the Commanding Officer himself and his quick reaction team; the QRT. They had to stop, as per plan, almost at the same place where women were assembled and hence they would take care of everything; genuineness of reason for stopping, or a drama of deceit by the women staged on the instigation of the terrorists. I moved ahead tearing the thick curtain of falling snow.

It was a snowy-misty day of 29 December 1992. The sky was overcast with thick dark brown layers of clouds hovering over the village. The temperature was minus five-six degree Celsius gripping the entire Kashmir valley into severe cold wave. At places it was snowing or raining and at places readying to snow. Most of the areas were covered with thick layers of snow and black tarmac road was covered with thin layers of snow; thin because continuously due to plying of vehicles it was melting, rendering the road slippery and dangerous. All around it was looking white, like a large shroud; as if the nature knew what was in the offing and hence preparing in advance.

It was heavily snowing in the village of Gund Hassi Bhat. Light flaks of snow falling from the sky were creating 'smoke screen effect' and restricting the visibility something like in the riverine plains of north India during foggy weather. The flakes falling on water proof jackets covering thick layers of woollen worn by soldiers and melting due to body heat, were indicative of 'warmth' our men were still maintaining in the back drop of the 'cold' environment all around.

The vast wetland-cum-lake of Hokarsar was covered with thin layer of snow and was creating illusion of small mass land of Siberian plains except for the presence of leafless trees. The migratory birds that had travelled from far north; from the other side of the Greater Himalayas to save themselves from the killing winters of Siberia to 'holiday' in comparatively warm climate of Kashmir, were confused whether Siberian winter had followed them. The trees, mostly of poplar and willow, looked sad since the snow had forcibly mounted on their head, body, branches but not on leaves; the trees had already shed them out of fear, before onset of winter.

The village was abnormally calm. The activities were minimal; movements of villagers insignificant and invisible, movement of traffic on the road almost nil. All was contra indicative to take it on face value. Some houses on the outskirt of the village were locked, some abandoned even without locking. It looked something had forced them to close the home and shops in a huff to move away. These were clear indicators of militants being in the village. The villagers used to abandon the place where militants were present or wanted to do something drastic against the forces, to save themselves from the cross fire and/or retaliatory action of the armed forces. In anticipation we had briefed our men; the soldiers to be extra cautious and extremely vigilant. I was moving fast while placing stops and pickets, to marry up with the neighbouring Company commanded by Major Kishor.

The above calm was shattered by firing from the terrorists on our soldiers when they challenged them to stop. They had jumped into the lake with lightning speed while firing at us and stunning us for a moment. Our heavy volume of fire had no apparent impact on the escaping terrorists. They kept on running and jumped into the water. Suddenly I saw Major Kishor and his soldiers from Charlie Company bumping into us; axiomatic indication that the village had been sealed. In fact they were the one who were chasing the terrorists when they saw them running to escape out of the cordon. But, it looked; our targets had already slipped out of our cordon.

Actually, as we came to know later, the women who were trying to stop us were really under severe distress. They signalled Major Kishor and his Company too in similar but more frantic manner as they had done to my Company convoy. Concluding the same thing as I had concluded that this was likely to be entrapment for delaying our cordon at the behest and on instigation of the terrorists, Major Kishor also did not stop. Then women beat their chest, cried and begged for stopping and insisted for an audience. They lay themselves on the road to block the movement of convoy of Major Kishor; some grabbed the vehicle of the officer and got dragged in the process, in all-out effort to stop him and his soldiers. The officer signalled the entire convoy to stop, as it was planned to stop somewhere there only; not necessary where the women wanted, and came out fuming at their audacity.

But his entire paradigm had changed when he heard what they had to tell. The women fell on his feet and requested him to chase the terrorist immediately who were running away, seeing the army convoy, after abducting some youth from the village. The women, subsequently were joined by some men who had hid themselves out of fear of the terrorist, told him that the terrorists had forcibly taken their children; some even minors to convert them into 'Mujahids; the fighters for cause of religion'. They indicated the direction of their move; towards the bund.

Major Kishor instructed his JCOs to deploy the Company as per plan. He along with his team, immediately, chased the terrorist who were running towards the bund of Hokarsar Lake, in the south-west direction of the village. The terrorist had no inkling and so were the villagers; that the army actually had come to cordon off the same village. Instead they thought army was moving to some other place and by chance; with god's grace, it was passing through the area at the time of their need. The terrorists had never imagined that the other company; Bravo led by me, would already be there on the bund. The terrorists ran towards the bund to escape; only to get entrapped between my and Major Kishor's Company.

I ordered my MMG detachment to fire, who were not ready yet nay; not even laid the gun which takes some time. It was not their fault I had yet to decide their exact place of deployment which was to be on this bund somewhere. I ordered the Havaldar heading the detachment to deploy the gun immediately at appropriate place so as to cover the entire lake and fire ahead of them so that they were 'bracketed' between the wall of fire of the gun and us. While running behind the terrorists, I instructed my radio operator to pass the message to all that we had encountered the terrorists and that all should be alert. We challenged them to stop from swimming away, come back and surrender. But they did not look back and kept on swimming away.

They were still well within our range; in the range of personal small arms like AK-47, carbine, SLR and surely under the fire of Light Machine Gun; the LMG. Tactical deployment of MMG was a long term precaution; if they slipped away from the range of small arms. We; I and Major Kishor, ordered our soldiers to fire on them. They dipped in the water and started swimming underwater, sticking out their heads only to inhale and exhale, intermittently.

The MMGs of both the Companies were laid in the meantime. They started firing ahead of them. The terrorists, were scared for their dear life. They stopped, shouted, pleaded for mercy and raised their hands. They started moving with raised hands towards us shouting they wanted to surrender. We stopped firing. I told my soldiers to take proper positions with precaution. Major Kishor, being senior, automatically became spot commander for the detachment of both the Companies present there. That is how it happens in army, without fuss.

The terrorists were moving towards us very slowly but slyly, as if tired or injured. They came up neck deep, chest deep and then waist deep. Suddenly they all feigned as if slipped, then got up and rained bullets on us; all five of them, in an extremely co-ordinated manner and then started running-cum-swimming back away. It was replied by heavy volume of fire from us, as a result of spontaneous reaction. They had wished and calculated we were naïve. None of us was injured.All had taken due precaution; as professional soldiers are trained to take. But more it was God's grace and good luck because they were not poorly trained.

But almost all of terrorists were injured. We could have easily killed them and could have given them water burial but that was not the aim. We wanted to capture them alive for two reasons; not to destroy life if aim could be achieved without killing and to extract vital information; hence the hesitation in raining bullets to kill them. Their actions looked sluggish despite their all-out effort otherwise to still run or swim away. It looked as they were badly injured and loosing grip of the self. We stopped firing despite their trying to run away from us because we wanted them to come back.

We decided to open our MMGs which together could effectively cover up to a kilometre of range, so as to fire ahead of them deep in the lake; creating an impregnable wall of fire and making it impossible for them to move ahead. They were well trained militants to our luck. Yes to our luck, because they understood invincibility of the fire ahead which a novice might not have. Any move ahead was like voluntarily falling on the lap of death. The MMG is a very lethal weapon, they knew. When at its best, it can fire almost thousand bullets per minute. Once the ammunition belt is mounted, it launches incessant death flying all over; in the form of emanating bullets. Now they had only two options; surrender or sure death.

Now they turned back again; towards us, presumably to surrender. We waited for all the five but with more precautions. They swam towards us, stood on their feet and moved holding their weapons in their hands up above their head. One of them was in pain and looked as if he would collapse. He threw his weapon; no it fell from his hand due to loosened grip. He had collapsed; his hands saying 'Farewell to Arms'. Another one had collapsed; his weapon falling into the water and he floating his face down. They both struggled in semi-drowned position. They were already injured for sure but it was due to our first or second time retaliation; can't be said for sure. Due to freezing temperature, the blood was not oozing much. The third one, who looked youngest among them, could not bear this. He threw his weapon, cried for mercy and moved with empty raised hand for surrender followed by fourth. But we did not lower our guards. We remained watchfull.

The remaining one; the fifth one had not disclosed direction of his intention. He then was again about to be in waist deep water; a position ideal to fire. We warned him to throw his weapons before moving ahead; he did not. We warned him if he did not throw the weapon he would be killed; he did not. He was probably the Commander since he had stared at the two who had run to surrender and muttered something incomprehensible to us. He had decided to do '*harakiri*'. He let lose all ammunition in his magazine of AK-47 on us; spraying like water flowing out of fountain. All of us ducked, as a matter of instant reaction, not knowing who his target was. My heart pumped more blood all over, increasing the adrenalin level in the body. Then several assault rifles blazed, simultaneously and spontaneously by so many; all of us in the vicinity. He collapsed like mosquito shrinks after being 'Hit' by powerful pesticides; the grey matter disgorging from his skull like lava from a volcano.

Out of the two about-to-surrender terrorists; the youngest one, cried like a child. He jumped out of water and collapsed vertically on the bund in prostrate position; face down, showing a symbolic complete surrender. It was not yet sure whether he was injured. The other one, who had long beards; looked as if never shaved from the time of its sprouting, came out his hands up and expected to be arrested; his expression remorseless and body language defiant. Major Kishor ordered soldiers in the vicinity to arrest him, check for injuries, any weapon or grenade on him. He had a China made pistol; magazine fully loaded. He was disarmed immediately. He was lucky; no injuries. The terrorist in prostrate position was lifted by soldiers, checked for arms, ammunition and injuries. He was also lucky with no injuries only bruises. Deep water cover had saved them. Other two were not so lucky and one had refused to be lucky. Both the surrendered were tied with rope but held for some time before moving to a secured place.

We waited for some time to see if the terrorists in the water have any life left or they are dead or still pretending. No one can even pretend to be dead without oxygen. Their faces down for long dipped in water were a symbol of their departure from this world. A few men were desperate to fish them out and frantically requesting me to allow dragging them out. I told they might be feigning, wait and do not be desperate, life is precious. One of the NCOs, who was a boxer and dare devil type opined sarcastically:

'Sir, they have already started their journey to the *Jannat;* the heaven, to be in the company of, as they believe, virgins.

They were sure the virgins would be waiting for their arrival properly decked up in the most beautiful dresses. After all they have died fighting for 'the cause of Allah' in Jehad, as they claim or believe.'I told him not to make fun and have patience when its matter of life and death.

Hearing the firing for so long, the Commanding Officer who was not far, was extremely restless. He wanted to talk to either of us and frantically enquired as to what was happening from our radio operator. Though everything happened within a few minutes, it felt like hours for those away, including the Commanding Officer. Since both of us; the Company Commanders, remained badly preoccupied, we could not attend his call until now. All messages were through the radio operator. Now Major Kishor gave long brief to the Commanding Officer over radio in detail. He, as I heard, among other things informed:

"Three militants killed, two captured alive and search for their weapons still on in the water. Encounter over and it is safe now to move in." The Commanding Officer had begun his move towards us.

Major Kishor told me to do rest of the operation at this place. Major Kishor moved towards poplar grove along with the captured militants; who were tied and being taken by men under armed escort, in case they still tried some stunts.

After some time I told my selected men to enter in the water and fish out the bodies and the weapon of the terrorists. It was freezing and anyone who had entered into the water would have become defunct for rest of the operation. Even a few minutes exposer in this water may cause hypothermia. His clothes would be soaked in freezing water and he would have to remove all of the clothes to put on dry one. Hence they entered with minimal clothes on them so that residual could be put on after removing the wet one. It looked an act needing more courage than fighting the terrorists and facing the bullets. But our brave men were never found wanting. There were more volunteers than I could have permitted.

All the three bodies were fished out but no weapons retrieved from the water despite sufficient effort. The base of the lake was extremely marshy and weapons might have got embedded; sinking in to loose slush. More men volunteered for search of the weapons. A few were allowed to enter. Two AK-47 rifles of the terrorists, with two magazines each but hardly any ammunition left in them, were retrieved from the lake. So they had stopped firing not because they wanted to surrender, but were rendered helpless; without ammunition.

The environment was deeply wounded; like the terrorists. The roar of Kalashnikov, Light Machine Guns and Medium Machine Guns had shaken the air and frightened all. The pouring snow was looking like pall of gloom falling to embrace and cover all around. The ever barking dogs were nowhere to be seen. The chirping birds were hiding away at unknown places. The air smelling of gun powder would have been suffocating for many but was only too familiar to us. The water near the banks from where the bodies were retrieved had turned slushy, muddy, bloody and dirty; as if reflection of the grey matter spewed from the broken skull of one of the terrorists. My men looked anxious and exhausted but relieved, as if thinking; 'thanks God! It was none of us.'

I ordered my subordinate Commanders to readjust the pickets and form search parties. I told them to arrange for lighting fire at appropriate place so that the men who were drenched in freezing water could warm themselves and dry their cloth. My JCO informed me that I was also drenched up to my thigh and need to dry my clothes. My soldiers informed me that in the heightened environment I did not realize that I had jumped in the lake and moved quite ahead up to thigh deep to fire on them. I told them that I would dry my clothes once the Commanding Officer's visit was over who was about to arrive.

Suddenly I heard a long burst of AK-47 coming from the grove; from the place where the terrorist were taken to secure them with rope by anchoring in the tree. As a spontaneous reaction, I ran towards the grove thinking all kind of bad things like; some terrorists might be hiding there and they might have fired on Major Kishor and his group. With me ran a few of soldiers of my company. There I saw the bearded terrorist fallen flat; his body having several bullets pierced through. Before I could ask, I saw one of the soldiers bruised and being assisted by other soldiers to stand up and regain his composure.

'What happened sir?'- I asked furious looking Major Kishor.

'Bastard, a real mother f****r. He tried to snatch weapon from our Jawan and tried to run away. Real son of a bit**' -Major Kishor was fuming and unusually agitated. He was not able to gather words for time being and kept on looking at the terrorist's broken skull and the blood oozing from all over. One of senior Havaldars, who had also fired on the terrorist, told me that the terrorist tried to free himself by getting in to scuffle, tried to snatch the rifle and run away. He was over powered, fired upon and killed. It looked he was a *fidayeen;* a suicidal terrorist, who either wanted freedom or death but never in the custody of the army.

"But he was tied in a rope?" I wondered.

"Yes sir. But he was pleading to us to free him so that he could read his religious scripture in the memory of his departed friends. I was against freeing him but Saheb (Major Kishor) told us to free him to respect his religious sentiments and allow him to pray for his friends. He thought, after all, where the unarmed terrorist could go from our invincible cordon. The terrorist took out small thick polythene from his pocket, un-wrapped the book from it and started reading. We could never guess his nefarious design and perfidious intent. He suddenly grabbed our Jawan and tried to snatch his rifle. Despite the dare devilry and treachery of trust in the name of faith, he could not succeed. Then he violently pushed the

Jawan and tried to run away, we fired on him and he collapsed. It seems, despite our effort to keep him alive, he wanted to be killed."- The NCO narrated.

When caught, some always wanted to be killed. And last was among them.

"Trips (my nick name among my seniors) you want to kill the last one alive?"- Major Kishor asked me in fit of rage.

"You don't want to take him alive and interrogate?"- Came out the spontaneous, mechanical counter query on unexpected, impromptu question. I was sure he was not serious but I cocked my assault rifle and placed the muzzle on the temple of the lone surviving terrorist. Major Kishor moved away. It looked he did not want to see their faces; dead or living.

The young *'Mujahid'* became stone, lifeless before death; a statue. I had not seen any expression on any face like his. From pink it became red then pale and finally turned grey; as if entire blood had been sucked by vampires within a few seconds. His eye balls stopped moving waiting to take the shot at any moment. He even had no energy left to plead for mercy. For the first time I saw him properly. He was hardly twenty or in early twenties; young, medium built, fair but soiled top to bottom in mud. He had thick black coiled kinky hairs; uncommon in Kashmiris, which was now muddied and wet. Like most Kashmiris, he was not putting on Pheren but jeans and jacket with trendy sports shoes; good to run faster.

I removed my rifle from his temple without pressing the trigger and moved a bit aside. In his already drenched and frozen body there was no heat left. Unlike our bodies; which were emanating steam from the drenched areas, his was not. Suddenly I saw vapour emanating from his frozen pants in the groin area.

He had urinated.

After I moved a bit away he collapsed, as if death gave way to life sans vitality.

In the army everything goes simultaneously at different level by different individuals or among different groups; death and dance, sorrow and celebration. So was here; a group of men had prepared tea for all in the close purlieu. It was the best thing they could have done. The Commanding Officer had arrived and he was also offered tea. He was looking very happy and elated not only because we had gunned down dreaded terrorists of Hizbul Momeen but more because the feat was achieved without a single casualty to our side; not even an injury. He congratulated all of us and appreciated the tact and courage displayed in the eyes of death by us; the Company Commanders and the men. It was a miracle that despite so much of firing from the terrorist that also from such close range no one was injured or had died.

We reached the spot where dead bodies were kept. The Commanding Officer was taken aback to see only one survivor. He asked Major Kishor, "How come four are dead instead of three as informed by you? I have already informed the Brigade Commander that two are captured alive."

"How does it make a difference whether one is dead or all are dead sir? All are traitors, all are having war weapons, all picked up weapons against the sovereignty of India, all have vowed to disintegrate India and all have tried their best to kill us. All have waged *Jehad*, all think we are *Kafirs*; not worthy of existence on the earth. All are fighting for so called 'Independence'. What else is needed in their credentials to qualify for death? I am sure the Brigade Commander also won't want them to become 'state guests' who are fed on state's exchequer; Gushtaba, Pilauf, Biryani and Wazwan? I wish none of them were caught alive, to be a cause for abduction of innocent people, for exchange in lieu; a drama enacted in connivance with some Kashmiri politicians to release these traitors, whom we capture by spilling our blood and giving our life."

The Commanding Officer was stunned; never expecting such a reply. He tried to pacify and reconcile:

"It is not that way. I am thinking he may conclude something else."

"Why should he conclude sir? We do not do anything illegal or illegitimate. Circumstances dictate how we react on ground. He has also been a Company Commander and a Commanding Officer. He knows what happens on ground and what harsh realities are."

"OK. Well done"- The Commanding Officer didn't want to listen more and wanted to move ahead. He put his hand on the shoulder of Major Kishor and tried to pacify by touch.

I explained the rest to clear all the doubts:

"Sir, this particular terrorist was killed because he tried to snatch the rifle of the escorting *Jawan,* scuffled with him and tried to run away. He was a suicidal terrorist; a *fidayeen*. I guessed he never wanted to be in the military net while alive. He wanted to kill himself or get killed by us but after inflicting maximum damage on us. Had we not fired he would have run away and it wouldn't have been acceptable to the Brigade Commander or any one of us here. He was a fanatic. Just see what he has drawn on the holy book?"- I indicated to the drawing of AK-47 with bullets flowing from it and hitting a crowd of vermillion and sacred thread wearing men indicating, apparently, Kashmiri Brahmins but broadly all Hindus.

The lone surviving terrorist was in dazed state; unable to talk, unsure of his future, afraid; he would live or die. Rest all lay lifeless. The doctor, a Captain; our regimental medical officer also had come with the Commanding Officer. He checked all four of them lying on the ground.

"Dead"- he pronounced.

The Commanding Officer looked at the weapons of the terrorists, that they call 'Kalashnikov'; both the AK-47/56 assault rifles made in China, imported or smuggled by Pakistan and pushed into Kashmir along with the terrorists; that they call Mujahids. The Commanding Officer also spoke to the lone survivor, briefly.

All the terrorists were between the age group of 22-28 years; the youngest, who was surviving, was 22 and the eldest, who tried to snatch the weapon and was just killed, was 28 years. The lone surviving terrorist was also the highest educated among them and was a Kashmiri. He was in state of daze, looked bewildered and spoke incoherently. He was shivering badly; due to cold or fear or both, could not be said for sure. The doctor checked him and advised that he should be allowed to warm up by lighting fire to regain his physical strength and the doctor also injected and administered some medicine to control his blood pressure which had plummeted abnormally to dangerous level. When the doctor was administering the lifesaving drugs I teased him. We were room-mates and were good friends as well.

"So you have also become 'friend' of the 'terrorists' like me?" I teased him as many used to tease me for being empathetic to locals.

"I am under Hippocratic oath to save life. I will be friend to even enemies; including Pakistanis in the war zone, if they fall under our captivity in an injured or sick state. You can't do anything to me. I am doctor; trained to save life irrespective of whose life it is."- He shot down my sarcasm to death while giving life to the terrorist; charmingly and smilingly.

Besides medicine, the terrorist was given warmth near fire to save his life. After some time the surviving terrorist was better and disclosed more about him and all those killed and lined up. He also identified place to recover an UMG; Universal Machine Gun with belt drum.

'Three of the dead, including the one who was trying to snatch the rifles, are Kashmiris and fourth; the one who died the last in the water while fighting, is a Pakistani'- the survivor now identified.

"Who is the commander?"- I asked.

'The one who had died fighting in the water; the Pakistani'- he declared indicating to the last one died in the water.

After visit of the Commanding Officer, while moving away together from the grove where dead bodies were kept, Major Kishor smiled at the Commanding Officer reminding him of Laila and Majnu and our success to catch the later.

The CO disclosed:

'The owner of the house, where these terrorists had plonked themselves for food and alleged celebration had come to me and was falling on the feet. He was not tired of explaining how his enemies had associated his daughter with these terrorists, who forcibly used to enter his house and demand or snatch everything they wanted. He was telling they were nuisance. Nobody liked them but all were helpless. I pitied on him and did not bother much whether he was harbouring them or they had forcibly occupied his house and were demanding things for themselves. After all, I feel somewhere they; the local people are helpless. The parents of the boys, who were being taken by these terrorists, were equating us with angels; sent by the Almighty to save them. Today's operation was a great success. I appreciate all of you.'

The brigade headquarter was informed and police were called to take over the bodies for further disposal. We waited for the police to arrive and take over the dead bodies. I looked at the dead bodies. All were now covered with fresh, white and pure looking snow; as if on Almighty's order nature had sent the Qafan; the shroud. A few circular blood spots were visible on the thick layer of snowy shroud; indicating from where death had entered to snuff out the life. I became a bit philosophical thinking everyone will die one day but certainly in different circumstances. God's grace is equal and the same for all; who gets what is one's own destiny and doing. An Urdu couplet ran on the screen of my mind;

Tera Karam to aam hai Duniya ke vastey,

Ab kis ko kya mila ye muqaddar ki baat hai.

"Your (God's) grace is the same and equal for all; who gets what is his destiny (and doing)."

Later we had lunch and told men to have lunch and be ready to move back by 3.00 pm. The Commanding Officer ordered that the villagers should not be bothered for anything. The Commanding Officer opined that the information about the assembly of the terrorists was very accurate but reason was different. It was not celebration but abduction for new recruitment.

We moved back to our location with one addition; the surviving terrorist. He was detained and taken by us for further interrogation; which was no less revealing and interesting than the encounter. It was going to be longest interrogation, at least, for me.

In the evening I tuned 'Azad Kashmir Radio' (POK) and Voice of Kashmir (Pakistan). Whenever time permitted, I listened to their Evening News; a source of great entertainment, broadcast in very sweet voice in chaste Urdu, with best voice quality in the area. All India Radio and Radio Kashmir Srinagar were pathetic and poor cousins of their western competitor; in terms of quality: and in terms of lie and propaganda; a naïve child. Some believed the sympathisers of *Mujahids* and pro -*Azadi* forces who dominated the Srinagar Radio Station, had intentionally degraded the broadcast quality, to allow space for propaganda of Pakistan and POK broadcasters. The broadcast of 'Azad Kashmir Radio' (POK), if translated from Urdu into English went like this, convincingly:

"Our correspondent has reported that today Indian Army carried out cordon and search operation in village Gund Hassi Bhat of Badgam district of 'Gulam Kashmir' (meaning 'Enslaved Kashmir'; a name given by Pakistan to the area under Indian sovereignty). Five innocent youth, who had come to meet their relatives, were caught by the Indian Army. Three were shot dead in cold blood, one was beheaded. One youth was taken as hostage. A dozen of women were raped. In anger and outrage the women and children blocked the Srinagar-Gulmarg highway, women laid themselves on the road; not allowing military convoy to move. The Indian Military men dragged the women to clear the road by disrobing them publically and tossed the children aside."

I was sure, Goebbels; Hitler's propaganda minister, might have felt inferior if he had heard chicanery of these channels; converting the lies into truth and truth into lies so effortlessly.

****

Burial ground at the base of Hari Parbat. All terrorists/insurgents killed during military operation near Srinagar area were buried at this location. Many call them "martyrs". The board (only the line in English) reads:

"Lest you forget: we gave our today for tomorrow of yours".

Chapter 2

Love, Loss and Illusion

Then, at last, came the third detainee for interrogation; the twenty two year old lone survivor among five hard core terrorists. Four out of five were killed by us in a deadly encounter two days back in the village Gund Hassi Bhat. I was eager to talk to the lone survivor, beyond completing the formalities of filling the interrogation report, to understand his persona. I was interested to peep into the psyche of the terrorist, his inspirations and the causes that he perceived to be justifiable-reasons for becoming a terrorist. After regaining the composure from temporary comatose, during informal interaction on the day of encounter, he had sounded interesting. Although he was looking different but I could instantly recognise him due to his thick black curly hairs, oval face, sharp and comparatively short nose.

He was allowed to have bath hence looked relatively happy, lively, smart and clean; no muddy clothes, no soiled hair, cleaner teeth, clean shaved face and fairer complexion.

But he was putting on the same cloths; the royal blue jacket and sky blue jeans. Despite washing, stains of mud and blood remained on them. The blood of his fellow terrorists, who had since died in the encounter, had fallen on his jacket. Pair of sports shoes in his feet was the same. He wished me 'good morning sir' in English and displayed effortful faint smile, as if doing everything only to ensure I am not displeased. I smiled back and enquired how he was doing now. Sensing he had not recognised me, while adjusting my papers on the table, I asked,

"Have you seen me before?"

He looked at me carefully and then said, 'No sir'

I was puzzled how could he forget me; his aborted death. I reminded him of the moment when I had placed the muzzle of my rifle on his temple when he was brought near four dead bodies of his colleagues. Remembering those moments he shuddered, then looked at me again and said hiding deep anger and despise for me:

"I remember the incident but don't recognise your face sir. During those moments, I was blank; my brain was not working."- he said truthfully or to show passive contempt to me, could not have been ascertained.

I told him to sit down on the ground close to my chair, as other two before him had done. To make him mentally comfortable, I asked if someone from his family did not visit and whether they did not give him some additional clothing: since, as I could see, he was putting on the same old clothes. His reply was in negative. He told me that our soldiers were kind enough to give him soap and allowed him to wash his clothes, alternately, in two days. He also thanked me and my men for providing him warm water in icy winter to have bath today.

I was surprised because invariably members of the family of the detainees used to visit our location, as soon as they had come to know about the detention bringing in additional clothes, soap, shampoo and other articles of essential needs. At times these articles were allowed to be handed over and at times denied. The details of detainees were informed to the village-head of Gund Hassi Bhat, besides police and other concerned civil authorities. He told me, there was no one in his family, most likely a lie. It neither was important for me, officially, to verify his statement nor was I interested. But at individual level he had aroused tremendous interest in me due to the past circumstances under which we had caught him, a few words he had spoken and the contents of the items I had recovered from him.

That day in the morning, after two days of Gund Hassi Bhat operation, I was instructed to write the interrogation report of three detainees. Among them one was from the Gund Hassi Bhat operation and two were from some other operations. The report was a pre-requisite for handing over the detainees/ terrorists to the police for further disposal. The adjutant gave me small chits about all the three, separately, mentioning vital but very few details about them to be filled in the interrogation report.

Based on interrogation, confession and material evidence, all were to be classified 'RED'; hard core terrorist. "RED"(assumed) was for possessing prohibited arms and ammunition, waging war against the state, indulging in secessionist activities, carrying out attack on the armed forces and committing other heinous crimes under IPC and/ or other applicable statute. Rest of the details were to be filled by questioning the detainee on the spot. Along with the Interrogation Report, the detainees were handed over to local police for prosecution/release. The report was written when the detainees were no more needed by the army or the maximum detention period permitted in the rule book was exhausted.

After getting brief from the adjutant, I had told my office

assistant; a combatant soldier, to inform the quarter guard commander to send the detainees under escort, one by one, in their order of seniority of detention. I told my office assistant to place a small table and chair in front of my office, in the open sun so that I could enjoy, bask and relax in the sun which was rare here due to tight schedule of operation and rare visibility of the sun during winters.

Ideally the report should have been written by the interrogators but it was given to me as 'load shedding' by my seniors to reduce their burden. The interrogation report consisted of all possible information about the terrorist like his name, address, education, training, organization, crimes committed, weapons possessed and recovered besides the most important aspect; his classification. The classification was done in colour code names based on evidence. If the detainee was found 'innocent' or still a 'suspect' or a 'terrorist', he was classified as; (let us assume the colour codes) 'green' or 'grey' or 'red' respectively. I was also given arduous task of going through the recovered and seized subversive material; posters, pamphlets, hand bills, photos, audio and video cassettes and translate them into English, particularly if these were in Urdu and Kashmiri. I used to do it with help from some knowledgeable and reliable sources including local people.

The first two detainees came one after the other. Their report similar to scores I had filled in the past. Their bio-data followed by terrorist organization they were affiliated with, their own position in the hierarchy, level of training, place of training; Indian Kashmir, POK or Pakistan, arms and ammunition recovered from them. In other column: route followed for egress and ingress, how he was brought in to militancy; voluntarily or forcibly, by conviction or coercion etc. The same story told by all of them, in same way that I had become conversant and familiar with the places of training camps in POK, as railway stations on my way to my home town; knowing beforehand which one would come next.

This terrorist was unique. Most surprising was that he was caught in encounter as a terrorist but still he was extremely critical of militancy, terrorism and Pakistan nay; even separatist leaders and their agenda of freedom and Jehad. He was not only Pakistan trained but well educated, spoke good Urdu/ Hindi and reasonably good English. I had seen he, in previous interactions with my colleagues, had displayed sharp intellect and understanding of the environment. After filling the usual columns I reached the column of 'material evidence' before 'classification' in to the category of 'green, grey or red'. The 'material evidence' column struck me, reminding of something unique I had recovered from him.

We had recovered a walk-man, a couple of cassettes on his identification, besides the Universal Machine Gun (something like our MMG but not part of Indian Army's arsenal) from him; after he had recovered from temporary comatose that day. Assuming the cassettes to be some propaganda or subversive material, I went through them and enjoyed. It contained self-recorded (copied) Ghazals and songs of assorted singers. Among them most voices were known to me; Ghulam Ali, Jagjit Singh and Chitra Singh, Begum Akhtar, some others unidentifiable, may be some-not-so famous artists of Kashmir or Pakistan; but all were mesmerising. Since I was very fond of Ghazals and so were a few of my colleagues, it multiplied my interest in him.

Before filling these two important columns of Material Evidence and Classification, I thought of searching his 'heart and mind'. Hence I prodded about his choice of Ghazals; as we both were of almost same age group and had a lot in common including some of the singers. Captain Shaant Singh, one of my seniors was also very fond of Ghazals of Jagjit Singh and Chitra Singh. One of Captain Shaant Singh's choicest Ghazals I had discovered in this cassette also. He repeatedly played Chitra's one Ghazal several times in a day so much that it got automatically imprinted in my memory without effort since his room was adjacent to mine and dividing barrier;

a plywood wall, was as fragile as the Ghazal itself. Most of us were bachelors, staying in field conditions with minimal formalities. Captain Shaant Singh was in love with a girl back in his home town in mainland and wanted to marry her but there were hurdles in the way which made him very touchy. Senior Officers used to tease him:

"Captain change yourself, else you will also be burnt with the 'house'"- referring to his frequently played Ghazal sung by Chitra Singh which went thus:

Kabhi to khul ke baras abr-e-meharbaa`n ki tarah,

Mera wazood hai jaltey huye makaa`n ki tarah

Mai ek khwaa`b sahi, aap ki amaa`nat hoon.

Mujhe sambhal ke rakhiyega, jism-o-jaa `n ki tarah.

As I understand, it could be translated like this;

"Someday (at least one day) pour like a generous cloud

(As) My existence is like a burning house

May be I am only a dream, but I am your possession

Keep me secured, like your own 'being' and emotion."

Keeping in mind his cassette, I thought of starting with an emotional and curious question. Abruptly and without reference to the cassette I asked him smilingly: "So who is your 'Amaa`nat; possession' and where does she stay?

He was taken aback and could not clearly gauge what the question was and gave a blank and fearful look as if he had missed some important question of the interrogating officer.

"I have nothing left with me sir. I have handed over everything to you?" he said defensively.

'But someone requests you to keep her like your own Jism-o-jaan; body and soul?'- I added to his amazement.

After searching his brain thoroughly and my face blinkingly he shuddered but could not find a word to respond.

When I told him the reference, the cassettes and its content his face blushed like a young bride's face when her veil fallen off unexpectedly in the crowd. Trying to gain composure he smiled, looked hugely relieved, became emotional and shyly told me that it was given by his girlfriend who had since been moved out of the valley for further studies. He disclosed that from the moment her parents came to know about his disappearance, they concluded the obvious; that most likely he had gone across for training to become a Mujahid. Hurriedly they packed her up, sent her to undisclosed city in mainland India so that her connections with him were permanently snapped and nobody could relate her with him.

"It is 'Shakespearean tragedy' for you. You have lost both the worlds: the 'love world': the girlfriend and 'chosen world'; Mujahid-friends?"- I prodded.

His eyes moistened; for loss of 'girl friend or 'Mujahid friend' couldn't have been ascertained.

'If I tell you the truth of relations about people whom you are calling my 'friends' you will not believe me sir'-He said in a sad and broken tone.

Uncaring about sincerity of his statement, I prodded him by saying that he must be missing the company of his friends, who were now in the *Jannat*; the heaven, in the company of soft touching , delicate, young *Hoors*; the beautiful virgins since, as they believed, they died fighting for the cause of 'Allah' and accordingly, they might have been rewarded. In contrast he had a bad luck and had to sit close to a 'macho' like me.

He became serious, his eyes and irises widened and said;

"Sir, kindly forgive me for saying so but do not relate their act with cause of 'Allah'. I believe dying for cause of Allah will surely take one to the *Jannat*. I do believe in the theory of *Hoors* and *Jannat*. But they will never be in the *Jannat* for the acts they did. I am grateful to the Allah for gift of life and thankful to you for rescuing me from those monsters. They were not human but beasts; that have destroyed my life."- He wanted to say more but, it looked, he stopped; thinking long sentence might look sermonic and annoy me.

I was taken aback since I felt he was moving on the wild path, very different from usual pleas by most of the terrorists caught by us. All follow the same path of blaming it on someone else for them joining the insurgency. But he was hugely different; he was calling his ex-colleague beasts.

'Don't you consider it disgraceful to call your friends of yesterday demons and beasts; with whom you wined, dined, danced, fought and were caught for the same cause of "Azadi" and "Jehad". I retorted to touch his nerves.

"Sir, you have reasons to say what you have said but I am different. I do not drink. I am blaming no one like others but myself for being a fool. I am a victim of my own poor judgement. Joining militancy was my own choice but leaving it was beyond my choice. By the time I realised it was too late I was already in the net; on the path of no return."

I was surprised, not on his revelations but his frankness. I did not want to say anything but his silence left me with no choice. By past experience I had learnt that they used different techniques to befool the interrogators. Contrary to my gut feeling I tried to snub him:

"This story churning may be new for you but I have heard it several times and listen to every second day. You plant IEDs to kill army men and security forces; you kill anybody who is opposed to your idea of 'Jehad' and 'Azadi', you all did your best to kill us just two days back. You recruit youth forcefully to take across and get them trained, you carry out extortion and killing at will, you rape hapless girls and extort money from their family; all in the name of *Azadi* and *Jehad*. But when under the net of the security forces, you start blaming someone else for your act and plead helplessness to get empathy and leniency in your treatment".

He sensed my disgust and contempt for such explanation that his words have generated. He turned his eyes from my face to the closest point on ground. I continued-

"Now you will tell me that you were indoctrinated and intoxicated in fundamentalist-ideology by Maulvis, Pakistani Military men in civvies in the name of *Azadi* and *Jehad* during your training in POK and that you were shown videos and given lectures to become a Mujahid, fight for religion; which is in danger and fight for *Azadi*. You will also tell me that you were forced by agents of ISI against your will to become a Mujahid."

"No sir, I will not tell you all that. I, with extreme enthusiasm, excitement and zeal had voluntarily gone across, against wishes of my family. But what I saw in the training camps created repulsion and revulsion in me."

I was further surprised to discover enough courage in him to disrupt an army officer. I knew it was not audacity but somewhere his courage of conviction and my openness that had invigorated him to say something. He continued-

"I could never get convinced what they tried to teach me in the backdrop of their character and act. Within a few days of my stay in the training camp at POK, I was disillusioned and started disliking their theory of *Jehad*, their doctrine of *Azadi* and their utopia of 'puritan' state. But the most I hated was their character, nay; their characterlessness and their falsehood. Today I could gather courage to say all this because I know my worst is behind me. Now anything will be better only."

"It sounds bizarre when I remember that you were caught with them firing on us and now telling me something contrary. What made you so angry about them?"

My words made him a bit hesitant but after some time he continued-

"Sir, I have been ruined. I lost my family, my studies were disrupted. I lost precious three years of my life; which

I want to forget that they ever existed in my life. By now I would have completed my post-graduation; most likely in English Literature."- His throat choked with emotions and tears rolling down his cheeks. I showed interest in his words by aptly looking at him with sufficient doubt about sincerity of his statement.

"How strange and unbelievable it is? You along with other four fired on us and tried your best to kill all of us. You all emptied your magazines and now you are telling me that you have been ruined"- I asked with a bit of surprise.

"Sir, I was helpless in the company of those demons. Had I not pretended to fire on you all, I would have been killed by them. But believe me sir, I had fired very few bullets and that also aiming none; it was above in the open sky. If you would have retrieved my rifle from the lake you could have seen it." He tried to justify his claim by indicating proof of his action and intention.

It was difficult to verify what he said. Moreover it had no value operationally. As it is, we suspected some of the rifles and magazine could not be retrieved due to depth of water, slush and sub-zero temperature of the lake.

"So you had shown 'mercy' on us by sparing our life?" I took deep breathe while asking.

"You had shown mercy on me, sir. What mercy I could have showered on you? You could have killed me but you did not. I am grateful to Allah for giving me new life. I am grateful to you all for keeping me alive. I was fed up of that life, their company, their activity, their conduct and behaviour, which was very humiliating toward me. They were epitomes of the ills; a human being can be trapped in. They extracted and extorted money from our own people; the villagers and troubled them with all kind of hassles. They forced people to cook for them in the mid of the night by waking them up at gun point. They raped girls and no one had guts to resist them. If someone tried to reason with them, they cited Maulvis and their explanation that a Mujahid is entitled to any thing he desires and that no one can deny them. They killed anyone who resisted them and invariably the reason was not ideological but personal. If they had grudge with someone before becoming Mujahid they would take revenge by the gun they had brought in from Pakistan, even if the target is a Muslim. What is Jehad, what is religion and who is a Muslim; they never understood? Their understanding of all the three was a perversion. The Hizbul Mujahideen cadres snatched our guns and killed some of our cadre only because they thought we were Shias. The fight of freedom is fraught with internal trivial fights. The life is not worth giving for such a cause. But my realization was very late."

He wiped his tears from his eyes and cleaned his flowing nose from thick hanky and paused to take deep breath; which was forced by bodily need due to his continuous sob.

"What was strange in their character that made you antagonist of the very ideology you had dedicated your life to?"- I asked him to solve my puzzle.

"Sir, in 1989-90 there was a rage about 'Azadi.' After their training in Pakistan, thousands of Mujahids with their weapons had entered Kashmir valley. They openly displayed their weapons and fired at will. The existence of government of India was limited within their office premises and writ of police or CRPF only within their barracks or within their post. Army was not called in till then. The Mujahids had decided to declare 26 January 1990 as the date of declaration of 'Independence' from India and preparations were going on in that direction. Selective killings of Pundits had become routine matter. Pundits were leaving valley in hordes; most of them without displaying any sign that they were leaving it forever.

Almost all Kashmiris thought now they were going to become Independent. The pro-Indian people also started rethinking their loyalty to India. Those who were not in favour of secession from India were afraid that if Kashmir became independent, they would be considered 'traitors' and might be killed or persecuted or ill-treated. Everyone wanted to be more loyal than the rest with the Mujahids. That was from where the mad rush had started. Most of the youth were dreaming to be part of 'Jehad'. The stories told by Mujahids were so fascinating that any youth would have loved to be part of the folklore. I, contrary to advice of my mother and family, was frenzied with the fever of freedom, and one day sneaked away from home to be part of the youth who were going to Pakistan for training."

"How did you go across? Who assisted you?" I asked just to allow him to continue.

"There was no problem going across those days. Many Kashmiris were part of ISI network who initially selected and latter facilitated recruitment of youth for Jehad. Anybody could opt to become Mujahid. One of the bakers known to me already had come back from Pakistan with Kalashnikov after receiving training. He was treated as an angel. Every one visited his place to pay obeisance. I was impressed and he was one who facilitated my move across."

He continued-"One day without informing any one at home, I left for Srinagar early in the morning on the pretext of going to the University to obtain some information for my further admission in undergraduate classes. I reached Srinagar and roamed around at the old bus stand, as told by my contact and waited for someone to come and accost me. I was told that the agent would not take my name but name of the Mujahid who was sponsoring me. Accordingly one middle aged person approached me and whispered the name of the Mujahid. I said in affirmation. He told me to follow him."

"It was late morning of Oct 1989. I was led in a stationary mini bus in a corner. I felt good when I entered since the bus was almost full with all young men. I sat in the rear seat and looked trying to glance over the enthusiasts. Slowly a sense of guilt started gripping me, particularly for not informing my mother. She would go mad, not finding me around. She might guess in wilderness including that I might have been killed by security forces. My inner conflict continued. The bus started moving towards Baramulla. With the increased speed of the bus my sentiments also accelerated. I felt giddiness and thought of getting down, but it was a bit late. Slowly, I became fearful when I realised there was unusual calm in the bus despite all young men between 16-25 years of age sitting there.

Soon I realised, the unsuspecting men who had accosted me were not as simple as I had thought. Their activities and gestures were highly frightening. I shivered within, not sure what I had done was right or wrong. I started having second thought. I tried to get down first at Pattan followed by several attempts at whatever stops came by pretending that I needed to urgently go to toilet and that I had no change of heart and nothing was abnormal but they were smarter than I. They knew such change of heart was common among youth, at one point of time or the other, very early or a bit late. Whenever I requested them to allow me to go to the toilet, they told me to hold it until we reached Baramulla because it was a nonstop bus and other passengers would be unduly troubled."

The story was interrupted by my office assistant, who intervened to ask where I needed soup or tea. Out of civility I asked my sitting companion the same question. He perceived the courtesy was more than enough and he did not cross the line of having soup or tea with his captors, though I had asked him genuinely and wanted to share. He thanked me and politely refused saying he was honoured merely by my offer. I did not deem it right to have anything when someone was sitting and hence told the office assistant not to bring anything.

He resumed his narration;

"Crossing a few check posts after scanning and frisking, the bus reached Baramulla but did not stop there at the bus stop. It was taken to a diversion at a secluded place ahead of Baramulla. We all were told to de-board the bus and immediately taken in a car having curtains so that we were not able to see where we were heading for. At the halt we were given lunch and told to go to sleep until evening. In the evening we were served rice with vegetables as dinner and in the late night taken in a vehicle to unknown destination. After a few hours' drive, we were told to get down. It was late night and was dark all around. Only shining thing was freshly fallen snow on the ridges. It was very frightening"- He paused.

"Except the driver and co-driver; who were agents, rest four of us were alike; recruits for Jehad; with or without our consent. We were not allowed to talk to each other until we had reached the training camp in POK. The journey was similar to detective stories of fictional novels and we were handed over like commodities from one to the other agent; that they called guides. We were given dry eatables, some Pakistani currency to be used in case of separation from the group due to one or other reason, and a code word; to be told to the guide on other side of the LOC for identification. We were also indicated the locations of Indian Army posts and educated how to bypass them through thick forests of coniferous trees and under growth of more than 10-12 feet grass and fern. After staying for three-four hours in a vacant shepherd-hut, we were led by a guide to cross the LOC. On the way I was so tired and afraid that I felt as if I would freeze and not move. The guide terrified me by reminding that if I did not move, I would be caught by Indian soldiers and then I would be tortured beyond imagination. Only fear kept me mobile and alive in those treacherous terrains and hells' winds"

"OK"- I said just to allow him to continue. His way of description was quite captivating. His way of revealing the secrets was very enchanting, style engaging and body language and gesture conveyed sincerity of emotions. His Urdu was almost Hindi and easy to understand mixed with most appropriate words from English. He was proving to be a great communicator.

"The environment in the training camps was completely alien and nothing 'Kashmiri' except a few things like; the climate, terrain, topography and of course: the youth around; most of whom were from lower middle or lowest strata of Kashmiri society."

"Were they volunteers like you or abducted."- I showed curiosity.

"Most of them were volunteers who were motivated by some trained Mujahid or agents; mostly Kashmiris from this side of Kashmir. However, most of the trainees were barely literate or semi-literate. There were very few who could comprehend correctly anything taught to them beyond weapon training."

"What else was taught?"

"Besides small arms training which consisted of firing, opening and reassembling the Kalashnikov; IED fabrication, planting and remote activation of explosives, physical training and tactics were also taught. However, maximum time was dedicated to motivate and indoctrinate the recruits about the freedom and holy war, or in their word: 'Azadi' and 'Jehad'. Two things were most emphasised: 'Freedom' from the 'Hindu' occupation and 'atrocities on Muslims' in India. Jews and Hindus were painted as the worst enemies of Islam and Muslims. Videos and films were shown about the atrocities on Muslims all over the world and the cadre was warned that if they did not prepare to fight for their religion it would be eliminated. We were shown videos of Palestine and how they were fighting for their freedom."

"How was it related to India when no one is doing anything to vacate Kashmir from Muslims? Rather Hindus; several lakh Kashmiri Pundits have been driven away en-masse from their mother land of several thousand years by terrorists who are exclusively Muslims, How was it relevant, at least, in the context of Kashmir."- I asked to understand the relevance.

"It has nothing to do when you see from Indian context but for them it is not limited to 'Azadi' it is beyond; it is the 'Jehad'."- He gave short answer and left it unexplained.

"How"- I quipped.

"Sir, it is like this. One day one strict looking religious person with long beard and Afghan type dress and head gear came and explained us the value of Jehad. He described in detail why Jehad is important. In his opinion, had there not been concept of 'Jehad'; there would not have been 'the true religion'; Islam itself, because Arab Pagans who were something like Hindus only, tried to destroy it before its spread. Even if it existed it would have been only in the deserts of Saudi Arabia. He described in detail how the 'faithful' spread the 'true faith' among Persians by destroying their 'rotten culture of worshiping fire', how they eliminated or converted 'non-believers' from Persia. And see today, he described, Iran is a Vibrant Islamic country. Then it is 'Jehad' which created a race like Afghans, else they were also 'Idol worshipers' and meek; part of Hindu-Buddhist cult. Then Division of 'Hindu India' and carving of a Islamic country of Pakistan, in his opinion was also a part of 'Jehad', which further extended boundaries of Islam and shrank the 'non-believers'. Now further we have to extend the boundaries closer to the coasts of Indian Ocean and finally 'drown' the 'Kafirs'; non-believers, in the ocean. We, a few chosen and educated among the trainees were shown the maps depicting graphically how Islam had spread gradually in the sub-continent."

"And the most important thing was that most of the 'Mujahids' went to sleep during his long lecture, since, as I guess, either they were not interested in all such theories or didn't understand."- He looked up on my face to emphasise this point.

"Very nice and fascinating story it is! It should make you proud as a Muslim. Why you have grudges against them?"- I asked hiding my disbelief of what he claimed to have been taught. It was amazing to listen to his revelations and his understanding of the history. Arabs were Hindus before advent of Islam was news and a new knowledge to me.

"I would have also been convinced but for the truth I saw in them. During day time many of them were devout Muslims, puritans with flowing beard; five times Namaaz a day. But during night, they were more liberal than liberals. Not all but some of them were exactly opposite what they taught. A few of us were privy to their private life, I was one of them; cursed to see and be part of all. They watched blue films, drank and listened to vulgar music. Women were not allowed in the camps and they compensated their lust of sex from boys. The life was hell for me and a few like me who would never disclose what they went through for fear of shame. They knew nobody would have believed their version, and their disclosures would be taken as 'defamation' and they would be decimated by the Mujahids roaming around."

"And this was exactly what made me to hate the group I was put into. I wanted to get rid of that life so that I could be relieved of the bondage. I doubt that even you will believe what I am telling you."- He removed his focus from my face and looked down.

I had heard many stories but not like his. Most of terrorists were not so forthcoming; at least never spoke badly and defamatory about their mentors' character. Lot many questions came to my mind but did not ask since I didn't want to go into irrelevant details. However, I was still inquisitive about his hate for the group he was part of.

"But that was in POK during your training. Why did you want to be away from your companions who were killed by us?"-I was looking for some strand to solve the puzzle.

"One among the killed was a Pakistani from tribal areas of North West Frontier Province. He was very disdainful of Kashmiris and talked derogatory thing about Kashmiri people in general and about me in particular. He always ridiculed me to be 'girlish and meek with low fighting spirit'. He used to ridicule me by saying that I was shrewd, intelligent like pundits from whom my forefathers; Butts converted to, and

I carried their other qualities as well; timid, having no spirit to fight, unduly tolerant but haughty and arrogant about education. He often said our genes needed to be changed to make us fighters like Pakistanis and Afghanis; the Pathans, the Pakhtuns and the Punjabis. Such words generated a very deep sense of hurt in me. I started disliking them and wanted to get rid of them and their activities. But had I tried it out-rightly and directly, I would have been killed the moment they would have come to know about my thoughts. So I strongly and effort fully pretended to be with them; with my body, soul, emotion, idea and intellect."

"Sir, the mess Havaldar has sent the message that all the officers have reached officers mess and are waiting for you for lunch."- My office assistant informed me, disrupting my most interesting interaction with a Pakistan trained militant under our captivity.

I had heard some of these things from a few previously captured terrorists also but neither they were able to communicate so well nor in so much of detail. But most revealing and striking was his revulsion and reasons for hate to the extent of wishing them to be killed. A genre of 'Jehadis' was in revolt against their mentors; their activities, their preaching and their disdain for race of Kashmiris. I was realizing how 'typifying' can be treacherous and self-deceptive, how it can be false and paradoxical. I knew Kashmiris were no way poor fighters. His story was touching; a story of lost opportunities, a story of disillusion, a story of broken love, a story of transgression of personal choices, a story of sexual exploitation and a story symbolic of destruction of a generation.

I had all the details which I had to fill in the interrogation form. Everything what he had told me just now had no place in the form. I wrote small gist of it all. But still I thought of asking him whether he had told all this to the previous interrogators; my seniors.

"Did you tell this during interrogation?"

"I have told them briefly. But what is the point telling them sir? Will they believe it? They were asking only about weapons, training, my subversive participation etc. Since you asked me and gave me a long audience I told you my tragedy; tragedy of a person whom you call a terrorist and they call a Mujahid." He said while trying to gain his composure.

Then suddenly he asked me with enthusiasm and hope.

"Sir, Can you do a favour to me by returning my cassettes?"

"Sure. You will get them through the guard commander along with the walk-man and other belongings of yours at the time of your release from us. They are your '*Amaanat*; possession' and you must keep them 'close to your jism-o-jaan; body and soul'-as said in the Ghazal"- I assured him smilingly referring to the Ghazals and its contents.

"I am so thankful to you sir and I will never forget you in my life; for sparing my life, listening to my tragedy and for returning my 'Amaanat'; my girlfriend's only gift left with me, my invaluable memory. Else my life is really a burning house and it may get destroyed any moment"- His throat choked.

"But why didn't you tell your story to someone earlier? – I asked.

"Muh ki ba`at sune har koi, dil ke dard ko jaane kaun

Aa`wazon ke baa`zaron mein, Khamosi pahchaa`ne kaun."

(Everyone listens to what mouth says, but who would understand the pain of the heart?

In the market place of high pitch voices, who would recognize the pain of silence?)

I tried to figure out these already heard lines. Yes, this was also part of the Ghazals which he had in his cassette. I remembered it was part of Nida Fazli's composition in some serial on TV.

Thereafter he kept quiet. He was truthful or deceitful was extremely difficult to establish but he had touched a chord in my heart. I felt even if he was not truthful, he had told a true story of some one else. At personal level he had created some empathy in me for himself. I wanted to talk to him longer but could not. The CO and other officers were waiting in the officers' mess for me. For interrogation report nothing more was needed. I gestured the sentry to take him back to the cell, with a strange feeling; unclear why the order of taking him away was difficult to give.

It was his destiny. I was deeply pained to see beautiful young life getting destroyed this way. I filled the remaining two columns of the form.

Material evidence: UMG; 01, Magazines drum; 01, Ammunition; 135 live rounds.

Classification: RED

Writing the last one word "RED" would be so difficult in this case—I had never thought in my life. I had written it so many times so easily in the past.

I saw a young, educated, intelligent, bright boy being taken to cell of confinement. I collected all my papers, placed in the file and handed over to my assistant to send it across to the adjutant's office.

I moved towards officers' mess alone on foot in deep contemplation; how complicated is the life and the world, every individual is an interesting story, has a whole lot of emotions to part, a whole lot of pain to share. I remembered their encounter, their firing on us, their death and his survival; by skin of the teeth, my placing of cocked rifle on his temple, his urination, his fainting, his cassettes, his Ghazals, his drift from his girlfriend, her shifting, his broken contacts, his training, his disdain and his dreams. I realised the fallacy of generalisation. I assured myself; all is not exclusively black or white: at least Kashmir is not a dichotomy; even at the extremities of a terrorist and a military man. And certainly not at emotional and intellectual level. There is so much common; our Ghazals, our emotions, our love, our loss, our pain, our illusions and a lot which many know but very few accept and say.

****

Yeh fiza aaj Khamosh hai kyon?
Har jarre ko akhir hosh hai kyon?
Ya ham hi kisi ke ho na sake,
ya koi hamara ho na sakaa.
Maujen to hamari ho na sakin,
Toofan bhi hamara ho na sakaa.

Why is the air still?
Why every particle is conscious?
Is it that I could not be of someone?
Or someone could not be mine?
(I knew) The waves were never mine
Even typhoons could not be mine.
From 'Gunaaho Ka Devta' a novel written by
Dr Dharmveer Bharti

****

Chapter 3

A Grand Mother's Questions

When a young sepoy informed me about apprehension of a male in a female's attire, I felt as amused as curious. He was breathless, I guess, more due to curiosity, the apprehension had aroused than exertion of running. It was not difficult to conclude that the man caught was a suspected militant else why would he hide in a woman's attire and impersonate. It was obvious that something was seriously fussy about entire episode. He needed to be interrogated thoroughly. While moving towards the 'cross-dresser' several thoughts came to my mind and I wondered about ingenuity of the militants to invent the strange ways of hiding. It also perplexed me to think about uprising since convincing reasons were yet to be found, at least by me.

It was in a remote village of district Badgam. The village was isolated and surrounded by thick vegetation and trees. In close vicinity there were no other villages except a tiny hamlet across the orchard which, we were informed, was mostly inhabited by Shia Muslims. Hence, it was presumed, chances of getting 'catch' (militants, arms or ammunition) were scarce. It had been a general perception and assumption that Shia Muslims were not involved or less involved in militancy. But nothing was a general rule in the valley. There are so many shades; like a rainbow. I had been coming across people within the valley, including Muslims, who were dead against the insurgency; the senseless bloodshed, and even Azadi and Jehad.

Today was an operation ordered by the Brigade headquarters; more for area domination than with hope of catching some militants. We were hopeful even against our own assessment, presuming, we would not return empty handed. Otherwise also, our western neighbour across the LOC had pumped in so much of illegal and lethal war material that if we placed our hands anywhere, we were certain to get some weapon and ammunition. If not arms and ammunition, subversive and hateful literature against Hindus or India, were a possible catch. We all reached the location within pre-planned timings with only two out of the four companies participating. The Commanding Officer's crack team: QRT was also part of operation since the Commanding Officer had decided to supervise the operation himself.

The village was comparatively small, away from the urban centre; unkempt, neglected, dusty and under developed with extremely low literacy. Unlike most of our operations, which were planned during night and executed before dawn, it was planned before noon and executed in the afternoon after lunch. This was one more reason that most of us were at our best of agility and energy; impact of full night sleep, which otherwise was rare.

Beautiful serene rural landscape had increased my vitality. I was exuberating with energy and enthusiasm. We announced through our public address system, which was always carried by QRT, that all men above 16 and below 70 years of age should get congregated at the school building. The school building was as small and dilapidated as the village. There were very few men who gathered because most of them already were out for work to Badgam or to Srinagar; as carpenters, mason, welder etc. Some of them had gone to sell their articles like; vegetables, fruit, maize, corn, etc.

Villagers started gathering at the school building; hardly 50-60 people. Children of all ages hanged around the congregation with curiosity. This village, with scarce population and poor connectivity had very few military operations, contrary to villages well connected and close to the cities. Before starting search in my area of responsibility; which was half of the village but still very small, I thought to have a look all around and at the place of congregation. It was more to be familiar with place and quench my curiosity of talking to cross section of people and less to have anything to do with the congregation. Because to take care of the crowd there were other set of people.

I always was eager to interact with people; educated or uneducated, rich or poor, professionals or daily wagers, old or young, to understand their mind set, to know why this insurgency, when the nation and the constitution has given them so much, has bestowed much more than one can ask for. The nation has given complete religious freedom nay special rights and privileges as minorities, full political right without discrimination, doles of grants and funds in the name of development cutting from the share of mainland states. The state of Jammu and Kashmir has special status in our constitution. Then why was this hostility and insurgency?

There are states much poorer than Kashmir region or the entire state of Jammu and Kashmir. In fact by any parameter of wealth measurement, Kashmir is far better off than many states like Bihar, UP, Rajasthan, MP, Odisha, Chhattisgarh, etc. I always was eager to understand why they carry a sense of victimhood despite equal rights, nay; special rights and status, and despite soft treatment, hitherto, given to them. Hence I always wanted to talk to the people of all strata of the society.

When I reached the place of congregation, almost all children looked at me. Not because I was something special, but because I was another addition of strange people in their village; with some strange attractions like a radio operator accompanying me with a big wireless set on his back with high extendable antenna mounted on it, two three scouts with bullet proof jackets on, and AK-47 in hand. Many children smiled at me innocently; hardly knowing or understanding the real reason as to why this cordon and why this search. I doubted they ever understood real reasons for our arrival at and departure from their village.

Children, who looked dirty; un-bathed, unclean with blowing nose, dried snots and flaked boogers, soiled and unkempt hairs, wearing old and new Pheren, overused shoes with or without socks. Due to cold, their faces were dry with scaled skin but still pink cheeked and smiling. Most of them, it looked, did not brush their teeth. "The elders say", they disclosed, "If you eat apple after getting up in the morning, you need not brush your teeth. It automatically gets cleaned." The apple is aplenty in the valley, at least in the season. I softly pinched cheek of one of them and smiled, he smiled back with a lot of shyness but rest all the children had a hearty laugh, know not why? Probably because he was 'touched' by 'army'and a stranger, rest were not. Later they might tease him.

"*Che Kya chuie nav;* what is your name?"- I asked lovingly in Kashmiri, by now a bit of which I had learnt by frequent interactions with local population.

"Abdal (Abdul)" he said after looking at his friend, as if garnering support, then ultimately looking down. It instantly touched my chord and went in to my memory since I had a classmate-friend by the same name in my childhood.

"*Chu chukhu school ghasan;* Do you go to school?"- I asked in my broken and transliterated Kashmiri.

He nodded in affirmation instead of answering in words.

"*Subjects kya chuie;* what are the subjects?"- I asked.

"*Scienus* (science), *Hisaab* (maths), Urdu." he said heads down out of shyness.

Hindi?

Kihin; no.

"English?"

"*kihin;* no" he said.

"*Bachus English paraan;* I study English" another one jumped in with a lot of enthusiasm and sense of superiority.

"*Engishus manz kya chuk paraan;* what do you study in English?"-I asked in my broken Kashmiri mixed with Urdu.

"Everything"-and then elaborated meaning of everything."A for apple, B for bat, C for cat"- the boy said confidently. 'Everything' for him in English was literally 'A to Z.'

Another boy who was comparatively older in the group; a teenager, looked at me with soft smile and guessing my temperament to be cheerful and attitude open, said in Hindi:

"Sir but soon they will re-learn all this."

'How?' I asked.

'A for Army, B for Bullet, C for Catch, D for Death, E for……..'

But stopped abruptly noticing someone in the crowd signalling him to shut up by putting his index finger on lips. He shuddered, went cold, his smile disappearing abruptly. It looked he was reminded of whom he was talking to and what he was talking to.

"Who is he?" I asked with a smile as if nothing was offending and tried to bring him back to normal.

"My father."

'OK'- I glanced through the crowd. All were sitting quietly as prisoners of war.

I moved out of this small chat I had with children. Very close was the "spotting; identification" parade going on. This place had its usual entities; the Commanding Officer, his QRT, the Adjutant, the interrogation centre, the spotter, etc. I saw mood was extremely relaxed among officers. The Commanding Officer was having coffee with the other Company Commander and his staff officer. I wished him with a customary salute. He asked me about progress before offering me a chair and telling me to sit down.

"What about catch, any ANE; anti national element, arms or ammunition during search?"

"Not yet sir, but we are hoping and searching. The chances are very poor, since timing of this operation is not suitable for catch." I said defensively.

"OK, doesn't matter, what you would like to have, coffee/ tea?"- It looked he himself was not expecting much from this village.

"Nothing sir"- I said.

"Why?"

"I just had tea with the men."- I told him.

"Doesn't matter, have a cup of coffee, it is good."– he said being unusually informal which was not very common during operation.

I sat down and participated in the chat which was already going on among them about the overall situation in the valley, slide in militancy, catches of other units and other military formations; all in an informal way, relaxed. The topics ranged from role of Pakistan to the role of Islamic fundamentalists, governments failure to convince the world community about sponsorship of terrorism by our western neighbour, suffering of local people; particularly women and children, the impact it was having on their psyche, on the education of the children, role and conspiracy of fundamentalists in mass exodus of Kashmiri pundits, etc. They also discussed the dimension of the uprising and were convinced that it was not political but religious in nature. The literature seized and revelations of the arrested terrorists were testimony to it. Political demand was just a cover up for theocratization of the valley, they opined.

My coffee was over. I sought his permission to leave; following the military tradition of seeking permission of a senior for everything, if he is in the close vicinity.

"OK, then go and supervise search of your company. This village is small but surrounded by thick vegetation, tell boys to search surrounding areas also."-He advised me.

"OK sir."

I wished him, got up and moved away. My escorts and the radio operator, who were waiting a bit far from the officer's sitting place, followed me.

The weather was pleasant and the surrounding charming. The corn crop was at its last phase and vegetable grown in the field had started greying and paling since it was Sept-Oct. In contrast to the plains, the valley remains dry and deserted during winters due to extreme cold and snow fall. Trees were shedding their leaves, to prepare themselves to be bare, so that they could easily shrug off white shroud of snow forcibly thrust upon them. Trees shed their leaves before onset of winter so that the snow is not stuck on leaves and they do not die of snow bite. The vegetation too pale, dry and decaying slowly; since they know the future for next four-five month will be snow, rain and cold. It will not let them survive. So it is better, they must have decided: to pale, dry and go in hibernation gracefully, on their own.

I reached the eastern out skirt of the village where my

Company was deployed. Since the village was small, three search parties were deployed for searching the houses, with one villager each in all the search parties. Two search parties were ordered by me to look around for any militant hiding in the bushes, vegetation or field of vegetables and fruit orchards. They kept on searching in the bushes, overturned heaps of hay stakes, stacked in the field. A few women kept on working; collecting or cutting dried stems of maize, in the nearby field.

From earth to sky everything was so beautiful. I got lost in the nature and thought of our beautiful Kashmir valley. I wandered in the ancient world; initially exclusively resided by Hindus or pundits, then entered Buddhists, and later dominated by Muslims. It was hub of education, place of creation of world class literature, drama, philosophy, poetry and grammar. Even handicraft, silk, woodcraft, architecture and embroidery are unique. I remembered changing times; of dominance of Brahmi, Sanskrit, Sharda, Kashmiri and later Persian script. I thought of rich literary tradition of the valley, imagined its grandeur; place of assembly of fourth Buddhist Council by King Kanishka and birth place of 'first historian of Indian subcontinent; Kalhan, who chronicled history in his timeless treasure *Rajtarangini*. I imagined how many Rishis, Munis, monks, Sufis and even foreign scholars might have roamed around at the same place where I was standing.

"Sahib, we have caught one militant"- one of the sepoy from neighbouring search party came running, and breathlessly broke the news.

"Who caught him"– I asked.

"Havaldar Shinde"– he replied.

I along with my escorts and a senior Subedar moved towards that area. After reaching the spot Havaldar Shinde described me how all this happened. After hearing the story all were amused and surprised. He narrated:

"My group was searching in the bushes and vegetation

when I noticed three women working in the closeby field. To be sure who they were I looked at them. Two of them looked at me but the third turned around, faced opposite, showing her back to me. I thought she might be feeling shy of us and over looked the act of the woman. But while searching around, I noticed she was constantly keeping her back towards us. Then I observed her carefully; she looked exceptionally tall and well built. So I decided to go and have a close look at her." I could not stop my smile and the Havaldar understood the meaning of my mysterious smile he broke the eye contact looked down and smiled, saying, "No sir not that"

"Yes, I know she looked tall and well built. You are also tall and well built"-The suspect was already in our net so I thought of having some fun at the expense of captor and the captive.

I had spoken fact fully but with a mischief. He was well built; a wrestler, but not what I was taunting to.

He hid his smile, overlooked the taunt and continued, "When I watched her closely I saw long hairs on her leg close to the ankle and exceptionally thick hair on the toes. Her dress was also undersized and ill-fitting to her body. When I called her to look at us she did not. Then we decided to surround her. I called the other two women and made them to confront her and remove her veil of scarf from her face".

"And you discovered a beautiful woman?"- I asked.

"No sir. I was shocked; he had shaved his face, put on some cosmetics to look like female."

"You mean she was a 'he; a man". I asked and continued.

"Where is he?"- I asked ending the joke and getting into serious business.

"He is there in that orchard. When we discovered him to be a man, he tried to push us and run away, not even fearing that within our small arms range he would easily be killed. He also dared to break the cordon but was over powered by me and my team. We have tied him with tying rope in a tree with our men around."

"Very well done. Commendable. Was there any weapon on him?" I asked.

"No, but I am sure he must have hid it somewhere. The two women could not tell anything about him. In fact they refused to identify her/him."- He revealed.

"OK. Let me inform the Commanding Officer." I gestured to the wireless operator to come closure so that I can speak over radio.

In brief I told the Commanding Officer what had happened and what the possibilities were. The Commanding Officer came with team of interrogators, who were our own unit officers. He was equally amused to see a man of well-built body and five feet ten inch height in an undersized, tight, ill-fitting attire of a woman.

"Name?" –The Commanding Officer asked.

"Abdul Rahim."

"Fake or real?"- He further asked.

No reply.

"Tanzeem? (Organization)"

"Al-Barq."

"Training?

He kept quiet

"Hathiyar"(Weapons)?

No answer.

The Commanding Officer looked amused after seeing him in a woman dress and hearing that he was from Al-Barq. We had heard about this newly formed terrorist organization. This was group of not much of significance, adding into already oversized clan of almost 45-46 militant organizations.

Formed out of disgruntled elements from various already existing terrorist organizations; which dreamt merger of Kashmir with Pakistan instead of Azadi, Al-Barq was trained and supported by Pakistan. Al-Barq; literally meaning 'lightening of Allah' was the newest born baby in the already oversized family of Jehadis, fundamentalists and separatists organizations.

His preliminary disclosures were not different from others. Before 1990, for two-three years there was hardly any effective presence of might of government of India or government of Jammu and Kashmir. He was among the hordes of youngsters who were convinced or coerced (or had volunteered; no one can say for sure) by ISI/Pak agents and some of the Kashmiri zealots on the pay roll of ISI; to go for training in POK. Under the governments of 'sons and sons-in-law'; - as the Kashmiris loved to put it about, of the dynasty-founder of post-independence Kashmiri dynasty, "the anti-national elements had a free run in the valley".

"Take him for interrogation" the Commanding Officer thundered jolting me from my thought process and gesturing forward the team of interrogators. They were not from intelligence corps but had developed excellent techniques to extract result oriented and actionable information from the militants; invariably vital information leading to other operation and big 'catch'. Their method and tool ranged from conviction to coercion and allurement to excesses depending on response and degree of hardness of the detainee or the terrorist. One of the officers punched and kicked him while taking inside the interrogation centre.

"So you wanted to hide under the dress of a woman?"

He looked around and asked in a commanding voice to the soldiers:

"Give him appropriate treatment so that he remembers in his life; what are the dangers of hiding in the garb of a woman's attire?"

A few soldiers could not stop their smile and tried to hide it from the officer by looking other way; knowing the officer rarely revealed his lighter and humorous side of this kind. Most remained serious and none spoke. The 'cross dresser' was taken in the closeby building which was temporarily converted into interrogation centre. There he went through the 'welcome ceremony', which all militants had to go through.

There they sang songs of their past 'glory', told their 'heroic' stories; destruction of government property, their 'daredevilry' of planting IEDs and attack on the military convoys, the 'holy' act of killing the 'Kafirs', eliminating the hurdles of 'intellectually pervert' among Muslims who still had loyalty with *Kafirs*, their 'pilgrimage' to POK or Pakistan, the 'knowledge' they gained there, the 'gifts' they brought back to be used for destroying the 'evil' rule of 'occupying forces' of India. Of course all it was not without music, the music they themselves used to create; their cry, call, shriek, scream, squeak, slither, slink and kink on the floor.

After some time he broke down and revealed all his 'heroic' deeds; IED blast in Ompora near Badgam on the military convoy, firing on moving columns towards Badgam, extortions in the name of fund raising, encounter with the army in Sunoor Kalipore etc. He told the same story line of his voyage to Pakistan, which we were used to hearing so many times. He begged to leave him as he would take out his weapon and hand over to us. He took us in dense vegetation in an orchard, which was very close to the fields where he was caught. He revealed during interrogation that he belonged to the other village and had come to "collect" money for "freedom struggle" in this village and got trapped due to "surprise" and "untimely" cordon of the army. As soon as he came to know the army had arrived, he hid his weapon in the bushes, snatched a woman's attire from nearest house, covered his head and face with 'Hijab' and pretended to be working in the field with the other two women who actually were forced to keep on working in the field to give him 'cover' and 'company'.

The interrogation team with large contingent took him to the spot, where he had thrown or hid his weapon. His hand securely tied in a hand cuff rope, 'anchored' on a wrestler; armed men encircling him around; with AK-47 ready to fire, in case he tried some stunt like; to run away.

While entering the interrogation centre he had gone as a 'man' dressed in a 'woman's attire. But when he came out, he was looking like a ghost, his orientation lost, legs falling apart; moving with the support of the escorting soldiers, but still in woman's attire because there was no male cloth to dress him. He was taken in an army *Jonga* with a few protection vehicles in the lead and trail. He took us close to bushes and signalled to stop. He indicated the place where he had thrown or hid his weapon. Men searched out a packet from the bushes neatly secured. The AK-47; Kalashnikov in militants' parlance, was clearly visible. It was uncovered; one China made AK-47, two magazine and 50 odd rounds. Everyone was so happy. After all it was a double 'catch', militant with Kalashnikov, magazine and live bullets; all without firing a single bullet. Aim plus was achieved; from a place which we thought to be a 'dry land'.

"Well done Shinde." congratulated the Commanding Officer to the Havaldar who had caught the 'cross dresser militant'; as all loved to call him, irrespective of the words' descriptive meaning. 'It is your common sense and intelligence which had made it possible.' I added.

"Sir, we should search his house as well." I suggested as a proud Company Commander whose men had caught the militant using their sheer common sense and intelligence.

'Why not, we will wait here'. The Commanding Officer signalled me to carry out the job with my men.

We moved in a convoy of vehicles to the closeby village; the village of the terrorist we had caught. It was so important hence I decided to personally lead and supervise. We reached the house; identified by the terrorist as his. As soon as he got down, the curious villagers became curious onlookers. Seeing a 'woman' in an army *Jonga* was a shock and surprise for them. They also tried to figure out who the woman was. After they recognized the figure in the female attire, they became panicky. We spread out and started searching his house and surrounding areas. It was more like a hut than house. We searched each and every nook and corner of a two storeyed small house of three-four compartments.

Hearing the hustle bustle; a few words of yelling and whisper, an old, frail and sick looking woman emerged from a corner of the house holding a child in her arms. She was short, bent, malnourished, prematurely old and had stained and worn out teeth. As soon as she recognized her son in a woman's dress, she became hysteric. She yelled, wailed, shouted and cried for help from the neighbours. Said a lot in between but only "Khudayu; God" and 'Be`gunah; innocent' was understood by me. We were searching inside. I told men to take her out side for some time as it was creating disturbance in the search. Men took her out forcibly since she was not ready to move; like an obstinate serpent. She was entangling her in any object, coming her way, which was likely to give some hold. She kept on crying and wailing outside the house; soldiers not allowing her to enter the house.

Nothing objectionable, rather literally 'nothing' at all was found except a few old stinking rugs and a few potteries; all empty, without grain. Barely any utensil was in the house hold. The family was extremely impoverished and badly off. I wondered what they must be eating. I came out, asked from the villagers about the family. One of them narrated:

"Sir, this boy has two children; four years and two years old. The wife has recently died or committed suicide; is not clear. She had nothing to eat, nowhere to go. In 1989, when his father came to know that his son has gone *'Paar'* (other side) to get training to become 'Mujahid', he was extremely disturbed since the boy was already married and had a child. The boy's wife was second time pregnant. The old man used to cry most of the time. He was already very weak and frail. His health started failing and one day he died before seeing his son in the new birth of a "Mujahid". He was weak hearted person and used to work as carpenter. Now only old woman is left; the mother of this boy, who looks after both the grand children since there is no one else and he is hardly seen in the village.

"But there is nothing in his house, how the old woman supports herself and the small children?"- I asked.

"*kya bolenge;* what to say? -He has some land but who will till?" He replied fearfully in broken Hindi/Urdu and continued-"The villagers are merciful and give her something in lieu she does household chores."

The search party came out of the house signalling completion of search. We started moving towards our vehicles. The old woman was kept at bay by our men so that she did not create "ruckus" until we satisfactorily completed our task. I informed the Commanding Officer about search and its result. Nothing much was expected; so Commanding Officer was not disappointed. He told me to wind up and wait there itself since all had to go via this village only. That was the route of our return. He ordered to free the villagers held up at the congregation immediately, so that they could go for Namaaz, as requested by some of them.

The Commanding Officer ordered closure of the operation. "All stations, (every one under that radionet in that location) be ready to move within one zero minute. Lift the cordon, free the men at congregation and move to your vehicles."-He transmitted over the radio.

All stations replied in affirmation, in their order of protocol.

After some time all reached our location; the village of the terrorist caught by us. We all came close to the road and gathered near the vehicles.

The men who held up the mother of the terrorist also moved towards the vehicle leaving the old woman free. But the old woman also moved towards the vehicle in which her son was sitting, holding two small kids; one in her arms, the other toddling and holding her hand. All three wailing; the old woman for reasons she knew and the toddlers only because the grand ma was crying. Her Himalayan tragedy was so apparent. It radiated to hit all and me. I strongly resisted; I did not want to look "swayed away" so frequently. I pulled down my sleeves to cover the entire hand and closed the buttons; a drill all military men are told to follow just before the last light. But psychologically it was to find some cover from tornado of emotions of a mother whose son was caught under AFSPA by the army. But her pain was so strong; it penetrated the strong 'armour' of a soldier's uniform and touched my skin; just a fraction of it for a fraction of a second; even that looked difficult to bear. I looked at her.

She left both the children on ground, hit her own face with both her hands, beat her chest and ran towards our vehicle. The younger child cried again. The toddler did not leave her hand and ran with her, and due to mismatch of speed got dragged and cried. Helplessly she tried to tear her already ragged pheren but failed; her hands were too weak to tear it. She looked in the sky and cried; as if asking the Almighty why she was being punished for others sins. I looked at her again. With her open raised hands, she looked around; she looked at the crowd of villagers, she looked at us, and ultimately towards the setting sun westwards: as if asking to all, including the Almighty - "who is responsible for my devastation?" The rays of setting Sun focussed directly on her face; glimmering in her mouth. Her mouth wide open while crying, all her teeth visible, broken, worn out and stained. It was so unbearable. Her voice echoed. Only three words could be understood by me; from her wails. *Reham, reham, reham, begunah, begunah, begunah* and *khudayoooo, khudayoooo, khudayoooo*......................

It was a common phenomenon that women; particularly mothers, never believed that their son could be at fault or he can be a terrorist. They always put up defence that he was not bad and all this was an aberration; even when their sons were caught with assault rifles, found involved in attack and killings. And she was no different. She also thought her son was '*Begunah*; innocent', even if he had gone to Pakistan to receive training to wage war against India, even if he had brought arms and ammunition to fight for secession, even if he had handed us over an assault rifle, even if he had attacked the military convoys, even if he had collected money to wage war against Republic of India. Not her fault; mothers can never be 'bad mothers': Sons can be 'bad sons'.

Our convoy of assorted vehicles, consisting of more than fifteen, started moving one by one from the front. She ran towards our standing vehicles at the rear; bare feet, her tattered plastic shoes had ditched her, like rest of the world. She tried to grab the vehicle in which a person; terrorist for us and a son for her; a part of her own flesh and blood was sitting. My men grabbed her and took her towards the onlooker crowd of villagers. They commanded the villagers to hold her and control her. Men behaved sympathetically and gently. I could see many of them were struggling to hide their true emotions; like me. All of us felt in the same grid, same place, in same emotional state; all of us being from the same race: Human. The scientists have given it a difficult name; Homo Sapiens.

The Commanding Officer ordered to all, while sitting in his vehicles:

"Don't get in to hassles now. Hand over the lady to the villagers and bring him securely."- as if he was also trying to hide his helplessness.

Again the sky was rendered vibrating by her wails-

"khudayoooo, khudayoooo, khudayoooo".

The Sun had already started its journey to enlighten some other part of the world. It had vanished in the western horizon, as if feeling red faced; leaving a cupric aura at the place of its disappearance. Now the sun was nowhere traceable as if declaring –"even I cannot bear it". All the villagers were freed from the congregation. It was time for fourth *Namaaz; Namaaz* of *Magrib*. The public address system of the mosques of both the villages sounded being switched on.

"*khudayoooo, khudayoooo, khudayoooo*" the pain of the wail was deeper. I was looking at her and in my brain spontaneous replay carried on; the empty house, her empty potteries, her empty urns, and her grandchildren. I thought of her son, his training, his IED blast, his misadventures, his AK-47, his interrogation, his confessions and his detention. Nobody could help him or her; it's their destiny or own doing or others doing for which they were being punished? Army had to do a job, I had to do my job; with compassion to her and without compassion to her son.

"Sir, the entire convoy has moved. We are only one left behind."- driver of my vehicle reminded me.

He had been holding the door ajar for so long, for me to slip in the vehicle. I was so engrossed watching the woman and her tragedy, which had swept my thoughts completely, that I forgot he was holding the door open for me. In such moments, I invariably used to forget I am an army officer. My combat uniform and the rank on the shoulders were prominent reminders; besides my men around, of course. I moved in the vehicle like a robot, trying to figure out who was responsible for her tragedy. The driver closed the door gently; resulting into lesser sound of the wails. He drove off. For the last time I looked at her. She was, forlornly, still begging for help from one and all; with raised hands and open mouth.

And then the Muezzins, almost simultaneously, from both the villages gave '*Azaan*' over the loud speakers of their respective mosques;

Allah-O-Akbar, Allah-O-Akbar,

Allah-O-Akbar, Allah-O-Akbar.

Ash-Hadu-Allah Ila-ha-Illallah----------------------------------

(God is great, God is great, God is great, God is great. There is no one worthy of prayer except Him-----------------)

The wailing got drowned in the synchronized recital of *Azaan* from both the villages and roar of engines of the military vehicles. Slowly all sounds; wails, roar and the *Azaa*n included, faded as our convoy moved away: only to echo within; more violently, more loudly, more deafeningly and more piercingly.

****

Mahroom-e-haqiqat hain sahil ke tamashayee
Hum doob ke samjhe hain dariyaon ki gahrayee
Chalte huye baadal ke saye mein ta-a-kub mein
Ye tashnalabi mujhko sehraon mein le aayee
Ye jabr bhi dekha hai taarikh ki nazron ne
Lamhon ne khataa ki thi sadiyon ne sazaa payee

-Muzaffar Razmi

Bereft of realities are those sitting on the bank
I could fathom the depth of the river only when I sank
Following the shade of moving clouds
My thirst has brought me in deep deserts
The history has seen those excesses also
When 'seconds' committed sins & 'centuries' were punished.

SEP BAJIRAO RUYNDHAL,SC
OP RAKASHAK(SRINAGAR - 1993)

Chapter 4

Sepoy Roundal Bajirao Dharma: Shaurya Chakra (Posthumous)

15 Sept 1993: Narbal, Badgam

On 'Independence Day'; the 15 August (1994), when the President and ex-officio Supreme Commander of the armed forces of India, conferred "Shaurya Chakra" to Sepoy Roundal Bajirao Dharma (posthumous) in the glittering ceremony at Ashok Hall of the Rashtrapati Bhawan, my eyes became moist and I relived the day when Bajirao had made supreme sacrifice for our motherland. His childless young widow Mrs Kalpana Bajirao Roundal had received the third highest gallantry award of peace time, given to the martyr; who had made supreme sacrifice in the face of the enemy, fighting sponsored insurgency from the across. I remembered the day and every moment of it, like watching the same play in the theatre of war.

In the officer's ward of Base Hospital in Srinagar, I along with the Regimental Medical Officer; the RMO, a captain rank officer and affectionately called as 'doctor', kept on waiting near the bed of the Commanding Officer. It was a private room where he was just shifted from ICU. We were the first from the Unit and from the operation area to visit him. Sadly we had deeper and bigger grief which brought us to the hospital and made us to be the first. We had brought mortal remains of the martyr, from the same operation area, to be deposited in the hospital mortuary.

Our Commanding Officer was under influence of sedative, which was given to him a few hours back. We were expecting him to regain his consciousness any time now; as doctors attending on him had told us that the effect of the medicine would be over any moment. Without talking to each other, I guess, we both were reliving the horror and loss during today's operation. Occasionally we looked at each other, as if assuring mutually, the CO might open his eyes any time.

"Where is that bastard?" roared the Commanding Officer despite being injured and on the hospital bed, when he suddenly opened his eyes and saw us. He was referring to the terrorist who was holed up in a house during our encounter and who had, deceptively, fired and injured him.

"Sir, we have caught him but dead. He refused to surrender and refused to come out of the house." We almost said together, doctor withdrawing in between and allowing me to complete the sentence.

"But I wanted him alive." the Commanding Officer spoke in disappointed tone.

"We tried all possible ways to convince him to surrender but he kept on blowing hot and cold with the intent of deceiving us. Finally after four-five hours struggle to convince him and not succeeding, we decided to call it a day, as it was going to be dusk and we were running short of time. He wanted to keep us engaged until the sun set so that he got the benefit of cover of darkness to disappear from the holed house". I tried to summarize the reason for every possible question the Commanding Officer might have asked.

"So you destroyed the house and gave him live burial". he asked the conclusive question guessing the outcome in the given circumstances from several of his past experiences.

"No sir." I explained, "To get you closer to him deceitfully, on the promise of surrender so that he can inflict casualties on us, was not his last attempt of bamboozling us. He tried this trickery with us several times. But when we stopped firing and asked him to come out; either he responded by firing on us or by putting new conditions. After you were evacuated, the Brigade Commander arrived on the scene, he also tried his best to convince him to surrender, but in vain."

"What time did the Brigade Commander reach and how long did he stay?" The Commanding Officer became inquisitive.

"The Commander had been there for an hour or so. He also tried to convince the terrorist to surrender, but in vain. The terrorist tried to convince the Brigade Commander that if he came and talked to him, he would surrender. Contrary to Brigade Commander's eagerness to talk to the terrorist for surrender, we suggested him not to come closer, based on what he did when you agreed to come closer and negotiate with him. The Commander left after getting brief about our future plan of action from the Second in Command".

"So what did you all do and what was the catch ultimately?" He became more inquisitive. "Sir, when high risk operation like getting close, negotiating, convincing, etc. did not work, we lobbed hand grenades to incapacitate him but it was ineffective because the terrorist was highly trained and knew how to evade such impacts. When all this did not fetch desired result, we decided to fire High Explosive rocket. One portion of the house, despite our effort to inflict minimum damage, was razed to ground burying him alive in the debris. After ensuring that all possibly hiding militant had been silenced, we searched the house.

"OK." he said only to break the monotony and allowed me to continue.

"We found that there was only one terrorist lying dead in the southern room of the four room house, his rifle damaged partially, one destroyed radio set, two unused grenades, one first aid kit out of which a bandage was already used by the terrorist on his right thigh and a military map of J&K. Except the last, which was printed in Pakistan, all others were 'made in China.'"

"How many terrorists were there? Were they Kashmiris?" He interrupted.

"There was only one terrorist. The locals could not identify him. The spotters and our sources identified him as an Afghani, a self-styled area commander of Hizbul-Mujahideen (HM). They said he was mostly operating and creating trouble in Baramulla and Sopore area, but recently relocated in Srinagar to do something big, since most of the HM commanders here, either were killed or captured. And sir...."

I stopped since I was finding it extremely difficult to tell him something very sad. And he also, having no inkling that something like this might have happened did not give me opportunity to deviate from the topic of the terrorists.

"So the operation has been wound up and all reached the unit location safely?" He wanted to be sure about closing of operation and safety of all men.

The doctor and I looked at each other simultaneously. I kept quiet and the doctor, knowing my difficulty turned to the CO and disclosed-"No sir we have also lost one of our men."

"Don't tell me. Who?"- The CO sat up on the bed from his lying position not caring about his wounds with his eyes wide open.

"Unfortunately it is true, sir. He is Sepoy Bajirao Roundal."- The doctor said.

"From your Company?" The CO asked while looking at me, since I was 'Bravo' Company Commander.

"Yes sir." I nodded but did not elaborate knowing that the CO was among a few officers who knew almost all eight hundred plus men by name and by face.

"That's very sad. It is not acceptable". - he looked reflective and went into contemplation for a few moment.

"How and where did this happen?" I thought, would be his next question but it was not.

"Tell the Subedar Major to prepare for proper funeral. I don't want anything lacking or any lapses. Ask the Second in Command to seek immediate consent from next of kin of Bajirao to perform his last rites here or else arrange to send the mortal remains at his native place." He sounded as if he did not want to say or listen further after giving these instruction. I nodded in affirmation to denote his instructions would be conveyed and complied with and we left the room after wishing him to get well soon.

This operation was among very few where we had lost our own beloved soldier fighting with sponsored foreign mercenaries mixed with local youth trained across the line of control. But this was unique in one sense which had no parallel in my unit and known to us otherwise; a few soldiers or probably only one who had seen and knew that one of our men; Bajirao had close encounter with the terrorist, fired and fought with the terrorist, injured him and had also got injured, did not inform anyone anything about the incident. We only realized that someone was missing, during closing report, after end of the operation; when all the incidents including CO's injury, recovery of dead body of the terrorist had already happened. Almost half of the day; from the time encounter had taken place to the time of roll call for winding up the operation, Bajirao remained fallen; dead or alive in the bushes.

The absence of Bajirao could be only discovered when the strength of the men who had come did not match with those present and ready to march. Then the Platoon Commander discovered that Sepoy Bajirao Roundal was missing. A search was launched to trace him. Entire area was combed. Finally our men located his lifeless body with bullet injuries and his weapon; a self-loading rifle in his hand still clinched tightly, very close to his chest. It was not very far from the house of encounter.

It was obvious from situation analysis that Bajirao was among the first to detect the terrorist and surely first and only one to fire on him. His magazine was short of three rounds and fired empty cases of the cartridges of same number of self-loading rifle; the SLR, were found near his body: only ten metres away from where several fired cases of AK-47 of the terrorist were found. Obviously, there was exchange of fire between Bajirao and the terrorist. The SLR magazine was damaged, consequently had stopped feeding live cartridges due to malfunction. The terrorist had good luck; for that moment, and superior weapon; capable of spraying bullets, hence he survived and Bajirao lost. What Bajirao had much more than the terrorist, was; courage, grit and undefeatable will to fight.

We found after examination of the SLR of Bajirao that the magazine was badly damaged and cartridges got stuck in the chamber blocking the firing mechanism. It was obvious he wanted to fire more on the terrorist to kill him but could not due to malfunction of his weapon. Actually, the wound on the right thigh of the terrorist was of a bullet of SLR which was fired by Bajirao. When we had recovered the dead body of the terrorist we had found that he had done self-dressing of fresh bullet wound on his right thigh. The bullet was stuck up in the thigh which was later confirmed after his post mortem. The terrorist had butt marks also, indicating Bajirao had got into close combat and hit him with butt of the rifle when it stopped firing.

"But how nobody else could notice this all." Was a question which was bothering all of us?

It was 15 September 1993. We had moved early in the morning to carry out cordon and search operation in village Narbal approximately 15 km from Srinagar city, on Srinagar-Gulmarg road. The village is big enough and is located on the tri-junction of Srinagar-Baramulla-Gulmarg roads. We had moved early in the morning from our location at Haft Chinar; a locality in old Srinagar city, to cordon off the village before first light. As usual the cordon was effective well before the first light. It ensured that all ingress and egress routes were effectively blocked physically as well as by fire of automatic weapons. Search parties were formed to carry out house to house search to trace hiding terrorists, hidden arms, ammunition or subversive literature. I was commanding "Bravo" Company and supervising the search with my usual companions; the radio operator, the scouts cum escorts and a few more men. Later Senior JCO also joined me and it became one more search party just to add or oversee the entire search operation. After search in clusters was carried out, we moved towards a lone house on the outskirt of the village at the end of the link road.

This was a house at the end of the motorable road, having four-five compartments; with entry and exits both sides. After completing search of the houses in main locality, we moved towards this house following the road and entered to search from the main gate, unaware of the existence of other entry/ exit opening in the backyard in thick bushes. We had no inkling that there was someone in the house whereas the terrorist was watching every step of ours, very well aware what was happening around; the arrival of the army, the laying down of cordon, sealing the entry and exit for all and then house to house search by our men. He was tracking our movement and when we finally approached this house, he was in prospective trap.

When our three men, including Bajirao, entered from the main door and started searching and sanitizing every possible place in the house, the terrorist moved out from the rear door in the maize field. He might have planned that once the house was searched and the military men came out of it from the entry door, he would re-enter the house; undetected. But to his bad luck, I along with my group entered the house, just to re-search, as soon as the three men including Bajirao came out of the house. My party also started searching the house and remained within for longer time, just without any plan or design. In the meantime Bajirao and his companions moved ahead which led them to the hind side of the house. Since our three men were still inside the house, the terrorist had no option but to stay outside only and hide him inside the maize field.

But the terrorist ran out of luck since before our three men inside the house came out, Bajirao with his companions started searching the bushes. The terrorist was watching each and every one of them, but didn't fire, obviously not to disclose his presence or location, until detected. When the three men came face to face with terrorist, Bajirao shot him with his SLR. One, two, three round of SLR, I heard, followed by a burst of AK-47, but could not understand what was happening as I was within the house. The huge structure of the house was between me and the spot of incident. I guessed, as in some of such cases; some civilian might be running out of fear and our men, without assessing correctly or mistaking him for a suspect, were firing on him. I got extremely worried that some innocent might get killed, so I shouted to stop the fire immediately and ran towards likely spot of fire. Before I could reach or see anything another sound of burst of AK-47 was heard.

This was the burst fired by the terrorist, I realize after end of the entire operation, which had fatally injured Bajirao. One from amongst the bullets, hit the magazine of the SLR of Bajirao, which got damaged and jammed rendering Bajirao virtually without arms and ammunitions. Had he been having an AK-47, instead of SLR, he would have killed the terrorist in his first strike itself, since he would have had the liberty and choice of opening a burst instead of single shot. After all, it was clear, Bajirao was first to fire. But unfit for close quarter battle, single shot weapon, difficult to handle, long and bulky SLR; could not prove to the occasion. The long demand of army to equip all soldiers in counter insurgency operations with AK-47 had proved right, once again.

I tried to reach the spot from the other side of the house, but to my shock, the terrorist took pot shot on me. A burst of AK-47 grazed my helmet from very close to my left ear. Had I not been wearing the helmet, which at times officers do not wear in contravention of the SOP, I would have surely been injured; if not surely killed. Immediately I took one step back, cocked my AK-47 and moved forward to retaliate, only to discover the firer; the terrorist had disappeared in thin air.

Actually he had re-entered the house from the same rear gate from where he had come out in the bushes to hide when the house was being searched. We moved a bit away from the house and took covered positions to ensure effective sealing of the house, at the same time to secure ourselves from sure fire from the terrorist. The rest of the men from my group who were inside the house for search, I found out, had just come out hearing the firing. Before I could inform the Commanding Officer, he himself enquired about the fire, over the wireless, after over hearing the shots. I told him everything I could, of course all under duress since I was busy ensuring unbreakable cordon around the house and securing the positions of the men. At this point of time, I had no idea or inkling that encounter had taken place with Bajirao and he was injured. Everyone, including me, concluded that it was the terrorist who had fired on me and my party. The men who were in the group of Bajirao did not disclose what already had happened.

The Commanding Officer reached the spot with his QRT; the Quick Reaction Team and strengthened siege of the house. Major Nirbhay Singh, who was commanding another Company and was a few years senior to me, also reached the spot and took the lead in furtherance of action. The holed up terrorist was warned, ordered to come out and surrender through the megaphone but to no avail. We warned him further that if he did not come out we would storm the house and capture him alive then he would not be treated well. He did not budge since he was sure; surrender or capture he would meet the same fate and get the same treatment. He thought, for him, death was a better option which was to come after fight. When we got busy to chalk out our plan to capture him alive, he shouted from a hidden location from within the house that if the Commanding Officer assured and guaranted him about his safety and proper treatment; otherwise available to a surrendered person, he would come out and surrender.

The Commanding Officer was more than willing to concede. He assured through the megaphone that he would ensure that the terrorist got everything entitled to a surrerdered militant. The terrorist further requested that the Commanding Officer might come a bit closer since he was finding it difficult to communicate with him, a few important points which are vital before surrender. Overruling our advice and overlooking the apparent danger, the Commanding Officer came closer in an act of, daredevilry. The inevitable happened. He was fired upon by the terrorist by a precise aimed shot, instead of a burst; which could have gone awry, the terrorist might have calculated. But the Commanding Officer was not as naïve as the terrorist had wished. The Commanding Officer had taken due precaution with substantial risk; he was putting on bullet proof jacket and only partially exposed himself. The bullet fired to surely kill him only injured him.

It was a big setback for us. Commanding Officer getting injured was most demoralising thing for all of us. Not only it angered us but strengthened the resolve to capture him alive. The CO was immediately evacuated to the military Base Hospital in the Badami Bagh cantonment of Srinagar, approximately fifteen kilometre from Narbal; the village of encounter.

The atmosphere was very charged. More than anyone else I was shocked how the terrorist had managed to evade the detection during the search of the house. No one could conclude for sure how many terrorists could be there. Major Nirbhay Singh, myself and rest of the officers also came to the spot, leaving remaining search operation to the command of JCOs. We all gave and took feedback, discussed different strategies and possibilities. We decided to talk to the terrorist to surrender. If he refused or delayed the surrender beyond reasonable time, only then we would go for surgical operation or decide to raze the house as the last resort.

Major Nirbhay Singh strengthened his protective gears and decided to storm the house with a few men but he was stopped by us not to take undue risk when we had several safer options with prospects of better results. We decided to renegotiate his surrender. The terrorist agreed and again requested that the negotiator come closer for better and clearer communication. Major Nirbhay Singh went closer and tried to negotiate. The terrorist did what we had anticipated and were ready for; fired a long burst in the direction of Major Nirbhay Singh. Nothing happened except our strengthened conclusion that the terrorist was deceiving us and he had no intention of surrendering. He also knew that there was no way out but to fight and get killed. The best hope he could have nurtured was to inflict maximum damage on us before we damage him permanently.

The owner of the house was called and asked about the lay out of the house to be precisely sure of the inner lay out. We also anticipated that the terrorist might try to break the cordon by indiscriminately firing while coming out of the house to run away. Precautions were taken accordingly to cover all possible exits under cover of heavy fire. It was decided to lob grenades simultaneously in all the rooms to incapacitate him and catch him alive. This would save the house from any serious damage. But our effort only resulted into dangerous exposer and attraction of fire from the terrorist, who by now had proved was hard core, well trained and highly motivated.

We guessed he was an Afghan mercenary. But nothing could be said until proved.

We decided to fire high explosive rocket and damage/ destroy the house giving the terrorist a live burial. The owner of the house pleaded helplessly, begging one or the other officer including me who had different priorities at this point of time. He cried and begged to spare his house which he said; he had built with all his savings. We told him if he could get the terrorist out, we had no reason to damage it. He feigned ignorance about the terrorist being inside his own house. His lie or truth about his prior knowledge of hiding terrorist could'nt be ascertained since it was a matter of intention. But why, contrary to our orders, there was no one at the house or in the close vicinity at the time of search-was a question the owner could not answer. The experience told us, invariably, the owners knew about terrorist being at their house but did not inform us before or during the search. They do not tell due to sympathy with the terrorist or due to fear of the terrorist-difficult to conclude and may vary from one case to another.

We were also least interested in such trivialities and always gave benefit of doubt to the owners of the house assuming they were helpless. What an owner can do if a militant forcibly occupies his house and converts it into a battle field? Nothing, except informing the army and co-operating; which was never to be. Invariably, finding themselves between proverbial 'devil and the deep sea' the owners used to run away and abandon the house. I empathised with him as a matter of my nature and habit, only to invite difficulties in already demanding times. He started pursuing me to the level of irritation, when I had to plan and execute the impending operation. Finally, I called him and gave him my clear piece of mind, as matter of fact, explaining him how merciful we had been with him.

"Look, we are being very kind with you. The terrorist is holed up in your house. You should be booked for sheltering a traitor; an armed insurgent in your house, may be a foreign mercenary. But we are not touching you assuming you are helpless and the terrorist has forcibly occupied your house without your knowledge. But we also know it is not true always. You people give shelter, food and support and do not inform us even when we are around. You do not inform us even when you are in the know of the truth. You do not inform us when you are sure the terrorist is hiding in your house; with weapon and ammunition, putting our life at risk. Still we are leaving you being merciful. What more do you expect? Now get lost else easily you will invite extreme troubles for you and your entire family."

Our soldiers took him away to ensure he did not get injured during cross fire or rocket fire. The high explosive rockets need minimum range to get 'primed' for explosion and impact. So the area was cleared of all; who were not needed there at that moment, including civilians and soldiers. The two high explosive rockets fired to bring down the house did their job. One portion of the house was almost converted in to rubble within a few seconds. We waited for some time for some reaction but nothing came. The search group of selected men led by Major Nirbhay Singh and I entered the house and searched each and every part of the ruins. In one room the terrorist was lying dead; an AK-56, unused grenades, radio set, map and a first aid kit close by. A well-built, tall, fair, turbaned man in mid-twenties with moustache and beard in an off white Pathani suit was lying lifeless; denoting end of his mission and start of a journey to "Jannat"; the heaven, in the company of his several comrades already there.

The arms and ammunitions were removed and counted. His body frisked and examined by the doctor; "he is dead." the doctor declared. A few villagers including the village head were called in to identify him; which none could do.

"We do not know who he is"- all said after seeing the "martyr" who had come to fight the "Jehad" for their religion and fight for the 'freedom' of their "brethren" in Kashmir. All villagers abdicated him and disassociated themselves from any knowledge or affiliation. The identifiers; the spotters of our own sources identified him as an Afghan mercenary operating previously in Baramulla and recently shifted to Srinagar/ Badgam. The police; which were already called in and waiting for the dead body even before he was actually killed, stepped in. The body was handed over to them for further necessary disposal after due formalities.

The matter was reported to higher headquarters. With a sense of achievement the operation was ordered by the Officiating Commanding Officer to be wound up. During the winding up report the CHM; Company Havaldar Major, was not able to match the strength which had come for the operation. It was falling short of one. After the head count it was discovered that Bajirao was missing and the entire trail of events could be discovered.

****

The body was kept in the mortuary in the same Base Hospital where the Commanding Officer was undergoing treatment. Next day morning it was to be collected and taken to the funeral ground directly, instead of Unit location in the crowded area of Haft Chinar; old Regimental Centre of Jammu and Kashmir Light Infantry. Everyone was to pay his last respect at the funeral ground itself during the ceremonial "last post."

The general atmosphere in the Unit was of sadness, loss and to some extent; of anger. The Second-In-Command or 2IC was called back from his leave, as per instruction of the Brigade Commander. If the CO is injured, the Second in Command has to be present and take charge. But Second-in-Command's arrival from Delhi, place of his residence during leave, was to take some time; at least a day. So the senior most Company Commander; who had just reported back from instructional posting in an institution of training, was to officiate. The night had to be spent before the sun rose for another day to prepare for the funeral. In between the consent of next of kin (NOK) was necessary to conduct funeral at the location.

"The army moves on its bellies." Napoleon Bonaparte had said. No soldier sleeps without food even if he wants to, or he is not allowed unless advised by the medicos. So were the officers. All reached the officers mess as usual but with some gloom and sense of loss. Today very few affirmed the offer of drink from the waiter. Most of them joined my rank of teetotallers.

"The biggest culprits are the bloody politicos. They should be lined up and shot. They are the one from Delhi to Srinagar who mishandled everything about Kashmir and converted it into slush." one of them said referring dillydallying and messy dealing of Kashmir affairs from day one. "See today we lost a soldier. Why?, because he was firing from SLR; a weapon of 1970 origin. May be, it is a good weapon in war but a stupid weapon to fight militancy in close quarter battle."- said one of my seniors who had accepted offer of the waiter.

"It cannot fire more than one round in one go"-Said another on non-availability of AK-47 or similar weapon for all the men in the counter-insurgency operations and continued on SLR-

"So long and bulky that till the time you try to aim your one shot, AK-47 can fire a burst of ten. And unfortunately that is what has happened today. Bajirao took on the terrorist and fired the first shot injuring him in the thigh. But he could not fire a volley since the weapon does not have the capability. It is unfit for close combat. And when the terrorist retaliated, he rained bullets. Even if he was a bad firer, that he was, he could manage to pump in some bullet and the result is in front of our eyes."

"Same is the state of radio communication." another officer chipped in.

"DRDO is a useless organization." the third officer changed the target of bashing and continued - "they bloody eat, party and roam all over the world on public money in name of study tour and research. In their conferences hours are wasted and 'minutes' are recorded. They will only give us INSAS when its technology will become obsolete all over the world."

A senior Company Commander; himself a Maratha interrupted and targeted the Union Home Minister, who also was a Maratha. "But biggest jokers are the politicians. Have you heard that grump faced Home Minister speaking in the parliament? A few days back he had "informed" the parliament that there are no temples in the valley which have been desecrated. But the truth is so contrast that we are seeing by our own eyes from Habba Kadal to Hyderpura and from Baramulla to Qazigund. But the Home Minister says nothing of that sort has happened; liar, shameless, cheats of the nation, misguiding even the parliament. They lie on almost everything."

To cool down the high temper, the senior most spoke up- "look gentlemen, the problem is not with one person or the other or one organization or institution, the country has never respected soldiers. We are only one nation in the world which had been ruled by foreign forces for more than seven hundred years. The Arabs, Turks, Mughal, Afghans and the British, so on so fourth: the same attitude is continuing with politicians, scientist and bureaucrats. But all these come from the society only. So basically society needs to change."

He concluded, "Yaar you see everybody wants more Bhagat Singh, Chandra Shekhar Azad, Savarkar and Subhash Chandra like martyrs but not been born in their home. They should be in the neighbour's house, so that his comfort is not compromised, he need not sacrifice. Great nation are not built up this way." He quipped and continued:

"And then it is like war. We should be ready to accept casualties. No force in the world; mighty and superior can ensure 'Zero casualty'. Do not look for faults after the incident; they will occur."

Suddenly the mess Havaldar; a Non Commissioned Officer

in charge of officers' mess entered to inform that food has been laid. Despite interruption, the talks continued.

****

This was the first time I was attending a military funeral. I felt proud to be part of an organization, which bestows so much of respect to its martyrs. A lot many thoughts went in my mind. I realized why the word "military precision" for accuracy, punctuality and flawlessness. Different groups were formed one day prior with precise responsibilities given to every group vis-a-vis the funeral. Like who would go early in the morning to purchase flowers and get the wreath made, who would go to the funeral ground to arrange for wood, pyre, container for urn, etc.

The national flag, cap and belt meant to be symbolically placed on the mortal remains of a martyr, the drummers, the buglers, the band platoon, the men to fire guns during last salute, the pall bearers, the sequence of event, and what not; everything tied up so accurately. Even the minute details cannot escape their attention. After all there is standard operating procedure (SOP) for everything.

In the morning, I, being the Company Commander of the martyr's Company, requested the Officiating Commanding Officer to allow me to lead the group which was going to collect the dead body from the military mortuary at the Base Hospital. It was more of an emotional request than rational since all other officers were directly reaching the funeral ground except the doctor. He, knowing the medical fraternity and more importantly the formalities to be completed, was to go with a JCO and a few men to collect the mortal remains. Today again we went together. After completing all the formalities finally we moved in a convoy towards the funeral ground.

The body shrouded with white cloth; the Qafan and covered in national flag, the tricolour moved in a convoy consisting of five six vehicles. First, a Nissan vehicle mounted with a light machine gun, the soldier manning it ready to fire in any eventuality. Then the truck with the dead body followed by our light vehicle; myself and the doctor, other vehicles with some luggage and troops in combat order to tackle any eventuality. All these arrangements were kept in place to prevent or face any ambush/attack from the terrorists. They are not bound by any rule or morality. They may fire on funeral procession. The road to the funeral ground was an ordeal; slushy due to rain, broken, pot holes with a lot many turns. There were not many funerals of Hindus taking place since inhabitant Hindus; the pundits had fled the valley and Muslims don't burn their dead. Most of the Hindu funerals took places were of military men, or martyrs from other forces. Why should state government bother to make the roads? I told the men, after stopping the convoy, to tie the coffin with the body of the vehicle so that it did not fall out or gets dislocated. We moved on.

At funeral ground everything was organized. The unit religious teacher, Panditji, himself a Maharashtrian moved forward to receive the convoy. Rest all stayed in their position. All officers and a few senior JCO's had the honour of shouldering the coffin to some distance; as mark of respect. The buglers were lined up in their ceremonial uniform, the firers and the group of '*Shok Shashtra*'; group meant to lower the rifles upside down as a mark of respect to the martyr. Another group would fire the blank round to give 11 rounds'salutes. In front were standing the officers and JCOs, in their order of seniority to lay the wreath on the martyr.

An elaborate procedure followed Commanded by an NCO, all unit officers and JCOs in attendance. The mortal remains were brought close to pyre and placed on an elevated platform. The guards did *Ulta Shastra;* rifles upside down, followed by *Shoke Shastra;* rifles in mourning position. The wreaths were laid followed by salutes and all taking their original position. After "wreath laying" was completed, everything was removed; the wreath, medals, cap and belt. The national flag is also removed but at the last. The body was placed on the pyre; the firers had fired co-ordinated shots in the air as mark of salute; followed by *Salami Shastra* and *Shok Shastra*. 'Last post' was played followed by two minutes silence and 'the rouse'.

Two minutes silence took me in life time of imagination. I tried to concentrate to pray to the almighty for peace of the departed soul but could not. The turmoil took me away. Till a few months back he had been my Assistant, talked a lot, discussed his plan of life; admission of his newly wed wife Kalpana in D Ed: Diploma in Education, about good education to his children when they came in this world, parental care and even post retirement plans. He had come to me with invitation card before getting married. I had joked -"now you will become a mouse from a tiger." He had replied with equal wit- "sir, we army men are lucky. We have to be mice only for two-three months when we go to home on leave and are with our wife. Rest of the time we are tigers. But poor civilians who stay with their wives entire year are cursed to be mice entire life." He had dreamt of his son becoming an officer in the army. All had ended today; unexecuted. His family; his young wife in early twenties, mother and father: how will they bear it all?

Within few seconds, I saw all his life dreams going in flames. The ultimate truth was in front of us; a truth which is undeniable, unavoidable and inevitable to all. It will happen to all; today, tomorrow or day after: with utmost honour or with utter disgrace depending on what you did to reach here. Or which side you were with. All saluted; his juniors, his seniors, younger and elders. Soldiers also cry. Some eyes were moist including mine; with pain and with pride. Involuntarily, effortlessly lines of national poet 'Dinkar' flashed in my mind:

Duniya me Jeene ka sabse sundar madhur takazaa`,
Ai Shaheed uthne de apna phoolon bharaa janazaa`.

"Sweetest and best way to live in the world is to die for your motherland:

Your coffin; in a funeral procession, covered in flowers and garlands

(To be raised by your fellow soldiers on their shoulders and in their hands)"

****

SMT KALPANA BAJIRAO ROUNDAL
W/O SEP BAJIRAO ROUNDAL, SC (POSTHUMOUS)
RECEIVING THE MEDAL FROM THE PRESIDENT
ON 15 AUG 1994

CHM SHIVAJI JAGTAP, KC
OP RAKSHAK (J & K - 1994)

Chapter 5

CHM Shivaji Jagtap: Kirti Chakra (Posthumous)

28 January 1994: Nayadgam Village District Badgam

When I reached close to the spot of encounter I could not believe what I saw. Our senior most Company Commander of "Delta" Company, a Major, was being evacuated by our men amid intense firing from both sides; the army and the holed up terrorists. Two officers and a few other ranks were holding different parts of his body and carrying him away from the spot of encounter. He was seething in pain and shouting at one officer, taking his name, not to touch his injured leg because the hold and resultant movement of injured parts were compounding the pain which was already unbearable.

'Leave me here, you are twisting my injured bone' - The injured officer pleaded to the officer who was holding his leg. Tibia and fibula; the lower leg bones of his left leg were so badly damaged that both the bones were almost severed, and the foot with half part from above the ankle was hanging on muscles.

'Sir, you are in a completely exposed area. The terrorists may take pot shots. We are taking you to safer place.' Another Company Commander who was carrying him tried to explain with reason.

'I want that bastard's head, nothing else.' The injured Company Commander shouted with a mix of anger and pain about the terrorist who had fired on him and injured him seriously. Amid heavy exchange of fire between our troops and the holed up terrorists, he was carried to a safe place by our officers and men by putting their own life at high risk. The path of evacuation was in the line of fire of the holed up terrorists who had fortified themselves in a two-storeyed house. The injury was so serious and deep that the bleeding from his leg had left a trail of blood all the way up to the army ambulance.

'Sir, we will get his head for you. We will get every piece of his body. The bastard will be captured dead or alive, in one piece or in several pieces. But before that we want to take you to the Base Hospital immediately.' Charlie Company Commander tried to console him. The injured officer was immediately given injection of morphine to provide him some relief from unbearable pain. The doctor, our Regimental Medical Officer (RMO) who was always part of our operation team, looked extremely worried and opined that the injury might prove fatal if he was not evacuated to the Base Hospital immediately. He further warned that the time is of utmost importance else even if his life was saved, his leg might have to be imputed.

The dangers of taking him to Base Hospital by road were many. But two of them were most worrisome; rural road condition ready to eat up the precious time by slowing the movement and danger of terrorists ambushing the evacuation convoy. The terrorists always looked for such vulnerable opportunities. It would have been suicidal to take him to Srinagar Base Hospital by road. Although it was just 25 kilometres from here, it was likely to take more than one hour. Then the convoy had to pass through terrorist infested villages like Dharmuna and Soibugh. Even to reach Sharifabad, the nearest cantonment base from where other facilities could have been arranged, was likely to eat up substantial time. Hence, it was decided to take him to Sharifabad first by road and then from Sharifabad by chopper to the Base Hospital at Srinagar. Thanks to the quick reactions of the army system else it was doubtful he would have been saved.

Now, after the evacuation, the atmosphere had become more charged. We were not ready to accept such casualties. The resolve to capture/kill all of the terrorists became stronger and patience to hold on for any longer; weaker. Although the CO sounded a bit low, the Company Commanders and the troops were restless to capture the terrorists live or dead; at whatever cost. One of the Company Commanders wanted to use rocket and blast of the house.

This operation was launched on 28 Jan 1994 in the village Nayadgam (Naid Gaam), in district Badgam, some 20 kilometres south west of Srinagar city and almost equidistance from Beerwah. The deployment of the Battalion was split up and our three Companies were located at Haft Chinar at Srinagar along with Battalion Headquarter and a lone Company 'Charlie' commanded by Major Marathe at Beerwah. My Company 'Bravo' was located at Haft Chinar along with 'Delta' and 'Alfa'. Originally the plan was to cordon off village Wattal Pora by 'Bravo' and 'Charlie' Companies and Chatta Bugh by 'Alfa' and 'Delta'. There was no plan to carry out operation in the village Nayadgam which was on the way, while moving on foot, to the village Wattal Pora. But the destiny of Major Abhijit, CHM Shivaji Jagtap and the two terrorists dragged us to the village as circumstances took unexpected turn.

When Charlie Company was passing through the village,

a few soldiers noticed three-four people running to hide inside the village. The Company Commander of Charlie Company, Major Marathe informed the CO and insisted that he be allowed to 'cordon and search' the village. The CO was not in mood to change the plan midway but due to insistence and high chances of encountering the armed terrorists, he allowed Major Marathe to carry out unplanned and impromptu operation in the village Nayadgam. I, with my 'Bravo' company, had already moved to the village Wattal Pora, cordoned it off and had started search. Wattal Pora and Chatta Bug villages along with Nayadgam were on our radar for some time due to frequent visits of Hizbul Mujahideen cadre and their excesses on some of the villagers.

In one such case, it was reported that one youth of the village suspected by the HM cadres to be informer of the army was beaten up so badly that his body had turned blue. It was doubted that the battered youth would survive. His sister was also molested by the HM terrorists. The worst thing was that the youth was not allowed to move out of the village for medication. When during search, unexpectedly, we encountered the youth, we were shocked to see his plight; entire body was like blue pulp. He was not able to breathe properly. We immediately arranged for his treatment by our own medical team.

Unaware and unmindful of changed plan, my Company 'Bravo' under my command carried on operation in Wattal Pora. Charlie was now in Nayadgam on its impromptu adventure. Later, when during identification and interrogation, things began unfolding; Delta and Alfa companies were also called in at Nayadgam. I remained unaware of Charlie Company's sudden changed plan and subsequent changes resulting into entire battalion minus 'Bravo' being deployed at Nayadgam.

In Wattal Pora, when I was intensively busy supervising the search operation, my radio operator came running to me breathlessly, and handed over the hand set of the wireless carried on his back. He could hardly manage to say- *'CO Saheb'* amid his breathlessness. Later, I realised it was more due to his anxiety than physical stress of running that had made him breathless. As soon as I transmitted 'OK Over' signalling I was ready to receive the transmission, the CO transmitted SOS message sounding in extreme distress. He instructed me to close the operation of my area immediately and reach neighbouring village of Nayadgam. Before, I could ask anything further he transmitted the code signalling he wouldn't like to take or give any more messages at this point of time since he had to communicate with other stations.

Despite being at very crucial juncture of search and identification, I did not think twice to order closure of the operation in my location and shifting to Nayadgam. I told my Platoon Commanders to immediately close the operation, free the assembly of villagers and move in a single file to neighbouring village of Nayadgam which was hardly a kilometre or so. Although not very clear what had happened in Nayadgam, I could guess something had drastically gone wrong which was not being disclosed over radio net. I told the radio operator to monitor the transmission closely to find out what exactly the problem was.

The radio operator could not detect anything since after a few transmissions the radio net went in silent mode; no transmissions. It was obvious everyone was busy in action. However, my radio operator, through his improvised coded conversation in Marathi and Kannada could find out what had happened. As per coded conversation, one of our important appointment holders, a Non-Commissioned Officer was suspected to be either killed or captured by the holed up terrorists. Company Havaldar Major (CHM) Shivaji Jagtap had encountered terrorists when he entered into a house to search. Heavy exchange of fire was heard but he never came out of the house. Battle with the holed up terrorists was on. Hence, we were being called as reinforcement. I was shocked and so were the troops of my Company. The face of the CHM, with big impressive moustache, began revolving in front of my eyes. I could not believe that a well-built and stout soldier could be captured by terrorists. Hence I was sure either it was not true, assuming it to be misunderstanding/miscommunication, or the CHM had been killed.

Sound of firing started becoming intense, as I reached closer to the village. On the outskirts I re-enforced the cordon and reached close to the spot of encounter, but not bang on. It was unsafe and I was told to wait for some time, a bit far away. I was briefed very sketchily by Major Marathe, the Charlie Company Commander. The scene of encounter was very confusing and unclear and no one was sure about exact place of likely hiding of the terrorists, their number and type of weapons. They were holed up in a two-storeyed house having several windows in all the four directions. It was assessed that they were hiding on the first floor.

But it was very dicey to conclude with surety, only based on origin of fire from a particular place, where the terrorists were; since there was no restriction for them to come down or go up to occupy the ground floor or top floor. There was only one Jawan, with very little service and experience to count, who had entered along with the CHM and come out of the house alone. He was so dazed that he could not tell coherently what exactly had happened. Based on confusing and shaky details given by him, what commanders on ground could conclude, was not sufficient to plan surgical operation. But before me getting into the battle it was important to know what had happened before my arrival. It was important to know how our one of the best officers got injured and how one of our most experienced, battle-hardened, brave Non-Commissioned Officer was captured or killed. The Jawan had informed the Company Commanders that he along with CHM Shivaji Jagtap entered the house to carry out regular search. They were completely unaware about the lay out of the house and had no inkling that some terrorists may be hiding inside this particular house.

As a matter of practice there was one civilian from the village with each team and so with this team also to assist soldiers in identifying the house, its owner and to act as interpreter between the soldiers and the local population. When the team entered into the house, they saw somebody running up stairs. The civilian was extremely scared and wanted to slip out as if he had some inkling about presence of the terrorist. But he was not allowed. CHM Jagtap chased the suspects with the same speed as they had run upstairs to hide so that they did not get any time to hide.

The terrorists went up and tried to bolt themselves in a room but CHM Jagtap did not afford them that opportunity by firing a few bursts on the door from his assault rifle. Scared, the terrorist left the door open but hid themselves somewhere in the room which had heaps of quilts/blankets at one side and bed on the other. They entrenched and readied themselves to fight it out with the army men. The CHM exhorted the Jawan to follow him and instructed the villager-civilian to come closer and explain for him the lay out of the house. When he decided to storm the room, the buddy Jawan suggested that instead of Shivaji being in the front, the civilian should be told to enter first since it was least likely that the militants would fire on a local; his own kith and kin.

The Jawan might have been right in his perception since using local civilians as 'vanguard' during search in dangerous circumstances was not uncommon in some Units. But the CHM did not allow that and scolded the Jawan for suggesting to put an unarmed civilian's life at risk. He thought it immoral to do that keeping in mind the safety of the unarmed villager: our own citizen. It was also likely, to save themselves, the terrorists might fire on the villager since terrorists are not known to follow any ethics. The experience showed us that during encounters innocents civilians were killed not only by army men's bullets but also by the terrorists' in the cross fire.

The CHM told the Jawan to follow him and instructed the

civilian to wait at the door. As soon as both the military men entered into the house with a whirlwind speed, a burst of AK-47 aimed at the door was fired by one of the terrorist hidden below the heap of quilts and blankets. But it was not clear who got how much and how serious were the injuries, since all these details were discovered in course of operation later; when almost entire operation was over. The other terrorist had placed himself very strategically at the opposite end of the room so that both could give covering fire to each other.

In the fight of life and death the buddy Jawan thought it proper to jump out of the building without realising at that point of time the CHM was already hit. He used his training of a PT instructor to jump from the first floor and landed up directly on the ground; not the best expected from a trained soldier. Some opined later, when he was expected to stand up with his buddy and fight, he gave preference to his personal safety. The civilian ran away from the scene, without entering the house, following the same route from which he had gone up to the door. Obviously, the civilian had no idea as to what exactly had happened, since he had never entered into the room, except that exchange of fire had taken place. The civilian was so shaken that for a few minutes he could not speak.

When he opened his mouth first thing he said was that the CHM had given him rebirth by not keeping him in front else he would have been killed. He thanked God and the CHM for him still being alive. Since the CHM neither did come out nor was visible, it was sure that he was within the house, most likely injured. Presumed to be two or three in number, the terrorists started firing in all the directions wherever they could see or guess any movement of the army men. They had secured a very advantageous position on a dominating rooftop of a big house and prevented any enforcement by firing at selective targets. It had become extremely dangerous now to move in or come out of the area of encounter without putting the life at undue risk. All, rightly, secured themselves wherever they were.

The Commanding Officer and other officers were on the periphery of the village when the encounter began. There were only two officers who were close to house where encounter took place: Major Abhijit and Major Marathe; Company Commanders of 'Delta' and 'Charlie' Companies respectively. The Commanding Officer reached close to the spot later but could not enter into the 'battle zone.' Although he was eager to come closer but was advised, keeping in mind extremely uncertain locations of the terrorists, not to come closer. In the given circumstances Major Abhijit was in better position to take decision with regard to further course of action.

Now the most important and urgent task in front of him was to enter in the house, whatever the cost, search for the CHM and evacuate him immediately to hospital. The Jawan who was with the CHM and had jumped out of the house was not clear, or he pretended so due to obvious reasons, whether the CHM was injured or captured by the militants. He said it was likely that the CHM had been captured by the terrorist and might be used as human shield to run away or as an 'instrument' of negotiation. Finding his versions unduly confusing and not worthy of precise operational considerations, Major Abhijit along with Major Marathe with select number of troops, decided to storm the house, rescue the CHM, capture or kill the terrorist and end the operation without wasting any time. Time was the most crucial factor assuming the CHM was seriously injured and needed urgent medical attention.

He explained his plan to the CO whose permission was needed to implement it. The CO, like most of the commanders in the army, placed his trust in the leadership of his ground commanders and gave his go ahead with a caution to take utmost precaution. As per plan, the buildings around the house were to be occupied by our troops to give covering fire and kill the terrorists if they tried to run away or capture alive if possible. But going very close was not free from undue risks. Hence except the closest house, which still was unsearched and suspected to be harbouring terrorists, all other houses in the close vicinity were occupied by our troops now. After these deployments Major Abhijit decided to clear the house floor-wise; starting from ground floor to first floor and then to the top floor. Although, it was contrary to the preferred practice of doing it from top to bottom, he assessed, circumstances were not favourable for the conventional method. It was decided to form two teams; one each led by Major Abhijit and Major Marathe to clear the house.

They decided to fire in all possible spots to draw terrorists' fire to understand their location but in vain. The terrorists were highly trained and knew not to waste ammunition when target was not likely to be engaged or, when they could guess it was to find their location by inciting them to fire. Major Abhijit and his team could have not left themselves on the mercy of the terrorist. They were running out of time. Every moment was precious since they had to find out the CHM in whatever condition he was and take him immediately to the hospital. Finally, he took big risk of entering in the house from the ground floor and clearing it upwards; without exactly knowing how many terrorists and where all.

On the ground floor they could find nothing. There was no resistance either. Very cautiously the house clearing parties moved upwards. The risk was extremely high and the CO was having anxiety. He kept on asking about the progress through the radio operator since the officer and rest of the team were busy with the house clearing. The team very cautiously moved up to the first floor of the house. As per the lay out spelt out by the Jawan who had been there with the CHM, the team moved first to the same room where they had encountered the terrorists. This time they had to take into consideration the blanket at one side and bed to the other. As soon as they entered in the room, as per predefined role, both these stacks were to be neutralised by firing on them. An important precaution was to be taken that they didn't fire on the CHM who was likely to be used as human shield, in whatever state. They entered the room with a storm, aiming to fire in the direction of the stacks, but almost all of them slipped at the entry: it was blood all around.

No fire came from any direction of the room. But it was visible and clear someone had been dragged from the entry of the room at the first floor to upstairs on the roof top. The room was spattered with thick blood but not dried yet. There were footmarks and dragging signs going upstairs to the top (second) floor. Despite apparent indication of some dead or injured person being dragged to upstairs and lesser possibility of someone being on this floor, it was imperative to search each and every nook and corner of the room and declare it safe and 'clear.' The search party under Major Abhijit carried out clearing of the room.

From the scene-analysis and circumstantial evidence they could reconstruct a hazy picture of what might have happened. But all that they could see was 'absence' of any human being and not 'presence' of anyone, except human blood. So most vital part was still mysterious: 'where is the CHM? Is he alive or dead, where are the terrorists, they are alive or dead, how many are there, who all are injured, etc?' But yes one clue was found; there were empty cartridges all around near the door as well as near the blanket-stack kept at the right corner of the room. It was now understood that CHM Jagtap took the entire burst on his chest or so it fell on his chest, when the terrorists had fired towards the entry. But the CHM did not collapse without assaulting the hidden terrorist. He charged and fired in the direction from where the fire had come, within fraction of a second of taking the burst on his chest. It was obvious that the cartridge cases near the door were from the CHM's rifle and those near stacks were from the terrorists' rifle. It supported the description given by both; the civilian accompanying the search party of the CHM and the Jawan. Short but fierce gun battle had taken place between the CHM and the terrorists in this room.

Now came the most dangerous and suspense filled part:

clearing the top floor and finding the CHM; alive, injured or dead, and encountering the terrorists. The team wanted to go up on the top floor from two approaches but it was not possible after seeing and assessing the room and the house. They had only one option of going to the top floor via the stairs on which some one dead or alive but surely injured with bleeding had been dragged. It could have been the CHM or one of the terrorists who might have been dragged in injured state by his buddies to prevent his capture by the army while he was alive.

They moved up bracing the danger of fire from the terrorists. The terrorists were likely to be watching each and every movement of the army men whereas army men were clueless about the exact location of the hiding terrorist. As per plan two teams from the roof top of closeby neighbouring houses were to fire on the roof top and first floor of the target house, if noticed some movement, to keep the terrorist down so that the house clearing party could reach upstairs with lesser difficulty and danger.

As expected, a heavy and long burst of AK-47 rifle came towards the up-stairing team. All ducked. Fortunately no one was injured rather team leader was happy that they had drawn fire and come to know the location of the terrorist. The fire from the terrorists was a bit immature. Probably out of fear they opened it up before they had perfect condition to engage the advancing team of the soldiers. Immediately within fraction of seconds the team retaliated with multiple burst from more than one position. But the terrorist was really a hard nut and hardened fighter. He immediately after firing, ran, jumped, entered and disappeared in neighbouring house unmindful of heavy fire from the neighbouring roof tops; which obviously could not engage him. Everyone was stunned, more on the daredevilry of the terrorist and less on missing the target.

They could see the dragging marks of the blood towards a dump of quilts/blanket in the other corner. It was obvious that it was the place where someone has been dragged from the first floor. It looked some of the quilts/blankets from the first floor were brought up to this floor. Very carefully and cautiously the heap was un-layered.

All hopes shattered. There they found the lifeless body of the brave NCO who had chased and cornered the terrorists when he spotted them, unmindful of his personal safety. Here lay a great human being who had refused to use a hapless civilian as human shield in the highest tradition of the Indian Army. Here lay a man of morality who warned the local villager to be behind at safe distance lest in frustration the terrorist should fire on him and kill him. Here lay the leader who had led from the front and who had taken burst of assault rifle on his broad chest so that his colleagues were safe and his countrymen could sleep in peace. Here lay the gem of the nation whom the nation was to decorate with the second highest gallantry award given during peace time while fighting in the face of the enemy. Here lay a true hero who reposed trust in the nation believing that his widow, his three minor unmarried daughters and one minor son will be looked after by those for whom he had laid his life. Here was the military man who fulfilled his pledge, to the nation and its citizens, that he would lay down his life to protect them, their honour and territorial integrity of their nation.

But that was not all he had done. It was just beginning of uncovering of his bravery. In the other corner was hidden the dead body of the terrorist who had fired on him and in lieu, had paid the same price. The CHM despite being perforated by several bullets of the terrorists had shown the indomitable courage and resolute will to kill one of his perpetrators before breathing his last. Here was the body of his antagonist who wanted to run and hide behind the heap of haystack but was chased, confronted and killed.

There was nothing left to take the CHM to the hospital. In fact the life had said adieu to both of them long back, when they fired on each other. All the hopes were shattered. Major Marathe, the Company Commander, was in a state of shock. He never had imagined his CHM to die a sudden death. It looked as if no capture or kill of any number of terrorists would avenge the CHM's death. The message was conveyed to the CO, whose hope against hope also shattered. Shivaji's mortal remains were brought down to safe place since neither the operation nor danger was over yet. However one big question was bothering us—where is his rifle? It was suspected the militant who was still alive might have taken over the weapon and the residual ammunition of the CHM. After all the aphorism goes -"all is fair in love and war." The terrorist was to use every means to protect him and destroy us. One of his colleagues was already killed by the CHM.

Now entire concentration was to capture/kill the other terrorist who had just jumped from roof to roof from this house to the neighbouring house. The newly occupied house was big and was surrounded very closely from three directions by three houses. It was a great disadvantage for us and huge tactical advantage for the terrorist. Actually, it was obvious, he had been planning his move very meticulously and had calculated all possible move by army and had planned its counter well in advance. His risky jump from one house to another was a very well planned tactics. There was only one side from where we could have fired on his likely place of hiding in this house; from the north side of the house.

No sooner did he see army contingents moving to deploy north side than he started firing. No contingents from any other area could reach this advantageous location. When Major Abhijit and his team tried to move from the previous house after clearing it, he did not allow them to get out of the house and continued firing burst in the area of their move. Major Abhijit and his team were determined to reach tactically advantageous spot and, as leader of the team, he thought to take a chance. He tried to fire on the terrorist from his left shoulder so that his teammates could reach the desired place and then, the team together could engage the terrorist.

But his dare devilry had inherent danger: he was hit by the burst fired by the terrorist. The burst was so long and powerful that it almost slashed his tibia and damaged fibula bone just above ankle. It instantly incapacitated him. But he could manage to reach safe corner before he collapsed. This was exactly when I had entered the area of the encounter. To the terrorist's bad luck, unknowingly, I reached the spot where Major Abhijit wanted to be. It was possible only because I was coming from a different approach from northern direction.

Major Abhijit was immediately evacuated under extremely tense and dangerous environment. Now Major Marathe took over the command of the operation to catch/kill the holed up terrorists in the fortified house. The tactical situation was such that other than taking risky and bold decisions there was no easy option left. Major Marathe and his team decided to enter the house occupied by the terrorist from the opposite exit which had large exposed area to move astride walls of the two houses. The terrorist was in the advantageous position of height and was closely watching each and every movement of ours team by constantly shifting his place of firing and hiding. His tactics was 'shoot and scoot.'

Despite all-out effort to keep the terrorist pinned down, the terrorist managed to fire on them. His target was the Company Commander; Major Marathe. But the entire team could miraculously save itself. Major Marathe was not injured but another NCO; Havaldar Namdev Sawant sustained minor injuries. The NCO was taken off the team and arranged treatment in absence of the doctor. The CO had triple whammy and was extremely perturbed about turn of events today. This was not happening for the first time but such occasions were very few and far between, when we had one death and two injuries; one Company Commander sustaining serious injuries and one NCO being evacuated from the op team. Since there were casualties from both Charlie and Delta Companies, the CO ordered them to withdraw and ordered me to take over the rest of the operation. Despite Major Marathe's insistence to remain part of the rest of the operation, the CO told him to move away with his team.

Now, effectively I was the only officer who was in the real battle ground and was in a position to lead the operation. I spoke to the CO over radio and he sounded unsure of future course of action, seeing so many casualties; one NCO dead, one officer and one NCO injured, at least one of them very seriously. He asked me what I proposed to do since I was the only one who had to decide the course of further operation. He wanted to come to the spot but I told him not to make any such endeavour; not only himself but none of the men. First, I secured my position and readjusted deployment of soldiers within. To my luck my rocket team had followed me, unknowingly, while coming to this village. I carried out assessment of the situation and recommended to the CO to destroy the house by firing rockets and give the terrorist(s) live burial. In my assessment there was no other option since all other options had been tried and yielded only one result; casualties.

I gave my proposal to the CO over radio who was sitting some 200-300 meters from the place of encounter. He was hesitant in allowing use of rockets because of two reasons; one, it was likely to have collateral as well as extensive damage, and inherent danger of own casualty in a much closed space. The rockets need minimum 180 meters to travel in the air for getting 'primed or activated.' Any less distance may not allow it to get primed. Un-primed rocket is like a heavy dead-log which would not blast but fall like a big stone on the target. I convinced him by explaining lack of options, and if any, it was likely to have more casualties. Although I, was youngest among the lot of Company Commanders, he had tremendous faith in my judgement. Finally, he gave his consent.

My northern approach was open, at least for the soldiers

who already were in close vicinity. I could manage to sneak in one more detachment of rocket launchers in another location; a bit away from me. Now it was perfect for me. I wanted to fire rockets from two positions due to a very important tactical reason. The reason was if I had fired from one direction the terrorist was likely to move to the other side of the house and keep on shifting his position. So it was important that we fire from two positions simultaneously and not allow the terrorist the flexibility of shifting from one side of the big house to the other. The second location from where the rocket detachment was to fire was not in visual contact from my location. So the fire synchronization was difficult. It was overcome by giving fire order over wireless sets.

This way almost entire deployment would become aware when rockets were being fired and every one would take safety precautions. But before firing it was important to ensure that no civilians or army men were in close vicinity of hit point of the rockets. Already, the civilians had left the location. In fact wherever a house was being occupied by the terrorists it was surely known to the owner and generally known to almost all the villagers. So they took all possible precautions except that no one told the army men about the impending danger of the holed up terrorists. The army comes to know, most of the time, only by sudden encounter and consequent injury or death either or both sides.

Before firing rockets, as a last resort and warning, we announce over megaphone to the holed up terrorists to surrender and save themselves. We also ensured safety of the innocent citizenry from likely collateral damage. In such cases it was also imperative to ensure minimum destruction/ damage to the property and building. Rarely had it happened that any such terrorist had come out and surrendered. But still we had to do that and we did that and waited without any positive outcome. When after reasonable wait no response came from the terrorist, I ordered my firers to prepare High Explosive rounds of rockets for firing. To my assessment only two rounds were sufficient to neutralise any living being inside the house but I was not sure whether he was on ground, middle or top floor of the house. So I told both the rocket teams to prepare three ammunitions each for all the three floors for maximum impact. For minimum damage to the building it was important that we did not hit the walls but hit the window panes, so that the rocket entered inside the house and blasted. We identified our points of hit.

I ordered each detachment to fire the rockets over wireless for synchronised impact. I was part of one such detachment. The ear-piercing sound of their launch made us deaf for a few seconds. So we could not comprehend whether it blasted at the target or just fell like a log as suspected due to range constraint. Those away from us informed over radio that only one blasted at the target. I ordered second and third rounds of rockets from each of the two launchers to be fired. At least, as we were told by the CO and other stations who was away from the place of launch, three rockets blasted on the target. In spite of our efforts to inflict minimum damage, the house was extensively damaged and I was sure no living being could survive after three blasts. We waited for some time for the dust and smoke to settle down before entering to search, locate and arrest or lift the terrorist, if found dead.

Although, possibility of anyone being alive after the rocket fire was almost nil, we took due precaution in entering and searching the house. Neither I nor any of my rocket teams entered the house. We were away and had to hold the defences on periphery of the houses. The teams that entered and searched the house found the terrorist dead with his weapon to his side, with sufficient ammunition still in his magazines. His body was searched for any explosives, grenade, etc. and then his dead body was brought out for identification. The villagers as well as our own sources identified him as a Pakistan trained terrorist and a resident of closeby village.

But even after intensive and exhaustive search we could

not find rifle of the already dead terrorist. We could locate rifle of the CHM but its breech-bloc assembly; the vital part of the weapon, was missing. After careful examination it was found that the terrorist had taken out the breech bloc assembly of the CHM's rifle and used it in his own rifle. It was a matter of guess only that probably due to fire by the CHM not only one terrorist was killed but his weapon had also got damaged. So it was cannibalization of parts. The operation ended with two terrorists killed, two AK-47 rifles recovered. But we also lost one NCO. One officer was still battling for life.

It was going to be sunset by now. Whole day was so action packed and full of fight for life and death no one realised the time. No one could have lunch, etc. that day. The police were called to take over the dead bodies but they pleaded fear. They were afraid they would be ambushed and killed by the terrorist if they came to take over the bodies. They requested us to send across the dead bodies to the police station to complete the formalities of post mortem and handing over the dead bodies of the terrorists to their families. The dead bodies were sent to the police station in a military convoy.

We came back to our respective locations of Beerwa and Haft Chinar. The mortal remains of the martyr were deposited at Base Hospital at Srinagar, as per army rules to complete the formalities. It was decided to perform last rites of the martyr at Haft Chinar/old Jammu And Kashmir Light Infantry Regimental Centre (JAKLIC) next day after due consent from the family and/or next of kin. The funeral was extremely emotional affair. But by now I had seen a few and reconciled to the fact that to protect the territorial integrity of the nation these are the prices we have to pay.

On 26 Jan 1995, His Excellency the President, Dr Shankar Dayal Sharma, just before beginning of Grand Republic Day Parade, honoured the CHM Shivaji Balu Jagtap with second highest gallantry award of peace time; Kirti Chakra. In the august gathering of diplomats of the world and watched by millions of countrymen he honoured him for displaying indomitable courage, disregarding his personal safety and going beyond call of duty for territorial integrity of the nation. Smt Kusum Shivaji Jagtap, widow of the martyr, received the award from the President on behalf of his martyr husband. The Raj Path reverberated with commentators words of appreciation of the martyr's bravery.

Sixteen years passed since then. On 31 Jan 2011, I could see the widow of the martyr face to face for the first time when she was invited to be part of our golden jubilee celebration of raising day of the Unit in Pune. All awards, monetary help given by the government and the Unit, etc. were grossly inadequate to compensate for the loss of the human being who was a husband for one, a son for two, a father for four and a martyr for 1.20 billion Indians. The suffering and irreparable loss was so apparent on her face, on her premature aging, on her movement and most obvious on her silence. No one could guess how many million times she would have missed his presence; in the moments of pain, in the moments of pleasure, in the moments of agony and ecstasy, at the time of her daughters marriage or son's school results.

A soldier's wife is, probably, the strongest human being in the world; stronger than a soldier. She is like a lamp that has to sustain itself amid storms of life and cyclones of loneliness. Amid drought of emotional fuel, she has to learn art and science of sustaining the life; her own and her children's. It has to remain aflame amid all odds. I imagined the glory of the martyr who was given sent off with great honour, bestowed with the second highest gallantry award and was saluted like a setting sun on the horizon; his aura still dazzling. But the widow was like a lamp amid rain and thunder-storm that cannot put off until the new sun rises. She had to enlighten the path of her children and fulfil the commitment of guiding them through the dark nights. She had to take them across the stormy river of life.

I did not know what answer she would have given if I/

someone was to ask her whether she would choose a soldier as her husband in her next chance/birth. But I could hear her husband singing the Maratha Regimental Song in choir, which I had heard several times during various functions and Sainik Sammelans in the regiment and in the Unit. Today I heard him singing it alone smilingly, as if answering my question put up to his widow;

Mard aami Marathe Khare, Dushmnala bhare ka pare,

Desh rakshavaya dharm taravaya, kaun jhunjhas maage sare,

Vadla pari ami pudech chalto, jai shivaji garjuni ranaat jhunjhato,

Maratha kadhi na sagratuni hatey, maruni dahaas ek Maratha kate......

We Marathas are men of mettle, always unbearable to the enemies.

For protection of my country, for restoring the true values, No one can put us on back foot.

Even in cyclone we move ahead, reverberating battle fields with the name of Shivaji,

A Maratha never leaves the battle field; even when one dies it is after killing tens.......

****

Janjeer Ki Jhankaar par, shubh geet gate jayenge,

Talwar Ki Aghat par, nij jay manaate jayenge.

ai Ish Bharatvarsh mein, sau bar mera janm ho,

Kaaran sada hi Mrityu Ka, deshopakarak karm ho.

– Pt. Ram Prasad 'Bismil'

Amid jingle of chains, we will sing for our motherland,

Amid hits of sword, we will celebrate our victory.

'O' God allow me, to be born in India hundred times,

And every time let me die for my motherland.

Number 2769281L CHM Shivaji Jagtap was search party commander. While searching one of the houses, the CHM and his party came under heavy fire of militants hiding under wood and grass. CHM Shivaji Jagtap got injured in the first burst. Undeterred by the bullet injury and in sheer disregard to his personal safety, CHM Shivaji Jagtap gathered his last ounce of energy and charged on the militants, killing one of them on the spot and simultaneously foiled the escape bid by the other two before succumbing to his injuries. For displaying outstanding courage, grit and devotion to duty and sheer disregard to his personal safety after being injured in face of grave danger, to uphold the tradition of Army, he was awarded `Kiriti Chakra', posthumously, on 26th Jan 1995.

SMT KUSUM SHIVAJI JAGTAP W/O CHM SHIVAJI JAGTAP, KC (POSTHUMOUS) RECEIVING THE KIRTI CHAKRA FROM THE PRESIDENT ON 26 JAN 1995

Chapter 6

Death in a Cordon

Several times, my gut feelings pushed me closer to the CO, to seek his permission to check the coffin but every time I landed up suggesting something short of it: to check the credentials of the people who were going to be part of *Janazaa or* just to frisk them. We, like the CO, were equally concerned about the sentiments of the mourners, atleast in this case. Irrespective of the fact, how they perceived us, we were conscious that we were dealing with own citizens. I went to the CO twice with the apprehension, but both times he raised his hand gesturing not to disturb the mourners and not to search the coffin. I guess, like mine, his hesitation was also mostly due to his humanitarian approach of not hassling people part of the last journey of a revered cleric. The hesitancy was despite apprehensions about the credentials of people participating in the funeral procession. And partly it was, I guess, due to psychological pressure media had created on the security forces by publishing several 'stories' about 'excesses' of the soldiers.

Capt Anil elaborated above; remembering the first operation, the battalion had carried out in village Soibugh and continued:

It had happened a few months after imposition of AFSPAct in Kashmir when we were newly inducted in the valley. In the history of independent India, for the first time such harsh Act was imposed on the people of Kashmir. National and local newspapers were awash with special editions of stories and incidents of alleged 'excesses' committed by the soldiers on the local population including the women. In one of such 'stories' in a special edition of a national English daily, a soldier was shown with his assault rifle in one hand and pointing finger from the other towards the bulge; covered below the *Pheren* a woman was wearing. He was haggling and insisting with the woman to lift her *Pheren* since he suspected she was hiding some arms or ammunition inside her *Pheren*. Whereas, contrary to the suspicion of the soldier, the woman was carrying a baby far deeper below the *Pheren* nay, even her own skin: she was pregnant.

Such publications and adverse publicity, which were appearing occasionally in one or the other journals, had somewhere impacted the CO's decision making. Practically, both the parties; the locals and the soldiers, had valid reasons to perceive themselves to be victims of misunderstanding. At times women were used as conduit to smuggle arms and ammunition out of the cordon by carrying them under the *Pheren* pretending to be pregnant, and invariably, even innocent civilians were harassed by 'once bitten twice shy' soldiers, now perennially suspecting every bulge in men and women.'

Capt Anil had begun above narration about first operation in Soibugh on my inquisitiveness as to how the village of Soibugh reacted under cordon. Tonight again our Unit was going to carry out 'crack down' with a hope to catch Syed Salahuddin. We had just come back from CO's briefing about tonight's operation. The operation was planned in the village of Soibugh, very close to our Unit headquarters at Sharifabad (Sharief-Abad) and not far from Srinagar city. The village had become a legend due to several juicy fantasies and a few true incidents during various operations by other Units but more it was due to being native village of Syed Salahuddin. We, three or four officers, came back straight from the conference room after getting briefed about tonight's operation to the cosy room of Major Kamal chatting about the previous incidents during Soibugh operation. We wanted to laze around for some time and remember the miracle happened in the same village during one of our operations.

Although, except me, all other officers had participated in the operation, they were equally interested to hear the narration of Capt Anil; more due to his captivating way of description of unique things happened during the operation than discloser of new facts. However there was another reason why Capt Anil was sounding interesting to all; he himself was lost in the woods, though he was only one supposed to be with the CO. Rest all were with their respective Companies.

When I had joined the Unit, I was taken to all the posts around Sharifabad Cantt for familiarisation. The village of Soibugh was indicated to me down to the west of the Cantt; which was on a high ground. We overlooked the village down approximately 3-4 Km away divided by lush green farmland of assorted crops dominated by paddy fields and a few cluster of trees.

On my curiosity about the village, Capt Anil had started recounting the first operation they had carried out in Soibugh before I joined the Unit. I sat on the carpet to listen and they gossiped all kind of things happened during various operations; laughed on their own silly mistakes, locals' problem of misinterpreting our instructions, which created a kind of confusion during ops and likely outcome of tonight's operation. In fact talks were focussed on the main incident of 'miracle' of resurrection of a dead holy man from the coffin but casual references intended at having fun just propped up. It was going to be my first operation in the iconic village hence I was extremely excited and eager to know about the village, its geography, people, and of course most interestingly; the previous incident of unbelievable dimension: the resurrection. What transpired among my seniors was unbelievably and incredibly interesting story of death of a revered man during cordon and the dead man's resurrection from the coffin later. I forgot everything about tonight's prospective operation and heard the story before going for dinner and preparing for the imminent operation in the same village same night.

Capt Anil carried on his narration of the first operation in the village Soibugh thus:

One fine evening, the CO summoned all the officers to come to the briefing room. He was overflowing with strange admixture of emotions; extreme excitement, a lot of exuberance and bit of anxiety. He told us that the Brigade Commander or `Commander' in the story) had ordered him to lay cordon around village Soibugh in the early morning between 0300 h to 0400 h tomorrow. He gave a very elaborate briefing and plan of the cordon and search operation, revealing what the Commander had told him. As per intelligence report Syed Salahuddin, head of Hizbul Mujahideen was to visit his family staying in the village, along with a few of his very trusted aides. He was to move in the village during midnight and was to leave before dawn.

It was some cloudy day of July/August 1991. The Commanding Officer briefed all officers in the conference room before dinner like today and then ordered the Unit to be ready and 'fall in' for his briefing at 0200 h just before departure to the target village. The Commanding Officer wanted to brief the soldiers himself and hence, in addition to briefing the officers in the conference room, he began his briefing to all ranks at the PT ground at the given time; sharp 0200 h thus:

"Today, we are going to cordon off village Soibugh. The cordon should be effective before 0400 h. We are laying this cordon with a specific objective of apprehending Syed Salahuddin, head of Hizbul Mujahideen. We have very reliable information that he is coming to visit his family after midnight and is likely to leave before dawn. So we have to lay an impregnable cordon; no one from within should be allowed to go out and none from outside should be allowed to come in. Remember they are very clever people. On one pretext or the other they would try to sneak out but should not be allowed without my or your Company Commander's permission. Once the cordon is complete, I with my QRT and Major Nirbhay Singh with a few selected men of his company will straightway reach the house of Salahuddin. Major Nirbhay Singh would lay another close cordon of the house and be part of my QRT to enter the house to arrest him."

After confirming from the troops in military style whether they have understood so far, the CO tried to motivate them and continued with a mix of Hindi and Marathi:

"The Commander has reposed his great faith in our capability, in our professional competence and above all in our tact of handling a very sensitive issue. It is incumbent upon us to stand up to the occasion and prove that his judgement about us is right, that we are capable of handling the most sensitive issue, that we can capture the most wanted man, that we can pluck and weed-out poisonous plants without harming the crop. He wants that Salahuddin should be caught without harm or hassle to the rest of the villagers."

As usual the Commanding Officer did not forget to emphasise on morality and vanity. Chastising the men he thundered:

"We are not civilians or policemen. We are military men and different from the rest. Our conduct and behaviour has to be flawless and spotless. Local civilians do not have faith in any institution but if they have even a little, it is only in the fairness of the Army. At no point of time it would be allowed to be dented. Any undue misconduct, misbehaviour or ill treatment particularly with the women folk will invite severe and immediate punishment. Hence better you all have control over yourself, your faculties, your tongue, and all other parts of your body."

The CO carried on his brief. "And you all should treat the old and the sick properly. Make your judgement and allow the infirm and old at home. Most importantly remember even a terrorist is terrorist only till he is alive. Once dead he is no more your enemy. Even dead terrorist should be treated with due diligence." The CO ended his briefing in a very philosophical way sensitising all men about how to treat women, sick, old and the dead.

Capt Anil continued his narration:

Two columns moved on foot westwards; towards the village, to cordon its South and Eastern flanks. Two columns were ordered to take long detour by mechanical transport via Badgam to reach the north and west end of the village. Both were to cordon the village in sync so that the 'prey' did not get a chance to slip out of our net—Capt Anil ended first chapter of the narration while lighting his cigarette.

"Capt Anil, the CO angrily had called you over radio and ordered to come ahead instead of being at trail. What was that?" Major Kamal interrupted to know from Capt Anil.

"Oh sir, do not remind. It was among most serious goof up of my life. You know what actually had happened during that pitch dark night. The columns stopped for something on CO's instructions. As per briefing and plan I was with him with my associated troops. When the entire columns stopped, I along with my radio operator also stopped. The Commanding Officer and his aides were leading, followed by mine and then your column. When columns stopped in the cluster of trees I could see nothing except my radio operator, who was ahead of me.

The cluster was so thick that no light could penetrate inside. To top it all, it was a moonless night with clouds hovering over. I was feeling sleepy hence thought of utilising the cover to smoke a cigarette. It satisfied my craving that cooled me down from stress and anxiety. For a very long time when my radio operator did not move, I went closer to him and asked him why he had stopped for so long."

Capt Anil lit another cigarette to control his anxiety remembering those moments and continues:

"To my shock it was not my radio operator but a dried stump of tree. The radio operator and entire column had moved ahead. I was alone and left behind. Quite many frightening thoughts came to my mind that day. I ran helter-skelter helplessly in search of any soldier in the vicinity but in vain. A few minutes back I had handed over my weapon also to my scout-cum-escort when I had thought of using the opportunity to light a cigarette. I thought, today I have to pay heavy price for a cigarette, if something goes wrong. On the other hand I imagined what all conclusions the CO may derive not finding me with him." Capt Anil described beginning of his ordeal.

"Oh, that is why the CO told me to go behind at the trail and send you ahead." Major Kamal revealed his moment of surprise and continued to reveal what had happened thereafter.

And you know there was chaos when the CO wanted to talk to you over radio and you were nowhere to be found. The radio operator was in panic and continuously mis -fed the CO to buy time that he is moving towards Capt Anil. Finally when he could not find you anywhere, out of fear and frustration, he stopped taking calls of the CO, feigning to be having some trouble in reception or transmission. In between the radio operator ran front and back of the column in search of you rattling in typical Marathi *"hey Sahib koote aahe; hey* where is Sahib". The CO was wild but couldn't have shown his frustration over radio net. Hence he told me to find out what the confusion was. I moved back and forth to talk to the soldiers of your Company to find when they had seen you the last but none was sure. In the cover of darkness and unaware of my presence they passed all kind of comments and exchanged jokes. One of them joked that probably 'Sahib' has gone alone to convey the CO's advance regards to Syed Salahuddin with a message to surrender to avoid bloodshed; like Angad to Raawan in epic Ramayan. I couldn't be careless since I was worried about your whereabouts and well-being. After going quite far behind at the end of the trail of the Company and not finding you, I requested the CO to allow halt and permit the entire columns to sit down taking tactical position and wait until you were traced.'

Major Kamal sipped his hot-turned-lukewarm tea and continued:

Oblivious of worrying mystery of your disappearance, small group of young soldiers had fun while sitting on ground; not knowing what the issue was all about. They were mimicking in whispers the briefing given by the CO just before move and enjoying its exaggerations and interpretations in their own way, thus:

"Hey Baba, you all be careful about dealing with women OK. If you are caught misbehaving or ill-treating women, your 'tool' would be chopped off and kept in safe custody in the quarter guard. It will only be returned to you when you would be allowed to proceed to your home on annual leave. To be on safe side I am not even going to look at the women even if they stare at me. Like a Sharmily (shy young woman), I will look down and hide my face from the beauties around"

Another added, "And bachelors won't be able to get it back even during leave."- All laughed their heart out in muffled voice. They only realised that something had drastically gone wrong when they heard my voice ordering them to shut up and keep sitting quietly. I was not in a position to even pin point and find out who the 'Joker-interpreter' was. I was so worried about your whereabouts. Thanks! God you lit the torch to indicate your location.' Major Kamal described the entire incident of lost and found to the very person who was lost.

"Since I was unable to see anything or anyone, I thought someone would be able to see me, hence I lit the torch.' Capt Anil laughed to hide his squirm and carried on the narration of first Soibugh operation looking at me and sipping his tea while taking puffs in between.

The cordon was laid as per plan. We married up with other two columns coming from western flank taking long detour via Badgam. They cordoned off Western and Northern flank and we, with two columns cordoned off the Eastern and Southern flank; which was along bund of wetland cum Lake of Hokarsar. The village was calm and composed beyond usually expected during cordon and search by the army. There was no trace that someone like Syed Salahuddin was around. The CO assumed it to be calm before the storm and was confident about authenticity of the information. There were reasons for being cynical also about results based on such information since never had it fructified in positive result in the past. However every time the failure was not necessarily due to inaccuracy of the intelligence.

Ours was first operation but our predecessors had similar information several times followed by cordon and search and back to pavilion empty handed. They had given up on Syed Salahuddin and were of the opinion that it was almost impossible to catch him though they were reasonably convinced that he did visit his family in the past. But this time, as the Brigade Commander himself had taken so much of interest and was very sure about the accuracy of the information, the CO was extremely enthusiastic about carrying on the rigorous search of entire village. He was also sure that the cordon had been laid perfectly and that if the information was true, the HM chief would be caught today.

When the cordon was about to be completed, the CO moved quickly with his QRT and with Major Nirbhay Singh's team to cordon, search and, if found; arrest Salahuddin. These were moments of extreme anxiety for all of us. The things were so serious that almost all of us were sure of some big encounter with the aids of the Hizbul chief. Major Nirbhay Singh laid a closer and stronger layer of cordon around the house. In fact he laid the cordon inclusive of all the houses adjacent or touching the target structure. We were expecting some movement, some activity around the house. We were also expecting that people would be awake and there would be sentries around the house. But there was nothing like our expectation. If there were fore-warning elements about our arrival, we could never notice them. Still the CO did not believe the obvious. He convinced himself and told us that it was the calm of a hidden volcano before eruption.

The QRT led by me reached the entrance and knocked at the door. There was no response. We knocked, knocked and knocked. A middle aged woman opened the door fearfully; her hands trembling, but tried to look emotionless as if it was something routine for her. The translator; a soldier trained in Kashmiri told her in her dialect that we have come to search her house. She did not resist verbally but asked in Urdu blocking the entry "What for?".

"We have information that your husband Syed Salahuddin is hiding here." The soldier revealed.

"Does anyone hide in his own house?" She asserted with a deep despise.

"We are not here for scholarly argument, get aside". I ordered her in a stern voice lest crucial time was wasted.

"Am I not entitled some sleep and privacy? Every second day there is crackdown by one or the other force at whatever time they choose." She asserted suppressing her deep fear.

"We soldiers are also entitled some sleep but are deprived

off because of the traitors like your husband." Said the translator in plain Hindi knowing she knows Hindi/Urdu.

"You all know he is nowhere in Kashmir. He does not visit us. We are already in so much of misery. Somehow I am bringing up my children. But you all harass me every second day. Please do not disturb my children, they are sleeping." She kept standing at the door effectively blocking it completely.

It looked she is trying to delay us. It almost confirmed that the man is surely inside, else she wouldn't have resisted. I signalled the soldiers not to waste time in arguments sensing her to be buying time for her husband to hide or run away. Our Kashmiri translator snubbed her while entering with a whirl followed by me, the radio operator, Major Nirbhay Singh and rest of the QRT. Rest of the members of the family were huddled at on place. Most of them looked miserable and frightened. Every nook and corner was searched. The CO surrounded by a few of the QRT men and the radio operator waited outside with anxiety, hope and the best and the worst.

But all was blank. Salahuddin was nowhere. The CO could not believe it. He entered the house and we again searched every possible place in the house. Not satisfied and with deep disbelief, he came out blank; filled with feeling of failure, confusion and unsure of the reality.

Was the information false? He murmured. Or we have failed in laying the cordon in time or he slipped away coming to know of our arrival. Or worst; he is still within the house in his untraceable hide out? So many things came to our mind, in the CO's mind and every one's mind. But still all was not lost.

"We still have the possibility of his hiding somewhere in the village. So we should move quickly to assemble all villagers at one place; at mosque or school or just at open ground, for identification parade." I tried to console the CO.

By now it was dawn. The CO told me to order general search operation of all the houses within the cordon under the supervision of the senior JCO and move to carry out spotting and interrogation at the congregation. I with my scouts and escorts moved towards the mosque. The CO along with his QRT also reached the mosque to instruct the Muezzin or the Maulvi to announce about the cordon and order all the villagers to assemble near the mosque for identification parade. But to our shock and surprise, we saw a large assembly of men and women near the mosque gathered around a coffin.

A few of the women were wailing inconsolably; beating their chest, pulling their hairs and hitting their face in grief. It looked as if our arrival had added to their pain and grief. Whereas most of them; particularly the old and aged, were sitting quietly, occasionally sobbing. A few men were reciting verses from the holy book. Many small children were sitting around; most of them drowsy with sleep and rest sleeping. A few women were also sitting with their babies in the lap. We were impressed by the devotion of the followers. The attachment explicit could be a matter of envy for any dying man. A few young men were preparing to take out the *Janaaza* and were waiting for the Sun rise. We were taken aback on turn of events. We were here to catch the most wanted man from the village, nay from the valley and here the atmosphere became such that any such activity was not only emotionally untenable but to some extent against civilised norms. It looked it was our bad luck and bad timing for the operations.

The assembled informed amid cries and apparent unbearable grief that a very revered Peer from Baba Reshi Shrine (near Gulmarg), who was on visit to the village, left them and this world to be in the company of the Almighty. He was a mystic who touched and changed thousands of lives by his spiritual prowess, miracle and supernatural strength. He had great following in the entire valley but he was most revered in Baramulla and Badgam districts. The followers informed that the Peer had several times defeated death and had come out of the jaws of the demise. But this time the miracle did not seem to be happening. Finally, it seemed, truth of human life had caught on the mystic also.

One elderly man from the gathering informed amid sobs what the revered himself used to say -"Ultimate truth of life is death and ultimate truth of a mystics' life is a mysterious death."

He was all right in the evening. He had dinner, spoke about grandeur of Allah, the Quran, the teachings of the Rasool and went to bed cheerfully. No one knows what happened to him late night. The villager further disclosed that the Peer had called a few of them and revealed;

"The death is around. I do not know who would win this time. I have defeated her so many times in her so many forms and incarnations. She tried to deceive me but I deceived her. I have seen so many of my followers being slayed by her, but her attempt to come closer to me were all defeated. At times I wonder how long I can be winner when I myself tease her, enter in to her house and poke her. I am sure, I win only because the *Allahtala* wants me to guide you and serve you all for some more time; to show you the right path, to guide you to reach your chosen destinations. Else I do not see any reason for my survival when she is perpetually behind me with all her might."

The scene was of deep sorrow. The followers of the Peer were inconsolable; particularly women. They cried, hugged and consoled each other while they prayed to the Almighty to give him power to resurrect as he had done in the past a few times. They prayed that he defeat the death again as he had done in the past. What to do? Now, after our announcement there was likely to be more gathering. They were preparing for the Peer's last journey. The grief was so deep that nobody looked worried for anything worse than this; like even arrival of the army.

The CO became a bit confused, and so were all of us. But army does not remain or cannot afford to remain in state of confusion for long. The CO enquired in detail about the Peer and assured them of all help and co-operation relating to the last rites of the revered. The villagers informed the CO about the Peer's last wish of getting laid at rest in the graveyard at Baba Reshi near Tangmarg. The Peer desired that he be given a burial at a place where he had spent most part of his life as a mystic, where he found permanent peace in the serenity of coniferous evergreens, amid sweet smelling shrubs and blooming flowers surrounded by snow clad mountain ranges of Pir Panjal; a darling and mighty son of the Himalayas. He wanted to be rested at a place where his revered Reshi Baba Payam-Uddin lived forever. They requested the CO to have 'Deed' or Darshan (look) of purity on the Peer's face; completely covered in flowers and white beards. The coffin had more weight of flowers than probably the mortal remains of the Peer or so we perceived.

The CO was moved and told them to prepare for the last journey. He commiserated with the followers by revealing that he mourned death of the revered and would allow the funeral procession in normal way but they had to understand that the army had to do its job. He instructed the village elder (Sarpanch) to select a few men and give their details who would be going with the mortal remains of the Peer. He instructed that rest of the men to gather for identification parade.

The village elder (Sarpanch) gave a list of 5-6 men who were to accompany the mortal remains to the chosen place of burial; Baba Reshi, some 35 km away from Soibugh. No woman was accompanying the mortal remains of the revered. Some of us were of the view that before allowing the men to go with the mortal remains, all of them should be frisked and scanned. Even though it would have looked 'insulting', it was decided to frisk and put them through identification parade without them knowing it. Secretly a 'Spotter (identifier)' was told to scan while sitting in a closed vehicle with dark glass windows if any of the men resembled Salahuddin or his associates or have any association with any type of subversive activities?

The spotter; a local surrendered militant could not identify any of them as suspect. Either all were innocent villagers or, a few were, unidentifiable outsiders; but all Kashmiri. He guessed and suggested that they probably were followers of the revered from some other part of Kashmir since he had not seen any of them ever. We were informed by the spotters that none of them looked any closer to Syed Salahuddin. The CO told me to write in Marathi '*YANNA JAU DYA;* allow them to go' and sign on the palm of all men who had been allowed to go out of the cordon with the mortal remains so that our own soldiers did not hassle them and no unauthorised persons slip out. Writing in Marathi on the palm was the most secure way of giving permission and weeding out any infiltration.

Capt Anil carries on the narration taking it to the pinnacle of curiosity.

All Company Commanders were away on the peripheries of the village with their respective companies holding impregnable cordon. I was the only one among officers, in addition to Major Nirbhay Singh, who were with the Commanding Officer. I had dual role as Company Commander and the Intelligence Officer. I could read something brewing within the Commanding Officer about the entire situation but he didn't want to look doubtful or confused. I was also doubtful about mysterious death of the 'mystic' but could not clearly figure out the right course of action to deal with it. The wails and chest beatings were so moving and genuine that it was downright inhuman to suspect anything foul. Then we had done everything; we have secretly carried out the 'spotting' and open frisking of all those going out, we have not allowed any one to go out with face covered, we have allowed only those to go out who were not from this village but had come with mystic, etc.

Yep, one thing still was a matter of deep doubt; the coffin. I thought it was possible to hide some arms and ammunition in it but felt a bit mean of expressing the same. I was almost sure about the death of the revered since Commanding Officer himself was offered to see the face. Even I could see some strands of the white beards under layers of flowers spread out. With my doubts, I moved closer to the Commanding Officer and tried to indicate the possibility of some arms and ammunition being hidden in the coffin. He was surrounded by mourning crowed submerged in emotions of grief. He waved his hands signalling not to raise such issues at this point of time.

I wrote in Marathi "*YANNA JAU DYA*; let them go" on the palm of all the six cleared by us to carry the coffin and further to move out of the cordon to Baba Reshi. The mourners cried and uttered so many things in sorrow, in grief; in Urdu but mostly in Kashmiri. When the pain is deep it finds true expression in one's mother tongue only. One of the prospective coffin bearers, the eldest among the "*YANNA JAU DYA*" group clasped the CO's hand and kissed it expressing his deep gratitude and utmost respect and sobbed:

"You are a great human being. No one would understand what you did for us. Our several generations will remain grateful for your kind gesture. May Allah; the most benevolent and merciful, bestow His choicest blessing on you."

The processions moved away. The women cried in chorus and threw floral petals on the coffin. Men became cool and composed. The soldiers stood erect in silence and watched. The coffin was placed in a vehicle and driven away leaving pall of gloom and grief in the entire village.

We began our procedure of assembling all men and confining all women and children to their respective houses. We already had searched house of Salahuddin without any positive result so it was decided to proceed further after having breakfast. In the meantime, villagers were ordered to gather at the grand mosque. During breakfast all of us discussed possibility of Salahuddin hiding in some other house and planning different strategies. The village was so scattered that one Unit could not effectively cordon and search the entire village. Then there were porous areas like water logged low land of Hokarsar, wherein island with groves provide perfect shelter for the militants.

Each house was searched thoroughly. Each person in the assembly was scanned by the multiple spotters to identify if there was any one like Salahuddin. Everyone in the congregation was frisked if hiding any arms and ammunition. All results were negative. Both were exhausted; the chased and the chaser, the villagers and the army. Many suspects were caught; on suspicion, on identification by the spotters, on chain reaction of naming someone else to save oneself and so on and so forth. They entered interrogation centre praying to God to save them and came out thanking; despite so much in between the two events that they were allowed to 'come out' and be with their family. The in-between had 'so much' that one forgot everything. After all, they knew it could have been worse. But nothing came out; no arms, no ammunition, no militant, no Salahuddin. The CO informed the Brigade Commander very hesitatingly about the outcome.

"NTR"or "NOTHING TO REPORT"; three words in army parlance conveying nothing has been achieved or nothing unusual. The CO conveyed the three words with a lot of distress and disappointment. The Brigade Commander paused in disbelief but told CO to wind up. When dusk began spreading its wings, the CO ordered closure of the operation and told everyone to pack up and move back to the base at Sharifabad.

We came back in vehicles; there was nothing to maintain 'surprise'. After good bath, fresh up and dress up all moved to the officers' mess to have dinner, relax and rejuvenate. We were discussing today's turn of events when the waiter informed that the Brigade Major or BM; a staff officer to the Commander wanted to talk to the CO urgently: The CO went to the field telephone kept in the corner table and Major Kamal whispered within our circle smiling mischievously; "The Commander is not satisfied by the screwing he did in the name of Salahuddin.

It seems he has something more for tonight. Have dinner and be ready to move again like Nishachars (night wanderers; literally meaning demons), to get screwed." We all smiled distressfully. We thought we won't get sleep tonight also.

The BM informed that the Commander wanted to talk to the CO. The Commander came on the line which the CO was already holding. After customary exchange of greetings when conversation began CO looked lost; his eyes and mouth wide open for a few moments until he regained his composer. We all concentrated to hear and decode the conversation which went like this.

"Yes sir!"- The CO said his eyes wide open.

"---------------"

"Sir, I thought it was irrelevant. Yes one Peer, whom they claimed had come from Baba Reshi, had died during that night but it was before even we arrived in the village." The CO tried to justify something which the Commander thought was a blunder.

"---------------"

"Oh no. Unbelievable sir! How naïve of us and clever of them?" Then he heard a long talk from the Commander only inputs were 'yes sir'.

He just came back and sank in the sofa, closed his eyes for some time keeping the face upward facing the ceiling. We all felt very uncomfortable. It was not difficult to guess what they spoke and what had happened. We thought CO would be very upset and might leave the mess soon. But he did not. He like a true army man overcame all the perceived defeat and deceit. He opened his eyes smilingly hiding his deep pain and frustration within.

"The Commander believes we have been deceived again. The dead 'Peer Sahib' gone out of our cordon in the coffin had resurrected in the jungles of Tangmarg and for the world disappeared in thin air with his disciples only to resurface the other side of the LOC as Syed Salahuddin."-The CO disclosed gist of the Commander's talk The CO further said that the Commander was peeved as why we did not check the coffin and why we did not tell him about the death drama which we thought was irrelevant and insignificant. Anyway there is always next time for the army. The CO repeated exact words of intercept revealed by the Brigade Commander, as claimed to have been intercepted by Military Intelligence and Signal Surveillance experts:

"Peer Sahib shows his miracle, defeats death again; resurrects from the coffin. The Kafirs forced him into the coffin, Allah took him out alive."

Lightning struck us. So he had again slipped out of strong grip of the army? Was the dead 'Peer' in coffin actually alive Salahuddin? Were all the mourners feigning? The wails, cries, the sleepy children and all chest beatings were theatrics: unbelievable. Or it is some misinterpretation of radio intercept by the Military Intelligence? The CO disclosed further:

"The Commander has been informed that the signal wing of Military Intelligence has intercepted conversation of very high credibility where it has been disclosed that Salahuddin feigned to be dead, was carried in the coffin and resurrected at a safe place. There were celebrations both side of the LOC after he came out of the coffin." The CO told us what Commander had told him.

It was unbelievable. The CO was also not convinced. But all kept quiet for some time, as if remembering the entire episode once again. I recounted each and every sentence purportedly said by the 'Peer Sahib' before his 'death' and repeated by his followers to us. I remembered his last words as quoted by his disciples and we discovered very different and new meaning:

"The death is around. I do not know who would win this time. I have defeated her so many times in her so many forms and incarnations. She tried to deceive me but I deceived her.

I have seen so many of my followers being slayed by her, but her attempt to come closer to me were all defeated. At times I wonder how long I can be winner when I myself tease her, enter into her house and poke her. I am sure I win only because the Allahtala wants me to serve you all for some more time, to show you the right path, to guide you to reach your chosen destinations. Else I do not see any reason for my survival when she is perpetually behind me with all her might."

Capt Anil ended his fascinating narration of the first operation and resurrection in Soibugh. The anxiety had again gripped him. He lit another cigarette. Another round of cup of tea was ordered before moving to our respective rooms to get into preparation mode for tonight's operation in Soibugh.

I had forgotten that I was sitting in the 'Den'; room of Major Kamal. The story told by Capt Anil about first Unit operation in Soibugh was so captivating that I forgot that I was sitting here after briefing of the CO and tonight again we had to go to the same village for cordon and search operation. Captain Anil warned me not to get carried away with wails, cries, pain and praise of anyone. Perplexed and amazed I moved to my room to prepare for tonight's operation in Soibugh. Thankfully, this time, we had no information about Salahuddin coming to meet his family.

Chapter 7

Mozi: The Mother

July –Aug 1992: Village Soibugh in District Badgam

As soon as I swam out of the emotional turmoil the old woman had sunk me in with the offer of a glass of milk and by revelation that her son had disappeared after firing by security forces only never to come back, suddenly my entire paradigm changed. I went almost ten years back and I remembered what the professor had elucidated. He had said, while explaining part of the monologue of Lady Macbeth: 'Take my milk for gall'-is the cruellest of all the emotions in the soliloquy: cruellest because the breast milk signifies the motherhood, the future of humanity, the tenderness, the purity of relation, the emotional attachment of mother with the child. Here in her prayer to the evil spirit, Lady Macbeth's wish signifies her conversion from mother to monster; begging for vices in exchange of virtues, begging for wickedness in lieu of piety.

The professor was explaining the significance of Lady Macbeth's monologue in Shakespearian tragedy of *Macbeth in* our literature class when I was under graduating in English literature at Allahabad University. The Lady overpowered by greed, ambition, hunger and thirst for power was praying to the evil spirits to unsex her, thicken her blood and exchange her breast milk for gall, so that she could conspire and execute assassination of the king, mercilessly. So that, in the vacant palace, she could enthrone her husband as king; the victorious General who had saved the king and the kingdom in just concluded war.

Today, when I met this mother, I remembered the words of the professor. I was meeting antithesis of Lady Macbeth and her wishes, a mother; who had already exchanged her "gall for milk." Had it not been discovered later about her to be an "extra ordinary" mother, anybody would have thought of her an ordinary woman; busy whole day, doing house hold chores, no time for self, happy when husband and children were happy and sad when any of them sad. Her wrinkle and premature aging were touchstone of her yester years' hard work, of her struggle for survival, of agony she had left behind. Love, affection, forgiveness and generosity were amassed but concealed so well that it could deceive any personality reader.

I met this mother on a late morning of July/Aug 1992. We were carrying out cordon and search operation in Soibugh. Comparative a big village comprising of Bonapoora, Grattawalli, Krali and Beig Mohalla, very close to our brigade and divisional headquarters at Sharifabad and 6-7 kilometres from summer capital of Jammu and Kashmir state; Srinagar. To the north-west of the village is great wet land of Hokarsar. The village, it's geography, terrain and lay out were quite familiar to me since a few times, as young officer, I have been coming to this village and surrounding areas as patrol leader. But it was my first operation in this village.

The militants from this village were too smart for the army

since there was hardly any catch or recovery from this village. Several efforts were made by the paramilitary forces and later by the army to catch Syed Salahuddin, founder/reviver of Hizbul-Mujahideen and later anointed chairman of Muttahada Jehad Council, but in vain. Rather one odd time, our columns were attacked by grenade and firing. The dream of top brasses to catch Salahuddin was a nightmare for the villagers who were frequented by one or the other force in search of a man who was staying cosily in Muzaffarabad; occasionally visiting Rawalpindi and Islamabad to take instructions for further destruction (or liberation?) of his native land; Kashmir.

A trained Unani medical practitioner, he was born and recognised in Soibugh as Mohammad Usuf Shah, who had left his first wife in Soibugh with a few children and crossed over to Pak Occupied Kashmir or POK to organize and fight for the "Azaadi; freedom" of "Kashmir". The trigger; apparent and immediate among many was, alleged rigging of 1987 general elections of the state assembly. His protest and subsequent humiliation, allegedly at the behest of ruling dispensations: 'the inheritors of the two dynasties of Srinagar and New Delhi; the Abdullhas and Gandhis, was said to be the instant cause of his rebellion.

Soibugh was 3-4 km from Sharifabad, our Unit location. It took almost an hour if the entire Unit walked to the village for cordon and search operation. But it never happened. Half of the Unit generally used to come from a long detour via Badgam to ensure that the village was surrounded by the army from two approaches, simultaneously; so that holed up militants had minimum chance to escape. I was a young officer, with barely a few months' service. Paucity of officers in the Unit had ensured that I was given a Company to command, leading effectively more than hundred men including half a dozen JCOs in the operation.

Two Companies led by comparatively senior officers were ordered to take long detour via Badgam and reach the village from other ends by mechanical transport. Remaining other two Companies, including mine were ordered to move on foot to reach the village out skirts before 4.00 am. The CO and his Quick Reaction Team; known as QRT in military parlance, were to come with us. Hence we were to move at least one hour in advance to cover the distance of 3-4 kilometres from our location to the village of Soibugh. Hence we got up at about 0230 h to complete the routines within half an hour and moved at about 0300 h.

Street dogs in the valley are perceived to be one of the worst enemies of the army, by default, and best friend of the militants. Alignment of their barking can easily be assumed as path of movement of the army. It gives away all the surprise; the army tries so hard to maintain. Not surprising that the army has constituted "dog shoo(t)ing squads" inside the cantonments to shoo(t) away the stray dogs found roaming within the limits of the temporary or permanent cantonments. As soon as we left the cantonment limits of Sharifabad, the dogs started barking from far but alongside our moving columns.

I realised 'the dog's life' has more connotations than I knew or rather I was discovering some more. The genes in the dogs do not allow them to sleep peacefully or remain quite whole night; no, not even during day. Their hearing and smelling capabilities are much superior to human beings. But is that a blessing or curse, since precisely, this is the superiority which does not allow them their peace. They fight each other and bark at every foreign object they see or every sound they hear; which they hear more than any other animal. I wondered for what they bark and fight whole night as nothing on earth belongs to them; the land, the house, the street, the trees and what not. But still they fight and bark; day in and day out. I guessed the Almighty must be thinking similarly about us; the humans.

Since lighting torch or cigarette, making avoidable noise etc. were strictly prohibited during the movement, the entire body used to move as if it did not exist, or used to pretend as if the dogs did not exist despite their fierce barking. The boundaries of the dog kingdom were so accurately but tacitly marked that no sooner the previous group stopped than the next one started barking as if the charge of responsibilities were handed and taken over within fraction of seconds. There were no territorial disputes of rights; only some overlapping of areas of responsibility.

Soibugh had invariably been returning us empty handed, with bad memories, negative results and some misadventures. During one of the operations, our men were falsely accused of molesting a girl, apparently on the instructions from the militants; whom locals call Mujahids. In another incident, one grenade was lobbed on our withdrawing columns, when they were passing through a narrow lane of the village; injuring one JCO, a Subedar and two other ranks.

There were many over grounds sympathizers of militants in this village; mostly in the garb of political/social activists and as religious teachers, spreading ideology of secession and fundamentalism. Some of my men were sure that the *Muezzin;* the religious person who gave call or *Azaan* for prayer, had a code word for indicating arrival of the army, and that was the reason, they argued, we were not able to catch militants from this village despite their concentration being highest in this area. In code, because they knew army had trained its men in interpreting Kashmiri language and speaking plain Kashmiri was not a viable option when it came to warning the villagers or the "Mujahids" about arrival of the army.

We were moving towards Soibugh, on foot in a single file: one column behind the other or one company behind the other company. Since I was not considered seasoned enough yet, due to limited experience and exposure in the matters of military operations, I was kept at the tail; behind the other company. I was happy; for that reason and justified on the ground that it was more convenient for me, irrespective of its propriety. I felt better by being at the tail since it relieved me of leading the columns in the pitch dark night. It also relieved me of fear of leading it somewhere else. We had planned to reach the village before dawn and lay the cordon before any one was out of bed. It was a dark moonless night, rendering the visibility to next step only, that also only by guess. Such operations were deliberately taken on moonless nights or during the phases of second and third quarter of the moon months to avoid detection of the movement.

Dogs were barking from far; behind us, left and right of us and now ahead of us. Strange noise of unknown birds was reaching us from far. The low lying area and lake-cum-wetland of famous Hokarsar was very close from here; I was told by one of my men. Another more knowledgeable told me that, birds from central Asian region and from Siberia visit this place for their temporary inhabitation during winters. It was July/August, hence no foreign bird in the lake. Some local birds residing on the trees of the village at the outskirts, were giving call to their clan after seeing the aurora on the horizon. The sky was readying to undress the black gown and slip in the working attire of azure, declaring to the world that it is time to come out of torpor.

"Sir, we have reached Soibugh." said one of my escorts from among the vanguards.

"How do you know?"- I asked.

"I can see the familiar Chinar; the maple tree which stands as grand gate to the village on the bounds"

"OK. I hope you are not hallucinated." I pinched him.

"Sir, I cannot be wrong. We have visited this village so many times that I recognise almost all the faces, all the trees, even the barking sound of Soibugh dogs." He boasted.

"So start fanning out as briefed to the left of the road. Get the Platoon Commanders on the radio net." I ordered the radio operator and the CHM in same breath.

TRirrrrrrrrrrrrrrrrrrrrrrrrr.

Suddenly we heard a burst of AK-47 tearing the serenity of the dawn. Birds in the close vicinity flew in hordes to unknown destinations, as if declaring to all: "the place has become dangerous, leave it". Bird of assorted ethnicity in the lake of Hokarsar consented to their racial brethren and hovered over the lake to see what was happening; from a safe distance. A few men ducked but most remained still, knowing like a seasoned soldier the sound was a bit far: posing no danger to us; neither in our line of fire nor in our area of responsibility.

TRirrrrrrr--- Trirrrrrr---trirrrrrr

The sound of firing was coming closer, it was just anywhere from amongst us. Suddenly all ducked; taking position on the ground to assess the location of the potential prey; mistaking him to be predator, or who could have turned predator. I stood like a statue; motionless and frozen. Before I could decide and organize my faculties to react, one hand tried to pull me down to take the ground, over bothering about my security and safety. I freed my hand and scolded the scout—"instead of finding and running behind the firer you are trying to hide. Go get behind him." I ordered him.

"Sir, it is still dark and not clear who has fired and from where?"

Suddenly, I saw my radio operator running towards me.

"Sir, the Commanding Officer on line. he said while handing over hand set to me.

The Commanding Officer informed and instructed me– "two suspected men have tried to get out of the village, taking advantage of gaps in the semi-laid cordon. Our men have fired towards them not to kill but to scare them to stop but they have run towards your Company. Ensure they are not allowed to get out of cordon. Catch them and be clear if they don't have weapons don't fire at them. Complete the cordon fast and seal the village." was the gist of the CO's orders given in three transmissions through inherent one way traffic system of the radio.

"Atankwadi." shouted one of my soldiers assuming them to be terrorists as soon as he first sighted the shadows of two suspects running towards our area oblivious of our presence.

I cocked my AK-47 rifle as a matter of habitual and spontaneous action. I heard several similar sounds in the surrounding. All stood, waited and tried to locate. The two shadows ran fast from far under the cover of partly misty and hazy dawn. Deep fearsome sound of their breath was so intense that it felt closer than they actually were.

"Catch them, run." I shouted while myself running to chase the shadows.

A group of my men ran behind the suspects. I was in lead. Slowly my men overtook me; I began dragging my feet to stay behind, they kept on chasing the prey. I stopped to wait and in between instructed the senior JCO to supervise the deployment to complete the cordon, after marrying up with the neighbouring Company.

"Two suspected militants caught but without weapon." came the transmission for me to the radio operator on the Company's Radio net.

"Well done. Be careful and get them to the rendezvous." I complimented them and informed the CO about the success who in turn complimented me and ordered to get them for interrogation.

By now it was all visible. The Sun had lifted the veil of darkness from this part of the globe. A new day with almost similar routine was going to unfold in my life, I thought. A day where I had to see similar faces with similar grump, a day of cordon and search, a day of interrogation, a day of similar pleas of begging for forgiveness, a day of similar questions and similar answers, a day of similar lies to save precious life and blame it on the neighbour for joining militancy or forcible induction by ISI, a day of spotting, a day of mistaken identity, a day of cries and wails and shrieks, a day of chest beating by mothers and "pheran" tearing by fathers since nothing else could they tear; neither the soldiers nor their own destiny, a day of children's curiosity and anxiety, a day of children becoming guardians and bringing food to their fathers, brothers and near-dears sitting in the congregation. And if there was some change it could only be a death; a dead body in civvies or sometimes in uniform.

As per laid down procedure, which now had become routine effortlessly, search teams were formed; to search houses, orchards, kitchen garden and all possible areas of hiding of militants or concealing of arms and ammunition or objectionable propaganda material, consisting of four to five men headed by a JCO or senior NCO and having at least one elderly villager to act as witness-cum-interpreter. At times a police man also joined the team on our demand, if available, to be witness that the soldiers did nothing adverse.

Since Soibugh is a big village five teams were formed from my Company alone, besides the approximate numbers from other Companies also; making it to more than twenty. My teams, all headed by one JCO each except one, which I decided to head keeping the CHM in the team so that in case I had to move around, the CHM could lead. I deviated from the standard practice of officers not being part of search team and confining themselves to the command, control and supervision functions only; to keep myself intensively engaged and interact with the children, women and men, to understand their psyche, mood and feelings, which was of immense interest to me. The teams were earmarked, their areas of responsibility briefed; reminded of dos and don'ts, and dispatched.

Since two suspects were caught, we were anticipating encounter or arrest of some armed militants. The Commanding Officer had also been passing missives over radio about likely catch, raising the hope of catch and heightening the anxiety of encounter. I briefed and re-briefed men to be extremely vigilant and careful, search each and every nook and corner of houses, and look for hide-outs. I myself carried on with my chosen team, leaving it intermittently; to make my presence felt in other teams also, to keep their morale up by being with them, giving some instruction or exchanging some pleasantries. The search continued. The heightened environment in the morning itself had ensured that there was no smugness towards the task.

It was going to be ten in the morning. I had only a cup of tea and so were most of the men. There was no chance of officers' mess vehicle arriving since, as the radio operator monitored the conversation, it had broken down on the way. Initially I thought of sharing the packed breakfast with men, which they had carried for themselves, but later abandoned the idea and decided to wait for officers mess vehicle to reach the operation area. Fortunately the men; our war arms, had breakfast so they were better off and fully active. I was feeling completely exhausted and squeezed out. All of us were awake from two in the early morning, neat eight hours. Lack of sleep, long walk, chase of the shadow-turned out to be-suspected militant, were multiplying the fatigue and lethargy.

As a matter of standard operating procedure, we never used to have food or water from the operation area. The Commanding Officer was very chary about anyone taking any favour or hospitality from locals. Reasons were many, including possibility of foul play, but bottom line was "Army is army; it is not police or a civilian agency." Here one has to follow the rules in letter and spirit, even without understanding the spirit, and honour the traditions not necessarily after understanding the reasoning behind it. It has to maintain highest standards of professionalism, honesty, impartiality and most importantly; morality.

I entered a modest house, having extreme depth and narrow width. Along with me entered the village elder that was part of our team, aged approximately 50. Contrary to the most of the households in this area, there was no child near this house. Contrary to the trend, the housewife also was not sitting outside; instead she was doing her household work, with a studied indifference to the presence of army men. When male village folk are ordered to congregate at designate place for spotting or 'identification' as the locals call it, women sit together in the group providing psychological support to each other, trying to cope with the anxiety as to whose husband or son will not come back home but reach military barracks' cells instead. Many, a bit more courageous, will engage themselves in handicrafts or knitting; very few in household work that also limiting to cooking food for the members of the family sitting at the congregation or for the children.

Out of appreciation for her courage to stay inside home alone and probably to show respect to her advanced age, smile came instantly on my dried and thirsty lips. The women in her late fifties reciprocated with broader and very affectionate smile, left the work and got up, continuously looking at my face as if she knew me. She looked at my face longer than usual, as if trying to read something written on my lips. I felt a bit uneasy and moved faster inside, which otherwise I would not have done and waited outside, for the men to search the house. She followed me in all the rooms, along with the village elder and my men, as if anticipating to ask or say something.

The search party started searching every nook and corner; the bed boxes, almirah, drawer, roof tops, false ceilings, trunks, suite cases, the potteries filled with grains or dried vegetables: not leaving anything for suspicion. I came out in the gallery and stood casually in a corner feeling tired and exhausted. I tried to control my constant yawning and tried to keep my eyes open effort fully, but in vain. I muttered to myself instinctively, unmindful of anyone's presence or absence, overcome by my subconscious feelings: "I am so tired and sleepy. They should finish the search soon."

The woman, who already was looking at my face, tried to decode what I said but instead looked lost. Now she looked at the village elder and asked in Kashmiri as to what I said.

"He is tired and sleepy" translated the village elder to the woman, I guess, and continued -"Wants his men to finish the search soon" and explained to me this much. He also said a few words of praise, I guessed, about me due to an incident a few hours back where he had become extremely emotional with me.

While exiting a house, I had scolded a young Sepoy for leaving the door of the house unclosed after search, reminding him that stray dogs and other animals may enter the house and spoil/destroy things. The stimulus for my trigger was freshly extracted raw milk kept in a bucket and left unattended by the house wife, who had since moved out of the house during search. I had chastised the Sepoy, oblivious of presence of the village elder, to be sensitive and sensible. But this small unconscious gesture was heart touching for the village elder. He came to me with tears in his eyes, held my hands in his hand and said;

'Sir, *Khuda apko hamesha salaamat rakhe*; may Allah always keep you safe, you are great. Who cares about us Kashmiris for a small thing as safety of our milk; leave apart houses, articles and eatables'? – I felt elated and a bit embarrassed since, I thought; it was part of our conscience and for this no praise was needed. I was also a bit dismayed on realisation that unconsciously we conveyed and read so much. The village elder had been telling this incident to selected few house wives since.

I came out of the house of the old woman, sat on a stoned platform and waited until men came. My radio operator followed me as usual and said something unimportant which I ignored. I closed my eyes to feel relaxed but within seconds dozed off.

"Sir"- the village elder's deep voice interrupted my nap.

"Hoooon"- I woke up totally disoriented, eyes burning as if someone had rubbed pepper powder in them. The village elder and the woman were standing in front of me. The woman was holding a big, thick-walled glass of alloy seen only in Kashmir, special to Kashmir, capacity more than half a litre. I looked questionably at them.

"Sir, she has brought milk for you." The village elder said.

"Why?" I felt uneasy and perplexed due to unexpected turn of events, since most of local population covertly considers army as 'entity non-grata', if not outright enemy.

The woman smiled and stretched her arms to hand over me the glass. I was in dilemma and felt that the village elder's praise had brought this 'embarrassment' on me. How can I have milk where I am not supposed to have even water, that also in Soibugh? I remembered the mysterious and suspicious 'story' of feigned death, the coffin and the great escape of Syed Salahuddin from the clutches of the army, due to deception and theatrics of the same villagers, particularly the women. Emotional rather than rational dealing of the army of the 'feigned death' was bigger reason for the great escape. Then it was Soibugh, nursery and hotbed of terrorists, village of Syed Salahuddin, founder of Hizbul Mujahideen, head of United Jehad Council.

"HM militants are big conspirators also. You never know what is behind all this. Head has been positioned above heart by the creator Himself. Why to overlook and regret? We and even the top brasses know the chances of foul play through eatables are remote but army is different. It has everything for its men; everywhere even in the glaciers, so that they need not look from other sources for anything. It does not accept favours, gifts, nay, even hospitality. There need not be necessarily plausible and apparent reason for everything. The guidelines are framed, standard operating procedures created, keeping several circumstances in mind. Not necessarily all should exist here.The orders are very clear; no to all kind of favours and hospitality including water and food."- I thought and continued in my mind.

'And then what about "espirit de corps?" Men are also hungry, they are also tired, they are also sleepy and they are also thirsty. No, no, I should not be emotional either to honour her sentiments or to look friendly and trusting. We army men are not politicians that we need to please people for vote. I don't need it. I just had tea and biscuits; brought and prepared by my men. I can have it again; whenever I want. I sat like a statue bodily conveying I am not interested, I don't like the offer. I won't accept it'.

"*ye chu gav dud*"- She spoke to me directly in Kashmiri not bothering to look at the village elder for translation, condensing all her affection on the face; in the most convincing manner, fearing lest it is rejected, as if it is her need, not mine. She was looking at my vermillion on the forehead; which as a matter of routine was put on our forehead by *punditji* when we used to visit Unit temple before leaving the Unit location for any purpose, including operations.

"It is cow milk"- the village elder translated smilingly and hurriedly with great enthusiasm. She was clarifying and emphasising it was cow milk since Hindus have special respect for cow and cow-milk; that was the reason she looked at my vermillion—I guessed.

She kept on holding the glass in her stretched right hand and her chin in the left hand, thumb hidden towards throat and index finger on top of the chin, down semi-circular below the lower lips, in a typical style of Kashmiri people; when they want to show extreme affection. Her smile was undefeatable. Now I was in deeper dilemma and started thinking how to get out of it. I looked up. The entire team had finished search and was standing scattered in the vicinity apparently pretending to be waiting for me but actually to watch the end of the "thriller" which was happening in front of them live. The men had known that I had been coming across such offers of tea, Kahwah, etc. quite frequently and refusing politely. They knew that I followed instructions quite strictly and deviated rarely.

I got up and instructed the men to carry on the search of the next house; I moved briskly towards the next house, pretending to be very energetic, fresh and in a hurry. The village elder followed with the same paces followed by the woman with slower paces with glass in hand. Slower paces; yes, I could see with slant eyes her askance look and move, she doubting her own effort fructifying. Or was it to save the milk brim-full in the glass from spilling; filled so enthusiastically for a dried lipped young man who had knocked at her door to give all possible troubles to her, as perceived generally.

I kept walking fast as if she did not exist in the vicinity, only to be reminded by the village elder about the milk, the woman and her affectionate offer. My determination not to eat or drink anything from locals or from her, was already reaching melting point due to warmth of her pure, selfless and motherly affection. Now, I carried on my fast paces more because what men would think rather than what I should do for consideration of right and wrong. I slowed down, allowing men to be ahead and far from me; to reach the next house. The village elder and the women too started walking slowly in sync with my steps as if they understood what was going in my mind. Before I finally decided this side or the other, several questions pushed each other to be attended first in my mind:

"Why is she so insistent to offer me milk?" I asked the village elder. He, as if a professional interpreter, passed it on to the women and to me back and forth.

"You are hungry and tired."

"So are my men, you did not offer them, why me only?" Obviously she might not be having that much to offer to everyone but still I asked to understand what was going on in her mind.

"They can share whatever little I have. But it won't be sufficient for any of them." the village elder translated that she had said and continued:

"They all do not look as tired as you; they are not as hungry also. I saw them eating something from their back-pack before they started the search."

"But why you are so insistent about me. We soldiers are tough people; we are trained to bear it all. Within a few minutes our officers' mess vehicle with food will arrive. We have everything it's a matter of time. I do not need it. Keep it for you."

She stopped answering. She was not of the breed to get into argument. She had not studied intricacies of language and laws of logic like university educated; fighting over meaning of a word or hidden meanings between the lines. She was losing hope. She looked sad but not irritated or frustrated. I probably had hurt her. I also felt hurt by her silence. To caress my emotional wounds I started talking to the village elder to know about her. He elaborated in broken Urdu:

"Sir, she had a son of your age. A few years back he had gone to Srinagar for some work and never came back. The same day there was a lot of firing in different part of the city due to demonstrations by JKLF and other 'Azaadi' groups. CRPF was deployed to control the demonstrators; many of them with Kalashnikov. They blamed each other for first opening fire but both sides fired on each other. Many people were killed, including some from CRPF and a few missing. Her son neither came back nor was traced anywhere. Some said he was killed some said he had gone across LOC with several other youth for training but no one knew for sure. Some even said he had run away with some girl to Calcutta. She believes he has been killed else he would have surely contacted her under all circumstances. She says you are like her son."

Sudden change in the paradigm left my nerves fulgurated for a moment. A gush of emotions created turmoil in my heart. Thoughts and counter thought neutralised each other leaving me stoned and a deadwood. I looked emotionlessly far: on the horizon to find a response; in word, action or gesture.

Women; I had concluded while analysing the persona of Lady Macbeth, can be cause of war and reason of peace, cause of creation and destruction, a string to bind the world and a rope to strangulate. They have been prime movers of war and peace, the sprout of ambition in a man; turning a prince in to a pauper and a pauper in to a prince. They can change the paradigms. So had Lady Macbeth; converted her husband in to a predator from a protector. She has converted herself in to a witch from a wife, a monster from a mother, to fulfil her ambition of seeing her husband as king; asking for "changing her milk for gall".

Here I was seeing a mother who had already exchanged her "gall for milk". She had thrown away all the venom, all the grudge, all animosity; standing taller than all. Can a person be so forgiving, so magnanimous? How much she might have fought within herself to be where she is? I looked at her, not on her face but on her feet; like a soldier who begins assessment of a person not from his attire or hair style but quality of his/her shoes. Her feet under a pair of plastic shoes; soiled, dirty and partially torn and socks; wet, soiled and porous. Today this parameter would have failed anyone in assessing a person correctly. Army cannot be right in everything and every time. Grey coloured lower; Salwar, upper covered with faded green coloured Pheren, trite embroidery creating perforation and allowing one to see the kurta concealed under. I looked up, up and up; like a teenager in romance: shyly, coyly and slowly.

She looked so beautiful, strong, tall and huge and sweet. I looked at her hands holding the glass. In my emotional domain her conversion from old village women to a mother was sudden. Now, for the first time I realised she might be aching for holding the glass so long. I stretched my hand and took the glass, moved back to the same stoned platform in front of her house where I had dozed off. Sat down at the same place, looked at the milk; light pink, thick, and smelling aroma of earthen pot. It was not much for me as a food article; but a lot as an affectionate offer from a mother who was seeing her son in me. I could not believe I could look like a Kashmiri; my chocolate complexion was in contrast to vanilla and peach colour of Kashmiris even if the shape and size of nose was overlooked. She had overlooked all above to find me similar to her son. I cannot dishonour a 'mother.'

I drank it very deliberately to enjoy the affection mixed in it. Rarely I have had so delicious milk other than when my mother had been preparing herself and offering it with a lot of cajoling; in childhood. I smiled and told her it was very delicious. She smiled back with extreme affection and tremendous satisfaction; asking should she bring more. I remembered my mother my family. I thought of her son and his unknown destiny. I thought of the circumstances under which I and she; and many more were pushed into for which none of them were responsible. I had nothing to give back in lieu. Even thought of paying money would have been an upfront insult. It was not milk she was offering but affection and relation; between two human beings, between an individual and entire humanity. I felt filled from within but empty handed; nothing to return. I looked at her and told her- "Moz" (mother in Kashmiri) -"Your son is alive and one day he will come back. Allah is great he won't allow anyone to kill him." I gave only thing I could have: hope.

"A woman can change your paradigm as; a mother, a sister, a wife or just as 'the other woman'. My paradigm was changed; forever. Soibugh was no more a village of only terrorists, militants, fundamentalist and zealots, a village of sworn enemy of Indian state, a village of grenade lobbing youth on the moving military columns, a village of head of Hizbul Mujahideen; sitting in Islamabad and Muzaffarabad to conspire Jehad in his motherland. It could no longer be perceived a village of deceits who carry live men in coffin surrounded by condoling and wailing women beating their chest for the 'dead'. Now it was also a village of a universal mother: a great human being, a mother who was beyond the question of being Kashmiri or Indian, a Hindu or a Muslim. She was a citizen of the world: beyond boundaries.

****

Ik lafz-e-mohabbat kaa adanaa ye fasaanaa hai
simatey to dil-e-aashiq phailey to zamaanaa hai

– Jigar Muradabadi

"A word of 'love' is a small phenomenon:
Contracted; it is heart of a lover, Expanded; entire universe."

****

Chapter 8

Balaa: The Dead Soldiers' March on the Streets

The young boy had mounted on me and had gripped me so tightly that in the first effort, I could not free myself. He shrieked out of fear but the sudden and unexpected turn of events had frightened me. He incoherently mumbled something, as if under severe distress, which I could not understand. I tried to retrieve my AK-47 rifle which was now pressed below my body due to mounting of the young boy, but could not. I could not comprehend anything, hence concluded the obvious; he wants to snatch my rifle and kill me. Trying to regain my agility from the stupor of deep sleep, I shouted while throwing the boy away from me. My scouts and the radio operator violently and effort fully disengaged him from me. The boy was shivering out of fear and again gripped me from my waist, begging for mercy. We were at the outskirts of village Heing, waiting for the orders of the CO to start cordoning off the village.

It was just past midnight of a crescent moon night in the month of August 1992, when my soldiers came back distraught to inform me the 'audacious and silly' behaviour of the civilians throwing stones, sickles, hammers and knives at the military men, who were equipped not only with sophisticated weapons but also, practically, enormous power to kill, arrest and detain without assigning any reason to anyone. I was leading 'Bravo' Company, as Company Commander, consisting of close to 100 soldiers and half a dozen subordinate officers. We were moving on foot leaving our vehicles at the outskirts of village Hard Aboora, near Kasba Beeru; a subdivision of district Badgam and our Unit location.

We had to leave the vehicles behind to maintain surprise and move with great stealth. Other reason for leaving vehicle was poor road condition, rough terrain and too many hurdles in the way. But nothing was impromptu; all was pre-planned, elaborated in the briefing of the Commanding Officer when he decided to cordon off village Heing, based on inputs from intelligence sources. The intelligence reports were coming in that due to pressure on the terrorist in the cities and towns, they have shifted to the rural areas and even in the forests of Sutaharan; foot hills of a tiny mountain range of Himalayas. All the four Companies were moving from different approaches to reach the village at the same time, tie up over radio and lay the cordon before dawn, simultaneously.

On the way close to the village Hard Aboora, we were not able to figure out which bifurcation of foot track to follow since there were more on ground than shown on the military map. As the target village was still far, I decided to wake up some of the villagers to seek their assistance in finding the exact way. We tried to wake up someone from the houses at the outskirt of the village. But to our surprise there was no one in these houses at the periphery of the hamlet. All were locked. We had no option but to wake up someone from inner part of the settlement. I moved ahead and sent one JCO and a few men to wake up a villager who could understand Hindi/Urdu and could guide us. If need be, we would tell him to accompany us till our target village. Rest of the Company remained tactically spread on ground; a bit far away.

I was shocked to hear, what my men had to tell me on return when they tried to wake up some villagers. Listening to our call, several men and women who already were grouped, started throwing missiles; stones, sickles even axes. The men could barely save themselves from the shocking conduct of the locals, joined us back; showing foresight, and narrated to me. It was not difficult for me to understand the reason since I had been hearing about fear psychosis created by ISI with the help of separatist-fundamentalists in the minds of locals by spreading horror of *Balaa*. But before elaborating about the phenomenon of *Balaa* it is important to understand the background in which *Balaa* was created.

By 1992 Pakistan and her spy arm the ISI; Inter-Services Intelligence, had realised the disastrous failure of their sponsorship of armed rebellion in Kashmir. Several thousand youth from the vale of Kashmir were imported to POK/ Pakistan; mostly in their twenties: and then trained, armed, funded, indoctrinated in fundamentalism, feverish with frenzy of false freedom, brainwashed and finally were pushed back in the Indian territory of Kashmir again. On their return, sooner or later, they were either killed in encounters or were; disarmed, detained, prosecuted and jailed. The euphoria of 1989-90 was fast evaporating and a sense of frustration, failure, fatigue and even betrayal was engulfing the "freedom fighters" of Kashmir.

Betrayal: yes, because they were assured by Pakistani army and the ISI that if the 'freedom fighters' could create 'conducive environment' or enough pretension for intervention, Pakistan would enter and intervene in Kashmir. The game plan was to create anarchy, paralyse entire administration, force the government to deploy army, force the army to deal with iron hand, propagate all over the world about the atrocities of Indian Army and then intervene in Kashmir to protect the basic human rights of the Kashmiris violated by India. They were assured by ISI and Pak army, as many of the top captured terrorists had disclosed during previous interrogations, that Pakistan would send its army to 'liberate' Kashmir if Mujahids paralysed the administrative and constitutional machinery in the state. 26 Jan 1990 was scheduled as date of declaration of 'Liberation', when in the presence of world media and shoulder to shoulder with Pak army Generals, the Kashmiri Mujahids were to hoist flag of 'Islamic Republic of Jammu And Kashmir' in Srinagar. Mujahids did their job quite well; as they perceived it, but Pakistanis never came. As most Mujahids believed, the Pakistanis betrayed everyone; the Mujahids, the Kashmiris and themselves.

The betrayal was not small it was devastating; substantial number of youth from contemporary generation were ruined, if not by destruction then by deprivation. Yes, deprivation of unhindered education, peaceful and conducive environment and a sense of security. On the contrary, they had to see every day all-pervading military vehicles and all-pervading soldiers all over; in cities, towns, villages, streets, jungles, in schools, in playgrounds and even in their own homes and in their bed rooms, at any time. Now substantial number from the same Mujahids were looking for 'pretensions' to surrender to the same army to whom they had vowed to fight. It was not only betrayal, the Mujahids believed; but self-betrayal by the Pakistanis. Pakistan promised to replicate "Dhaka of Indian Army of 1971" in Srinagar in 1990, which never happened. The boys; the Mujahids did whatever they were told to do: murder, rape, abduction, torture, destruction et al.

But all went in vain and drain when Pakistanis did not come to liberate Kashmir, as promised. Instead even a weak looking government in Delhi headed by Mr VP Singh, handed over state to the army under Armed Forces Special Power Act; giving tremendous power of arrest, siege, search and kill. Finding themselves in the given situation, as some of them perceived: "the 'Mujahids' were thrown by Pakistanis in the `lions den' and exits closed from outside."

Now the ISI was playing psychological dirty tricks, to keep the morale of the Mujahids stable, by shifting its focus from direct armed struggle to propaganda, sabotage and espionage. A propaganda; to detach, divide and disengage the locals from the armed forces, a propaganda; to defame, demoralize and demotivate the Indian Armed Forces operating in the valley.

And the phenomenon of *Balaa;* literally meaning 'nuisance or pest'was among the latest of them; with a sophistication that '*Balaa*' are ghosts of killed soldiers.

The ISI and its overground agents; the separatists-fundamentalist, religious zealots and a few Maulvis were spreading a rumour among the rural masses that ghosts of soldiers killed by 'Mujahids' appear during night and roam around on the roads. These ghosts, the rumour mongers had spread, roam around on the roads, streets, in the fields, on the mountains and in fact at every possible place: anywhere they thought the army could be. These ghosts look exactly like Indian Army soldiers since they had died in uniform with their arms in their hand. Their spirits wander around to take revenge from Kashmiris. They possess men, women and children and kill them finally. These spirits come in groups to "assist" their living comrades in fighting the Jehadis. Hence the agents warned and decreed:

"Kashmiris should not venture out of their houses after dusk. They should sleep in groups closeby, with whatever arms/missiles like sickles, hammers, knives, meet choppers, axes, hatchets they could gather. They should never come out alone if some soldier like entity calls them; even if these `soldiers' ask for help: routes, village name, etc. They should not be given water since they feign to be thirsty and hungry. They are ghosts; they are the *Balaa*. They should be 'chased and shooed' away by throwing missiles and stones collectively"

The villagers were further warned:

"The ghosts; the *Balaa* comes mostly during nights and tries to wake up a youth on the pretext of asking for routes. No youth should try to help them or him but raise alarm. All collectively should attack such ghosts; the *Balaa*, by shouting 'Allah-O-Akbar' and pray to the Allah, the protector, to get us rid of the *Balaa*."

This message was more intense in the rural areas, near foothills, away from urban centres because of two reasons: one rural, illiterate folks were more vulnerable and gullible to such beliefs, two; the militants were taking shelter in these areas due to heat on them by the armed forces in urban centres. After gradual induction of more forces including the regular army to tackle the sponsored insurgency in the valley, the density of force level had become very high, particularly in the urban areas and in the vicinity. The hot pursuit had forced the insurgents to take refuse on the margins; the hills or foothills, forests, groves etc. The forces had also shifted their focus from urban to rural and were launching more operations in these areas.

This was forcing the insurgents and their mentors across the LOC to rework and rethink their strategy. The phenomenon of *Balaa* was to effectively bamboozle both the locals and the army. The design was to create fear in the psyche of unsuspecting and innocent rural folk about imagined *Balaa* on one hand, and on the other hand deprive the forces of small support, at times they needed in navigation in the rural areas, by portraying army men as *Balaa* in appearance, characteristic, description, and pictorial depiction.

The new imaginary *Balaa* was proving to be disaster to the psyche of the women and children in some areas. Men, women and children were spending sleepless nights either in anticipation of *Balaa* or out of fear of *Balaa*. They were also fearful that in mistaken identity of *Balaa* if they tried to 'shoo away' the military men by throwing missiles, it might prove cataclysmic. There were reported cases within army that at places villagers had thrown missile on moving columns of soldiers, assuming them to be *Balaa*, during night without any provocation, rhyme or reason, causing injury to some military men and subsequent retaliation by army men with disproportionate punishment. The hapless, innocent locals had one more worry in their endless woes; the *Balaa*, ghosts of dead soldiers running behind Kashmiris to 'kill' them.

The local commanders of the army were also worried as it was withering away all the surprise element; the army is so sensitive about, even before start of any operation. The retaliations by the army were also eroding the goodwill of locals, whatever little was created by all possible efforts. After a few retaliation by the army men and its unpleasant consequences the local populace had started realising the 'realities' of '*Balaa*' but large swathes were yet to uncover the deception of the ISI. We also tried during our operations and in the consequent congregation to educate people about the propaganda and illusion of *Balaa*, but to little avail.

Kashmiri society, like rest of the subcontinent, is very vulnerable to rumours, whispers and belief of miracles in the matter of supernatural. Two incidents are too interesting to digest the temptation of mention. In the autumn of 1989, as the local elders tell us, a 'miracle' was noticed by some 'maulvis' of *Salafi* sect; a sect preaching fundamentalist form of Islam and an adopted child of ISI in Kashmir, that word '*Azadi*' that is freedom and '*Jehad*' that is religious holy war, were found embossed on the fallen maple leaves. They propagated that 'Allah' had sent message of 'freedom' and 'holy war' through these leaves of Chinar; which were considered holy in Kashmir and that the faithful had seen it.

It did not seem to be a coincidence that during the same period thousands of youth crossed over to Pakistan Occupied Kashmir (POK) in a well-coordinated manner, received training in numerous camps in POK and Pakistan, received arms, ammunition and other paraphernalia of war and were pushed back in Indian side of Kashmir to fight for '*Azadi*' and wage '*Jehad*'. Another incident is equally interesting that goes back pre-independence. The local elders tell that name of Sheikh Mohammad Abdullah, the then struggling leader of Kashmir and 'founder of Abdullah dynasty' was found encrypted naturally in Arabic and Persian scripts on some of the maple leaves.

In the light of above, after analysing why the locals had thrown missiles, I decided to go myself and convince the villagers to understand the reality, get out of false fear, come out and guide us in finding the way. Further my presence on the spot would have ensured that nothing was allowed to go beyond control either side. I asked one of my NCO, who had gone through language course in Kashmiri and had attained reasonable competence in interpreting and speaking the language to come with me. The NCO, by virtue of that ability, was attached with me to act as interpreter to assist me in communication with locals; not knowing any other language than their dialect. I briefed him to announce as loud as he could to the men and women under fear of '*Balaa*' to know that we were army men and not *Balaa* and that they should not fear anything. We meant no harm to them and we wanted their help in finding the way to Heing village. But if they did not co-operate and tried to misbehave with us, I told my man to announce in Kashmiri; 'the repercussions will be very unpleasant for them.'

Before we could reach right vicinity worthy of any announcement, we saw a few men, women and even children gathered at the roof top of the highest building, ready with their weapons in their hand; stones, sickles, canes and other assorted domestic tools which could be used as weapons of offence. Fortunately, it was not moonless sky as usual but crescent moon was there to show us some shadows. In the background of stars and faintly lit sky, I saw a silhouetted women figure on the roof top walking frenziedly from one corner to the other tying and untying her scarf; the head gear.

I also saw a few figures moving close to her as if they were her bodyguards. We also noticed some men and women on the balcony on the first floor of the two storied building. We could guess it was a big gathering of psychologically battered people, sure of arrival of *Balaa* in their beloved village. When we reached closer and were about to announce what I had briefed to my interpreter, the frenzied women shouted at the top of her voice in a frightening tone, coming out of her deepest fear:

"wallai wallai yuir wallai, paku paku balay hay aayae,

paku daru balay hay aayae.

Ya khuda bachav! balay hay aayae."

The soldier-interpreter could hardly hide his burst of laughter, on the paradox of the situation, and told me that the woman was calling all the villagers to come and help her in warding off the *Balaa*. He translated her words thus:

"Come, come, soon come, the *Balaa* has arrived.

Come all of you immediately.

O god save us! The *Balaa* has arrived."

The woman, followed and supported by a few more persons, was repeating the above words frantically. Soon it became like a choir and entered in my vocabulary verbatim. We saw a few men and women peeping from other directions also, ready to pounce on the evil but powerful prey (or predator?); the *Balaa*. If we spoke something, I thought, feverish people would throw the missiles without trying to understand the reality. They were so charged, their senses so overpowered that they saw nothing but *Balaa* all over. I told my translator not to say anything and instructed one of the scouts to light the powerful commander torch and focus on the faces of these people, which could create blinding impact, at least for a few seconds. It was to serve two purposes: one, it would give us correct picture of number, location, position etc of men and women gathered and two; it would blind them temporarily, impairing their capability to indulge in missile throwing. In between we would explain them and try to convince them not to throw anything and come down or send one person to assist us.

What we saw in the search light was both; amazing and amusing. Men, women even grown up children all gathered at the roof top to face and fight the *Balaa*, armed with most "lethal" weapon they could find in the household. I commiserated on fate of these people and felt bemused at the irony: they didn't have weapons but ready to 'shoot or throw' with extreme aggression; we had lethal weapons but not ready to use and shying away to hide.

My trick worked to some extent. The ISI and its agents had forgotten to mention that *Balaa* carried blinding torches. So we had first round of victory. My translator announced in Kashmiri on top of his voice:

"Do not get scared, we are army men and not *Balaa*. Assist us in finding the way to Heing. We want your help. But should you try some misadventure with us, the results will be devastating for you all, I warn you." He continued after pause:

"I further warn all of you to show courage and try to understand the realities. We are living people, carrying real weapons and not fake one".

Many were convinced but not all. The woman who was possessed by fear and fright was sure that we were *Balaa*. Again she screamed in very frightened and frightening voice repeating the same sentences in Kashmiri inviting her neighbours, all and sundry to join her to ward off ghosts of *Balaa* who have befallen her house. She kept on tying and untying her scarf, pulling up and down chain of her pheren. Moving hysterically from one corner of the roof to the other, a few men following her as if to catch or pacify her. Her third shriek scarier than the previous was suddenly muffled and gagged by someone who thought, probably, of controlling the situation going from bad to worse. "Someone has realised the soldiers are getting restless due to shrieks and resultant chaos, and may resort to some other means to get us down"- I guessed. I told my interpreter to tell them to come down.

"Are you coming down or should we come up"- he told me to have said and warned them in Kashmiri.

"Sir, for God's sake please hold on. I have to control and convince my mother who is very frightened due to your sight. Give me few minutes we are coming." A young sounding voice travelled down from the roof top. He spoke in Hindi/Urdu. We waited, nobody came. Knowing now that somebody up there knew Hindi/Urdu, I thought of communicating directly.

"Listen. I am an officer assuring you of no harm. We mean no harm to any innocent person. After all, you all are our fellow citizens. Like you all we also have family; mother, father, brother, sister & some of us children also. We have heart and emotions like you. We are human being like you, do not worry come down. " I spoke in Hindi which was Urdu for them.

I saw a young boy in his teens, coming down the stairs, followed by his father and a few adults. The boy, who seemed to have better grasp over language than others, told me that his mother became hysterical sighting soldier during night. With extreme difficulty he had been able to control her to keep quiet for some time and tried to convince her that we were army men and not *Balaa*. But her doubt still persisted.

I could make out from his voice that he was the same person who had replied from the roof top. There were three-four more men in addition to an elderly gentleman whom he introduced as his father. His father requested us not to mind his wife's shouts, as whole day, in the company of village women; she kept on listening and talking about military, militants and the *Balaa*. The boy said that people in his village needed counselling about the superstition of *Balaa*. In a gesture of assurance I took him in my arms and appreciated his courage and pragmatism. Every day's rumour mill, among women folk of the village, exaggerations, multiplying whispers were creating havoc in the minds of rural folk. I spoke to the entire group and assured them that we were army men and that they should abandon the phenomenon of *Balaa* forever, which was an imaginary sickness of ISI.

I told them that we loved people of Kashmir and that we meant no harm to anyone except those who had taken arms against integrity of India or were working against the interest of our beloved country. I requested the old man to come with me and show us the way to our destination. The old man told me that he was unwell and suffering from asthma. His teenager son volunteered to come with us; to the dismay of the old man. The boy said that his father was suffering from a disease doctors call apnoea, besides asthma. So his father can't keep pace with us. He assured his father not to worry and walked with us. I assured the father and the group that we would take him with us up to the village since it was very dark everywhere and that the routes were unmarked, rough and unrecognizable. I assured them that the boy would be returned to them safely under protection.

My entire column started moving towards Heing; our target village, under the guidance of a young boy whose name I do not remember now. He was slim, fair, and of average height and sounded intelligent. He was articulate and really courageous else who would volunteer to be in the company of army men during night? I could easily fathom his fear and his poser to be normal contrary to his true feelings. On my part I was trying to be as friendly and as unassuming as possible to keep him normal. A few of my pre-designated men led the column as scouts ahead of all but still close enough to me and the guide to seek directions at the bifurcations, crossings and water channels. To make things easy for him I asked about his parents, siblings, education, his liking and disliking, films songs etc. The boy remained cringed to me and indulged himself in continuous conversation with me on all kind of subjects he could lay his hands on or, he thought he could speak or understand; from cricket to carrier and from my bailiwick to Bollywood. I kept on reminding him not to talk in loud voice. He kept on holding my hand, at times placing it on my soldiers.

All the conversation was in hushed voice. He asked me about my studies, education and how one became army officer. He enquired about pleasure of travelling in long distance trains, which deodorant I used, which heroine I liked, which cricket star was my favourite, etc. When he came to know that I am from the same city as that of Amitabh Bachchan, he became very excited and enquired whether I had ever seen or touched Amitabh Bachchan? When I told him that during elections of 1985 Amitabh was one of the candidates for MP's seat from my city, which he won, and during his campaign he had come to our place, he was thrilled and said that I was lucky to have met Amitabh Bachchan.

I was not able to fathom whether his continuous enquiry was a by-product of his unbearable anxiety or unquenched inquisitiveness. I could not fathom whether incessant rain of queries was to supress fear of a forlorn among army men or fascination of being so friendly to an army officer, or was it an effort of `flight' from the fearsome real world. But irrespective of the truth, I was also enjoying his enthusiasm and wanted to keep him at as much ease as possible.

Village Heing, as we had assessed, was approximately one and half kilometres from Hard Aboora. Under normal circumstances it does not take more than 15-20 minutes to walk this distance but today it took almost 45 minutes due to various obstacles; most potent being dark night. I was so engrossed in talk with my young guide that I did not realise we are so close to our destination.

I looked at my watch in the mini torch light. It was close to three early morning. We still had approximately two hours to lay the cordon. It was quite dark and we had to wait for dawn while lying doggo. I told my men to spread out, deploy themselves tactically, be vigilant and relax. The radio operator, who was like my own shadow even in darkness, was close to me besides the scouts, who were a bit far. The boy had done his bit and brought us, hopefully, to the right spot. In the dark we could not have afforded to send him back. I asked him what he wanted now. He expressed his apprehension of going back in the dark and told me that he wanted to stay back with us until dawn and then, he would like to go back to his village. He was afraid to move alone in the dark, lest he might be mistaken as militant or a suspect by the soldiers and fired upon or detained. Or even militants might hassle him as an informer or guide of the army, in case they bumped in him. I realised the vulnerability and consequent danger to his life and assured him that my men would go and leave him up to the points he wanted them to.

Knowing that we were very close to the village, I ordered all to stop at a place which was high ground, covered with tall assorted trees. I ordered my Senior JCO to deploy soldiers around to secure the place and tell them to remain vigilant but no movements. I was feeling extremely lethargic due to lack of sleep compounded by walk on the uneven terrain. I was feeling sleepy even while walking. I lied down on the uneven surface, stretched my body, and kept my AK-47 hugging to me. The young boy and my radio operator also sat close by; stretched and relaxed. Surroundings felt serene and quiet. No sounds; except some insects', strange and unknown beings', all unrecognisable. The serenity was disturbed by lone recognisable sound of our big and bulky radio set kept close to the radio operator; continuously hissing like a cobra, reminding us of hidden vitriolic environment around. It could never be silenced.

We were awake last night also. Some sleep during day was insufficient. The body was demanding more and nagging at every possible prospect; like an underpaid labourer asking for increase in wages whenever he thought it was opportune to say so. This whole night; partially passed and partially ahead we had to remain awake. I was possessed by sleep. Men were also in the same grid but a bit better since they had no botheration of attending conferences, meetings, briefings, and of course, no office chores. On the undulating ground I stretched and adjusted myself to comfortable position. I searched for a bit raised place to use as pillow and I got it. Now it was comfortable; shingles pebbles and dried wooden streaks never mind. I wanted to just relax, no sleep. The predawn breeze was a bit cold but the intensity of sleep overrode it; despite my effort to remain awake.

I looked around. Nothing was visible except close by figures; silhouetted. Men were asleep or awake; could be ascertained. The radio operator was sitting close to me with the hissing sound of his radio set; alert, giving me comfort of generalising the same about all men. Scouts also figured silhouetted; stretched in comfortable sitting position but alert. My guide, the young boy, close to me semi- stretched, probably tense. I told him to relax and if possible, go to sleep. After all he was also deprived of sleep today. He would be sent back to his village after visibility improved. I did not remember when I went in to deep sleep. But it was surely before the boy because when I had last seen him he was awake; whispering something with the radio operator.

I was woken up by a fearful and frightening shriek and felt I was tied in rope. Trying to come out of slumber, I exerted to pick my AK-47; a spontaneous action a soldier slips in, to ward off any danger, but in vain. Somebody had mounted on me and gripped me tightly. I tried to throw him away and shouted. The radio operator assisted me. It was the young boy; my guide. While in sleep he was emanating frightening but incoherent sounds and screams when my radio operator had woken him up by shaking him forcefully. Disoriented, the boy had jumped on me, gripped me tightly and was trying to hide himself behind my body. Almost all men panicked, thinking something had gone wrong or someone had entered in to scuffle with some of my men. Others thought some terrorist had entered into our lie doggo.

I gained control of myself and the situation; told the men in commanding voice to sit down wherever they were and not to panic. The scouts; my men who had multiple responsibility including doubling up as advance guard and my body guard, were offended. They scolded the boy, chipping out his already wounded psyche. I told them to leave it to me, go away and sit down.

"What happened?"- I asked the boy and the radio operator jointly. The boy was still under shudder and could not utter a single word. The radio operator explained:

"Sir, it seems he had some bad dream and when I tried to wake him up, he jumped on you."

"Sir, please forgive me. I swear by Allah, I had a very frightening dream. Out of fear, unconsciously, I tried to hide behind you to protect me." He was trembling with fear. Breathless, he was trying to synchronise his breathe with his speech.

"OK, but what dream." I asked trying to keep him at ease by suppressing my volcano of instinctive upsurge.

"Sir, I saw that I was moving with you and your men towards the village in day light. A few Mujahids fired at your column. You all took positions and started firing at them and they on you. I could not follow you and got trapped in the cross fire in the middle; all alone. I fell on the ground, bullets flying over me. I cried for help but none was coming. I shouted that I am innocent but none heeded; all engrossed in firing on each other. I cried, cried and cried.That was when I was woken up. I was so terrified that I jumped on you; all unconsciously, impulsively." the boy elaborated and continued, "You are only one whom I had been thinking would protect me if something happened."

I told him to relax, cool down and have some water. Men gave him water and tea from the thermos, which they had brought from Langar; the men's cook house, before marching.

I stood up, stretched my body; more to show that all was well than to get out of slumber, and looked around to assess the situation. Everything was the same: the serenity, the darkness, the invisibility, the hissing sound of the radio set reminding of the cobra like hidden, unseen, vitriolic enemy; except the horizon. The horizon was diffidently indicating arrival of aurora before predawn. I asked the boy, my guide what he would like to do: to stay put a bit longer with us or would like to go back to his village under protection. He held my hand and told me that he was confused and did not know what was right for him. He requested me to decide what I thought best for him. I decided to move him back to his village since he was very afraid after the dream and that in company of his family he was likely to feel more secure.

I chose three men to accompany him back up to the point he wanted on the way to his village. But before he left I wanted to assure him that dreams are rarely true; they are reflections of our subconscious and unconscious mind's churning or hidden thought. They are part of our fears, our unfulfilled desires, wishful thinking, our worst apprehensions or our best unfulfilled wishes. I tried to explain him psychology of dreams and cited Sigmund Freud's research and explanation on dreams. He looked convinced but still fearful. I placed my right hand on his shoulder in an assuring body language and told him that my men would ensure his safe return to his parents. He held my hand from both his hands and squeezed softly a bit longer as if trying to garner more premium of trust from me. I said in a revealing tone- "You are wise, brave, and trustworthy, you trust others. You have good intentions and have a clean heart, you mean no harm to anyone, and hence you will be protected by the Almighty." I told my men to contact me over Company radio net in case of any unusual development. They left; all the four.

There was no communication on radio from the Commanding Officer on the Battalion net about our movement closer to the village. It was still dark and I had to wait for my three men to come back after leaving the boy close to his village. I told the radio operator and my scouts to remain vigilant and tell all men to get out of slumber to be ready to move after receiving the communication, which was likely to come any moment now.

I again lied down at the same place and thought of the boy, his mother, his father, their trauma, their dilemma, their superstition, their *Balaa*, the game of politics, the ISI, the propaganda, the soldiers, their difficulty, and their misery, their deprivation of sleep and other minor comforts, their bravery, their sacrifice. I discovered similarities and dissimilarities in the conditions and situations of the locals and the men in uniform. They are in the same grid, same place, same situations, same conditions, same weather, same vagaries and exposed to the same dangers; only substantial difference being they are facing opposite directions, facing each other.

I thought of the terrorists, their misplaced beliefs, their fight, their premature death, their short life, their limitation and the trauma of the family after their death; the devastation, the wails, the orphans, the widows, the psyche of all those watching all this or forced to live all the horror. I thought of God, His loatheness to give equal wisdom to all men, His lack of wish of intervention, His grant of unlimited liberty to men to fight and kill each other in the name of one thing or the other.

"The terrorists had fired on our moving columns. We had retaliated. The exchange of fire had intensified. I could hear the cries of the civilians, the injured terrorists and a few injured soldiers. They were many but we were more. They had only Kalashnikov and we had assorted weapons including heavy calibres. They were firing, hiding running and getting killed. A few houses had collapsed and they had got buried. But a few new had surfaced. The fight was on. Some innocent men had got killed in the cross fire. The children, the women were crying but not seen. Their wails could only be heard. The sky was echoing only cries, wails, shrieks and screams. An old man with long flowing, hairs, moustaches and beards, wearing spotless white cloths descended from the sky and appeared on the scene.

The darkness disappeared, the sky glowed but the devastation became more apparent. The dead bodies: of civilians, terrorists and a few soldiers; the collapsed houses, the buried men, the wounded men, the crying women, the distraught children. He commands: stop it you stupid. What for you are fighting and spilling blood of each other, destroying my creations, my houses, my garden, my rivers and my mountains. Everyone is stunned, frozen and listens quietly. He commands further. I had sent you here for very short period to love each other, to play, to enjoy the fruits of my creation and come back to me to reveal the glory of being there. But you all are fighting, killing and destroying each other. You claim to be fighting for your right, your land, your religion, your identity, your future. You claim to be fighting for the right of your children, your brethren, your clan, your sisters, your mother. Some of you even claim to be fighting for me: for place of my dwelling, for accuracy of my name, about my form or formlessness, about accuracy of pronunciations of my name in the language you learnt. You fight that my name in your language only is correct and my name in others' language is not my name. You morons you least realise that all languages were created by me to overcome your limitations of learning."

He came closer, stood like a mountain and continued:

"You did not learn anything from your forefathers: they also fought like you claiming that they are the owners of the land. Some of them equated themselves with me and thought they are here, on this earth forever: calling themselves with fanciful names; Raja, Maharajadhiraj, King, Emperor, Badshah, Jahanpanah Alamgir and many more words you don't know. They fought, won and lost. Neither their victory nor defeat, neither their win nor lost remained forever. They died, their empires vanished, their children also died; nothing could they take with them from here. Their children; some of them became pauper from prince, commoner from king, beggars from Badshah, ragged from raja. But you did not learn; you still fight for the land which is not yours, for the language you don't understand, for the God you don't trust, for the virtues you want to instil in others but lack yourself. You kill my children for the beauty of their skin, for the taste of their flesh, for the beauty of their horn or tusk. You destroy my mountains, my rivers, my air, water and space, believing it is yours. You all are down stupid." he shouted.

"Stop it you silly, else you all will be destroyed soon".

I got angry and asked him, "if you are so powerful why don't you give them wisdom to understand it all instead of giving sermons?". All were silent only I was shouting trying to match His words. "And if you are so powerful why do you allow all this at the first place? Reply you, saint, God, Almighty, and owner of the world, whatever you are. Tell me, tell me, tell me." I shouted.

"Sir, it seems you are in some terrible dream."one of my men had shook me. I opened my eyes and saw all my men sitting spread all around; some with their weapons mounted in firing positions in different direction.

I realised, I was in dreams. I felt down stupid. It looked as if dreams are also contagious; the boy started it and they were still continuing.

I saw it was predawn. The darkness was losing the battle, the light slowly embracing the surrounding in its bosom. The horizon was turning cupric. I looked around. My radio operator was receiving some transmission and was engrossed listening, replying and acknowledging it. My scouts came closer and told me I was murmuring, muttering and at times squawking in dreams. I could not remember my transition from thought to slumber, slumber to deep sleep and then from deep sleep to dreams. I thought of Sigmund Freud's explanations on dreams. If you keep on thinking something good or bad very intensively, it enters into your sub-conscious mind and recycles as dream. Your wishes, unfulfilled desire, may come in your dreams. The things you terribly wished to happen but did not happen; may come in your dreams. Your fears are your dreams. Your wishful thoughts are your dreams.

"Sir, you see we did not realize in the night, actually it is a graveyard that is why all those trying to sleep are seeing terrible dreams. The boy also was terrified after seeing the dreams at this place." One of my men revealed.

I looked around. He was right. The place I thought was my pillow was actually a grave; not very old.

"Don't be superstitious, I had very deep, satisfying and refreshing short sleep." I rebutted, lest they also start nurturing some superstitions. Some of them moved away to hide their smile, but none contested my claim.

"Sir, the Commanding Officer has ordered to close in for the cordon of the village and marry up with the neighbouring Company. It should be effective within fifteen minutes." My radio operator informed.

"Has the party gone to leave the boy, come back?" I asked.

"Yes sir, we are here." One of them spoke while coming closer to me.

"Hope all was well." I enquired.

"Yes sir. Actually his father along with some other men from the village was waiting for him near the water stream, just other side. They thanked us profusely and requested us to convey their gratitude to you for taking care of his son." They informed.

"OK, tell the senior JCO and the CHM to take count, give me the report and be ready to move." I ordered.

I looked around. It was still dark but visibility had increased. The graveyard was full of newly dug graves. The graveyard; my home and bed for one night, was silent, the surrounding green, and the fields beautiful; crops pregnant with yields. I apologised to all on whose tomb we unknowingly had sat and slept. I thanked the boy; my guide for assisting me in the most trying situation, I thanked my men for being always vigilant and giving me luxury of sleep even in the most vitriolic environment. I thanked all; the nature, the surrounding; all visible and invisible and of course the sun for bringing a beautiful new day ahead in my life. I thanked the Almighty, the owner of the world, for ensuring that neither of the dreams: that of mine and that of my guide were true and wished that the appearance and sermon of the old man in the dream were true.

****

"Illusions commend themselves to us because they save us pain and allow us to enjoy pleasure instead. We must therefore accept it without complaint when they sometimes collide with a bit of reality against which they are dashed to pieces."

—Sigmund Freud

****

Chapter 9

Salafi Baba

May 1992: (New) NavTheed Village near Srinagar

He had urinated in his pyjama. I was puzzled whether this was part of his usual theatrics or was it result of imagined fear about his fate in the hands of an army officer whom he had unfairly treated, abused and bamboozled. He was under the interrogation of an officer whom he had spoken derogatory things about, in most undignified manner, on the presumption that the army men did not understand Kashmiri Language. Was he dreading the worst in the hands of those who wielded extra-ordinary powers, with regard to life and liberty of the suspects: the army men? And whose even misadventures, at times, were beyond scrutiny and probe?

"And yes. Are you carrying your Coffin, Qafan and Kabr?" I asked him, recounting his dialogue spoken during our first encounter.

'*Pani, Pani, Pani.*' he squirmed; sincerely or as part of his drama, couldn't have been said for sure since none of us had even touched him.

'You should have carried your '*Pani*; water', nay everything you may need including Coffin, Qafan and Kabr. You would never know when death will strike and you may need these things. So what will you do, who will arrange for your Coffin, Qafan and Kabr?

'Sir, *mujhe maaf kar deejiye. Mere bachche yateem ho jayenge*; (Sir, forgive me. My children will become orphan).' he pleaded.

Hearing above from a man whom I once had thought to be a good human being and a man who had kissed my hand showering elderly blessings, only brought the thought in my mind that one reaps what one sows. Our two chance meetings were so contrast to each other; in the first meeting I had gone to ask for a small favour from him and in the second he was begging for his life from me. In both the cases it was water which we were asking from each other. But both the encounters were coincidental; rather god's wish. Today, while I was interrogating him, I remembered the day when a small incident had taken me to a chance meeting with him, for the first time, in the village (New) Nav Theed; a north western suburb of Srinagar city.

The Sun was still preparing to come above the horizon. Thick woods, to the east of the village on the high mountain slopes, were weakening the struggle of the little aura trying to cross over and light up the hamlet. The filtered illumination peeping out of the window panes in the backdrop of orchards and alpine woods, as seen from the wobbling vehicle, was creating an illusion of million fireflies performing pendulum dance at the same place.

The stepped houses at varied altitude looked awesomely beautiful on the foothills while we approached from the Fore Shore road from south west, leaving Hazaratbal shrine behind and taking a semi-circular detour on the northern banks of famous Dal Lake. In the ambrosial hours, when water in the lake was comparatively calm, the beauty of the Hazaratbal shrine reflected in the lake was mesmerising.

From the down, the village also looked a piece cut from the heaven and placed on the extended lap of mountain in a corner of the 'paradise on the earth' to the far north of banks of river Jhelum. I felt very charmed and thought such a beautiful village can have only beautiful inhabitants.

While placing the cordon around the village in the early hours and engrossed in the fancy about the village to be a piece carved out of the heaven, I had fallen into hell; in a semi-covered and poorly roofed soakage pit. Naturally, the stench was unbearable but more unbearable was the psychological feel of slipping in a soakage pit. Had there not been my scout-cum-escort moving like a shadow, who just in time caught me by back of my collar and held on, I might have got completely sunk in the shit-socket. Fortunately, the cordons were almost complete and hence I started searching for some cleaning place, leaving everything else to my Junior Commissioned Officer; a Senior Subedar.

Looking for bathroom or cleaning place outside of any house at the outskirts of the large settlement, one of my scout-cum-escorts knocked at the door of a big beautiful house. A middle aged woman opened the door, only to be taken aback on sight of a soldier; an omen of trouble in the early morning. My scout, in an effort to make her feel normal, spoke with humility; uncharacteristic of a soldier, at least in this part of India. He informed the lady that the officer urgently needed to clean the part of his trouser. He explained her how I got soaked in the sludge and I needed to use her bathroom, if she allowed.

The woman did not respond to the request. Instead she spoke in Kashmiri to the bearded man in fifties, sitting in the drawing room apparently preparing for Namaz; as if handing over responsibility of taking decision to the man. Their muffled and chewed conversation in Kashmiri, meaning of which I came to know several hours later, went like this;

Woman: "*Ye Chi Army, Amis Chu bathroom istimal karun.*" (It is army. He wants to use our bathroom.)

Man: *Soun bathroom kyazi*? (Why our bathroom?)

Woman: "*Amis chu dab lagmut, aab khadus manz, saaf chus karun.*"

(He has fallen in to soakage-pit and needs to clean urgently.)

Man (trying to look normal): "*Yale yem yeth gaub hatyar che tulan thele kyasi chena bathroom kalas peth tulan.*"

(When they can carry such heavy weapons, why can't they carry their toilet on their head?)

Woman: "*Khaudaies path math wanta yethken, agar yeman phekri tarui kahar karnay.*"

(For God's sake do not speak like this, if they understand they will let loose hell.)

Man: "*Yemo kafirav chu gaday kahar tulmut*"

(They are already a hell; Kafirs.)

Woman: "*Rabas peth kar te chupa, namaz-e-fazruk waqt ha chu*".

(Please for God's sake keep quiet. This is time for *Namaz of Fazr*)

Man: "*Dauh karukh kharab kafirav, subhai namaz wakta.*"

(The Kafirs have spoiled my day, before morning *Namaz*).

Neither I nor my scout could comprehend exactly what they discussed but guessed it was to help us. I guessed they might be discussing some internal matter as to which bathroom should they take me to or might be feeling pity on my plight. However the escort-cum-translator, who was part of my group but not in fore front till now, looked aghast.

On the presumption that the upscale locality was inhabited by educated people who understood and spoke languages besides Kashmiri, by default, the translator-soldier remained in oblivion till now. His face red in rage; not able to speak or translate for me, he looked at the woman, at the man and then with unexpressed pity at me. He wanted to say something to the bearded man; probably some scolding or chastising but could not. Unaware of the meaning of the words spoken in Kashmiri by the Maulvi, I told my translator to remain in the background. The translator- soldier gestured me to move away from the house and look for some other house or place to wash smudged attire on lower parts of my body.

This was not for the first time we were being abused and cursed in Kashmiri on the presumption that none of us understood the language. But it was for the first time that our soldier-translator dithered to translate the spoken words by the Maulvi-like man in the upscale suburb of Srinagar. Hiding his deep anguish, the soldier gestured me to move away from the house despite knowing how urgently I needed to clean my uniform and my body after falling thigh deep in a semi-covered soakage pit. I was a bit puzzled as gesture by a soldier to an officer, instead of verbal communication, was unusual. In such circumstances my soldiers always communicated in Marathi but my handicap was that neither I had learnt Marathi nor Kashmiri till then. Having no inkling what conversation had taken place between the woman and the man and feeling uncomfortable on my soldier's gesture, I thought of talking to the man directly in Hindi/Urdu:

"Is there any problem? I wanted to use your bathroom just to pour water over my trouser without removing them. You know I have fallen in to a soakage pit. I could never imagine in a beautiful looking village and in an upscale settlement, soakage pits are left semi-covered."

Man (in flawless chaste Urdu with natural sweet tinge of Kashmiri in his accent):

'*Janab* (Sir), it's so bad and so sad, my heart goes for you. I wish I could help you. The water in the overhead tank is almost over. Even I could not do *Wazoo* (washing of hand and face before *Namaaz*). I am afraid your good self may get wet without satisfactorily cleaning as the supply may end any moment.'- he reasoned with sympathy sitting on the handmade beautiful carpet spread on the floor.

"Ohhhh! Soooo! This is the reason. I was puzzled what you were discussing with your wife so long."- I said with a sigh of relief of being able to know the contents of their discussion.

"When she told me about your problem I felt very bad. I was discussing with her how we can help you. I proposed to her to get water from the other bathroom but she told me the other tank is also empty. I feel so helpless. An army officer is asking for a small help and we are not able to provide that; water, which is flowing plenty around, matter of chance sir. By the way she is not my wife but my sister. I have come to meet her. I do not belong to this place."- He looked at me piercingly while holding his chin edge of salt and pepper beards from his right hand.

"OK, OK. I appreciate your kind gesture and sympathetic sentiments towards me. I also remember my home where round the clock we get water and never store; you open the tap and it flows."- I said with melancholic tone but nostalgic pride.

"Sir, you belong to which place in INDIA?" He emphasised on INDIA.

"Allahabad: confluence of two biggest and most revered rivers of the subcontinent; Ganga and Yamuna." I boasted with childlike superiority.

"Oh! The city that gave India its first Prime Minister; Pandit Nehru. His forefathers were also Kashmiri. In fact more than half of the PM's are from your city. You come from a blessed place that has bestowed on you so much of *Tehzeeb*; culture. *Khuda apko salamat rakhe* (May God keep you safe.)" He shook his bearded chin in typical Kashmiri style with his right hand while still gripping it tightly.

I was charmed by his affection. I felt elated and inflated.

My soldier-translator waited for our conversation to end with military discipline and with patience of an ambush commander; not showing any adverse emotion, holding his breath until right opportunity came his way.

At the end of the conversation when I gestured to move, the man got up and came close, held my right hand from the fingers, lifted it up to his lips and kissed the reverse side of the palm; supressing the stench the sludge soaked trouser was emanating. My liquidation was complete. I flew in emotions:

"I wish the very best to the gem of a person you are. I apologise for the trouble I gave today early in the morning. I wish all human beings were like you. I really feel sorry to disturb your routine. You all have to go through a lot of agony due to military operations."

He bowed from his neck and wished me *"Khuda Hafiz* (May God keep you safe.)"

It was still dark and I did not deem it right to knock at another door for personal favour. I thought it more appropriate to wait for some time and in between check the deployment spread around the village. But before right moment came for knocking at any other door for help or my translator could tell me what actually that man and the woman had said to each other, I received an urgent call that I had to rush towards Dachigam National Park since three-four suspects had been seen running towards that area. Leaving every other issue behind, I rushed towards the boundaries of thickly forested national park up eastwards with my buddies and radio operator. Since the area was so vast, wild and thickly forested, any search was like a wild goose chase.

A few more teams were dispatched to search the area. While the teams searched for the three-four human beings, I got lost in the wild; such mesmerising beauty even in Kashmir was not common. The thick greenery of alpine woods and fir-birch forest in a staggered height could be a chance. It looked like God's best implemented scheme; springs, lakes, wild animals, water sources, and entire flora and fauna looked awash by nature. It was freshness in perpetuity.

Even after a few hours effort, no search party could catch anyone but I was flabbergasted to see so many sources of water, the water works and a developed system to channelize water for potable use for the residents of closely areas. One of the engineers at the water works system informed that the ten villages (hence the name 'Dachi-gam; means ten villages' in Kashmiri) spread on the slopes and at the top of the hills were relocated to keep the area cleared of human habitation by late Maharaja of Kashmir in 1940 so that the water sources were not polluted and the same could be channelized for drinking purpose. Remembering the lack of water in the house where I wanted to wash my trouser, I wondered how it could happen when there were so many springs flowing in this area. The discovery had brought me relief; I was happy that I had seen a place and very good water source to clean my trousers.

I was Second in Command of a Company. The Company Commander; my senior was busy with some issues and told me over radio to freshen up, have breakfast, etc. and then come back to the congregation; the assembly of residents for identification parade, so that he could be relieved. I was to assist in identification parade while keeping control over the crowd. I called my assistant and asked him whether he was carrying my spare pair of uniform. To my good luck he was carrying. I felt very happy. I thought of not only cleaning the slugged attire and my body but also having a good bath. The place had not much of privacy but it was not in the glare of the public eyes either; there was none except my troops and a few water works department workers. It had plenty of cold potable water flowing in the pipe coming from the springs from the higher ranges of the mountain; source of the water work.

I told my escorts and my assistant to be around while I planned to have bath. Among my escorts was my Kashmiri translator. He had endeavoured a few times to tell me something but I could not pay attention due to other pressing issue. This time while I prepared to take bath he came closer, took my articles as I gave him one by one, and said:

'Sir, do you know what the bearded man and his sister spoke.' finally he got the chance to reveal the unthinkable.

"They spoke about how to arrange water for my washing, I guess." I said non chalantly.

"No, the bearded man abused us and spoke a lot of offensive things about us assuming, apparently, none of us understand Kashmiri."

"What? But you did not tell me there. Why? What did he say?" I asked him stopping my undressing and temporarily discontinued preparation to have bath.

"The woman was sympathetic and wanted you to use their bathroom but the man scuttled it scornfully. While scolding her he argued that if we could carry such heavy weaponry why couldn't we carry our bathroom and commode on our head. He also said that we had spoiled his day by showing our 'Kafir' faces early in the morning." While I looked at my soldier-translator's face in disbelief, he described the entire dialogue between them verbatim.

Remembering the dialogue I had with the man and intense bout of mutual praise, I felt silly and naïve in front of my men. I could not react to his interpretations. Sensing my state of mind to be non-receptive to his description and my silence unbearable, he tried to convince me by reminding how they were not discussing openly but in hushed and chewed voice, as if, gripping their lower lip with their teeth. I remembered to have heard similar words like 'kafir' and 'hatyar,' etc. and tried to connect with my translator's interpretation.

"Sir, can you believe the bearded man's interpretation

that there was no water in the water tank even after seeing the waterworks system here; on the very head of the village which is supplying endless water to the substantial part of the city? In fact I was unable to comprehend why you believed him so easily. We should have checked his tap." He argued to convince me.

"I never imagined a gentleman and spiritual looking person in his advance age will indulge in senseless lie. I also could not imagine about his audacity that he would lie to an army officer, who, if in doubt, can search his entire house, arrest him without assigning any reason and detain him for long for interrogation." I revealed over confidence as reasons for my leniency.

I felt deceived and duped but not depressed. I felt duped; not of my possession but emotions and trust. I resumed preparation to have bath without reacting. He took away my articles and waited with dried ironed clothes along with my assistant till I had bath. Forgetting everything I had a good bath in the open area, in the beautiful surrounding, from flowing water from the pipe carrying water from the top to the water works station, though I felt very cold. While I had bath my senior JCO; a Subedar came and went back.

After having good bath to my glory, putting on good talcum puff which my buddy had carried for me and adorning on clean pair of uniform I was feeling extremely satisfied and happy. I reached the place of the Company Commander to relieve him and cheerfully saluted Major Kamal; the Company Commander and my superior, only to get shock of my life. He did not respond to my salute; as if he had something already in his mind. He looked at me from top to bottom; my new uniform, my fresh pair of policed shoes, my freshness and my overall happiness and then at his muddied trousers. Hiding his anguish and controlling his flood of anger, he asked me whether I had bath. Unsuspecting any wrong I told him happily.

"Yes sir."

"Where?"

"'Near water works complex."

"Fu** off you silly. Disappear from my eye sight. No longer can I bear your sight. Fu** off."

I could not guess reason for his excessive anger. But I was peeved on someone passing the information of my bath to the Company Commander. Later I came to know he was fed the information with a lot of spice and exaggerations. I was just two three months' old in the unit and had limited understanding of doing a thing or not doing it in the insurgency environment. Coming from purely civilian background my understanding of military sensitivities was also limited. I wanted to explain to him why I had bath but he did not give me chance. I left the place; hurt, humiliated and scorned. The soldiers around tried to soothe me by saying in the given circumstances the bath was more of a compulsion than choice.

I straightaway went to my already assigned place of duty; the congregation to keep the assembled men under control for identification parade. Since the locality was an upscale middle class settlement, there were many youth well educated, well dressed who could easily converse in Hindi and English. The adjutant had sent across photograph of a suspect and requested me to scan through the assembled people and try to identify the person, if he was in the congregation. Despite my best effort to hide my endeavour of matching the faces with the photograph, one youth who was well dressed and spoke flawless English, could guess that I was scanning to locate someone. After watching me for long he gathered courage to strike a conversation.

"Sir, may I assist you in any way." He said smilingly.

"What assistance can you give me?" I asked curiously on unexpected offer from him.

"In identifying the person you are looking for and whose photo you are trying to match with some face." He said confidently.

"Do you know why I am passing close to you so many times?" I asked him seriously.

"No sir." He said smilingly.

"Certainly not because you are very handsome, but because the photograph resembles your handsome face." I said looking piercingly in his face.

The young man with pinkish face turned amber. He gasped for response, thinking why he invited trouble of asking me to help. All who were smiling around bore mournful face and looked down. The young man scanned his brain to respond before he is ordered to follow the soldiers to the interrogation centre. He feared if he looked upwards to me, I may signal him to get up and follow. I could not bear for long the turmoil he was going through.

"Unfortunately and ironically we are not allowed to get interested in innocent and nice people. Hence you are not of much use to me." I said smilingly breaking the suspense.

"Sir, you had virtually killed me. What face I would have shown in the society and to my near dears. Mere pick up by army has devastating impact on us. Many people here are against senseless fight. Many hold senior positions in the central government. I would be a blot if I am picked up by the army. I swear by Allah, I never will support cessation or disintegration from India". He inhaled violently from his rounded lips as if smoking cigarette.

"But you have fair share of militants and their sympathisers in your village. Don't tell me your village is 'Pak-Saaf'- I intentionally used the double meaning word to denote 'Holy' as well as 'devoid of pro-Pakistani elements".

"Sir, I liked your wit. Certainly our village is not 'Pak-

Saaf.' But we are helpless. What can we do? We are suspected by both sides. Our life is hell. Our self-respect is ruined, our honour is battered and bruised, our studies disrupted, our routine uncertain and our life expendable. You will never understand our pain. We cannot choose time of our food, our bath, our sleep and our studies, like you can do. It is army and the militants who decide it." He paused, thought and then went on to describe the state of affair of the people of Kashmir:

"We are like 'football' being played between two teams of military and militants: neither of them having any 'goal post' anywhere; near or far. The referees siding with the military are sitting in Delhi and coaches tutoring militants; in Muzaffarabad and Islamabad. It is a state of complete disconnect in a never ending game."

He touched my heart not necessarily because of the substance in the words but the description of the situation. It was so eloquent that I could not stop myself looking at him with awe. One should learn art of communication from people of Kashmir. They can convey most difficult things in most eloquent manner with utmost humility. They are capable of hitting you without hurting, if they choose, and accomplished in disarming you of your retaliatory tools; just by their spoken words. I could not even retort that 'coaches' are meant for siding with their team but 'referees' are always impartial. Instead, praise for his intelligent description came naturally on my lips:

"You are very intelligent, speak with elegance and possess tremendous moral courage."

"Why not sir? I belong to one of the most intelligent races of the world; Kashmiri Pundits. We wrote the first history in the subcontinent, created among the best literature, composed the best poetry, created world class education institutions in the ancient world when most of the world was roaming naked, constructed structures second to none in elegance and grandeur; I have to be intelligent. It is in my genes." He said smilingly and boastfully, lifting the spirit of youth around, leaving me speechless. It's not that I did not know what he said but he 'said' so was unbelievable in the prevailing environment.

"But you are a Muslim?" I wanted to clear my doubt which arose due to his description.

"Yes sir, I am. But no Kashmiri Muslim denies the fact that they are converts from Pundits, though a few affiliate themselves with Persians and Central Asian races also."

'But all such talks are decorative and good only for academic purpose. What we are seeing on ground is in complete contrast of your feelings and description. The deception of people around has forced me to see every one with scepticism, listen to them with suspicion and take even their appreciation with a pinch of salt.'- I said remembering the bearded man and his 'abundant affection' for me in the early morning. Today's incidents within and without had alienated me emotionally so much that I could not stop sharing my bad experience with them.

The young man and people around him looked at me, expecting to narrate some specific incident. When I told them about the incident and described the house, many of them smiled. The young man in conversation looked at his friends around and tried to guess smilingly:

'*Salafi Baba*?'

A few around him smiled and nodded in affirmation.

"So his name is *Salafi Baba*?" I asked.

They broke in laughter. The young man explained:

"Sir, not his name is *Salafi*, but his sect's name. They claim to be modern day puritans of Kashmir, who are working tirelessly for salvation of Kashmir under the guidance of our 'holy' neighbour. Their interpretation of religion is so impractical and contrast to the Kashmiri culture that tauntingly we call them 'Baba'. They are negating everything Sufi's taught us; mysticism, love, tolerance, unity of souls, monotheism and oneness of the Creator. They are teaching us cynicism, hate, intolerance, exclusivity of souls based on method of prayer and different Gods of different religions based on their names in different languages. By his definition most of us are not Muslims; we eat with more than three fingers, put on trousers touching heels, drink water in one go or in more than three steps or less than three steps contrary to their prescription. In their interpretation all this is *Kufr*; blasphemous."

After hearing such a long discourse I realised who the bearded man was and how I was befooled. Frankly I was hearing the word '*Salafi*' for the first time and was completely unaware of their tenets. My anger and strong feeling against the '*Salafi Baba*' also subsided after disapproval and despise of his interpretation of religion among youth for his conservative approach. I was looking for that man in the congregation but could never trace. I told the group of youth that I was looking for the man but not able to locate in the crowd. They smiled and one of them said:

'Sir, you are not the first military man looking for him. Many tried before you but failed. He is like wet soap; the tighter you try to grip, the more it tends to slip out. See how he kissed your hand and you could not catch him." All broke in laughter including me.

"Sir, you please come to my house and use our bathroom, wash your trousers and have good bath. The water flow never stops in our tap. We will feel nice to help you. You can have Kahwa/tea also." He offered.

Since I already had bath I thanked him for the offer. Talking to them had uplifted my spirit in more than one way. The identification parade was about to end. Search parties were still carrying on search of houses in the localities. I moved to the officer's mess for lunch which was close to the interrogation centre. I was also eager to know about the 'catches'/suspects.

Experienced men have said good and bad both have their chain reactions and follow ups. My day had started with a very good mood appreciating the unique beauty of nature around village New Theed but was giving me shock after shock; fall in the soakage pit, deceit of '*Salafi Baba*', the Company Commander's anger etc, The day was wavering with mood swinging circumstances. Here I was greeted with ridicule by my senior colleagues with a Bollywood song that was filmed and played on a bathing scene on Jeenat Amaan in film Abdullah.

One of them sang the song and all around broke in laughter. The news of my bath was passed on to each other with a lot of cumulative juicy concoction and spicy toppings, like; the place of bath was very close to the congregation of local civilian population, was very vulnerable for attack by militants and was seen by so many people around; contrary to the truth. I over looked all the taunts and allowed them to enjoy their concoction thinking in the environment of uncertainty, firing, fighting and death anything can be matter of pleasure for us. Initially I tried to give reason for what I did but finding everyone in non-receptive mood, I kept quiet. But I certainly was hurt on lack of trust in the wisdom of younger officers by the seniors. I thought such treatment of young officers might be one of the reasons for young not getting attracted to the army.

I noticed most of the suspects detained from the congregation were interrogated and found to be uninvolved in any kind of subversive activity. This was among very few operations where we returned empty handed; no catch of arms, ammunition or militants. The operation was wound up before dusk. I had no regret of meeting the '*Salafi Baba*' but deeply missed company of dynamic, pragmatic young man who had coined the 'football' analogy which I was to use in the prologue of my book and which had truly touched my heart. The youth of this village had earned respect for entire Kashmir in my eyes. But most important part of this operation was yet to unfold somewhere else.

The time passed on and our battalion was ordered to move to Qasba Beeru (or Beerwah); a sub divisional headquarters of district Badgam.The area had become hot bed of militancy due to pressure of armed forces on militants in urban areas and consequent shifting of the latter at far flung areas. Frequent crackdown in big urban centres had forced the militants to move to the peripheries; outer and more secure rural areas like Beerwah, which has more militant friendly terrain and natural cover to hide. The higher headquarters of the army had the inputs that besides terrorists who remained underground, many over ground fundamentalists in the garb of religious teachers and Maulvis were roaming around spreading venom of intolerance in the Rishi-Sufi land of Kashmir.

The landscape surrounding the small town is extremely beautiful; hills, water channels, orchards of apple, walnut and almond continuously supplemented by willows, poplar and various other varieties found at lower altitudes of Himalayas. Substantial part of the road from Srinagar to Beerwah is common to Gulmarg; silently revealing' the journey is no less charming than the destinations'. It gave me understanding why Kashmir had so many Rishis, Sufis and philosophers. It is perfect setting for poets, romantics and philosophers to indulge in pursuit of their goal. Our location was on the slopes of a hill dropping down westward towards Sukhnag Nar; a water stream rolling down from snow clad ridges of mighty Pir Panjal.

Our unit was ordered to occupy an apple processing and packing unit set amid apple orchards, originally owned by a Kashmiri Pundit; an ex-MP (as some locals told us) from the area but now fled from the valley abandoning everything including the orchard. The big orchard spread in several acres had several varieties of plenty of good quality apple besides almond and walnut. It had several huts also probably for their staff and guests but now occupied by us.

My Company was ordered to move first and establish itself. Another Company followed. Third Company was ordered to move to Khag. But since shifting was a bit time taking, the unit began operating in the surrounding area by sparing and mustering appropriate strength from all the three locations. Suspects and terrorists caught during this period were taken to battalion headquarters at Sharifabad. Eventually when the rest of the battalion shifted to Beerwah, they brought the detainees with them. Among them were two Hizbul Mujahideen cadres from Mirgund caught from deep inside the groves of water logged low land of Hokarsar and, on their identification, their mentor; an over ground preacher in his fifties.

The preacher-Maulvi was such a great crook that our interrogators had given up on him. His antics were perfectly theatrical with conviction of reality. Whenever they tried to interrogate him he would feign to be sick, thirsty, and oblivious of surroundings and even feigned to not to know that he was in captivity of the army. He would feign to be calling for his children, his cow or goat and would laugh, cry shout in the same breath. He would talk, behave and act as if suffering from dementia. His melodrama was so perfect and appealing that some of the officers had started believing it to be true. Doctor checked him several times and declared his all parameters to be perfectly in order, including his brain. Whenever they tried to interrogate, he would start teaching them grandeur of the Almighty, revelations in the holy book and similar things.

One fine day when several officers were sitting in Adjutant's office in jovial mood, after CO's conference, the Adjutant smilingly raised the topic of the Maulvi, his theatrics and instructed me to interrogate the Maulvi and submit the report. He specifically told me to give the Maulvi some corporal treatment since all the mental treatments given to him were returned by the Maulvi with interest, leaving our interrogators crazy. I knew it was a tactics to cut my 'Charlie' and make me look silly. These are the tricks tried on young junior officers, at times for fun. The body language said it all. I already had taste of treachery of another Maulvi at New Theed so I wanted to tread cautiously. I took two soldiers and went in the detention cell to see the Maulvi who was turning nuts out of our officers.

Seeing each other we both became speechless; neither could he believe his destiny, nor could I; the reunion. He was the same Maulvi who had kissed my hand in New Theed and then before assembly for identification parade, had disappeared in thin air; the same person whom youth had christened *'Salafi Baba.'* Scene of his deceit ran through in my brain like a movie in theatre. Suppressing my true emotions I smiled and politely asked him:

"Oh, Maulvi Saheb, You? How come they can detain gem of a person like you? What did you do to be here?" I exclaimed indicating to dirty floor he was sitting on and continued:

"O God, faithful say your justice system is flawless then why this angel here in the hell hole?"

'Khuda aapko Salamat Rakhe. Uske yahan insaf hai tabhi to aapko bheja hai mere fariste!' (May God keep you safe. His courts have justice that is why he has sent you here, my angel.) - He laughed and then cried, wiped his tears and then preening his beard said further:

"Khuda janta hai us din jab apko pani muhaiya nahi kara paya to mujhe kitni taqleef hui thi"; (God knows how bad and sad I had felt when I could not arrange water for you.) Good people always meet good people and bad people with bad people. See ultimately, I have the privilege of being in your benign company again." Very sure that I would have never come to know what he spoke that day and what the youth of the village revealed about him.

"Truly." I said holding flood of my anger within, on his chameleon character.

"Oh! He is most merciful and benevolent, omnipresent and omnipotent. He is owner of the world, creator of the universe and master of all beings. He is witness to everyone's good and bad conduct." He sermoned contrary to his conduct and tried to create fear of God guessing the imminent that was to follow.

"Truly?" I felt like hitting his face but stopped as if someone had caught me at the last moment. I hid all my true emotions and thought of playing his game;

"Do you really believe He is master of all including the Kafirs? Do you believe that He is one with different names in different languages? Do you really believe that He gives salvation to those also who pray not necessarily as you preach? Do you believe that even if prayer is not said in a specific manner, putting on specific clothes, facing specific direction, also reach Him? Do you really believe that he is the creator, father, protector and master of all even if they do not believe in his existence or believe that He has some other shape and sizes? Do you really believe that all; good as well as bad is within Him and nothing is beyond Him including the dirty animals and insects." -My body language and emotions were so apparent he couldn't have missed them. He shrank within. I paused for so long that he had to say-"Yes."

"Then why do you think 'dirty Kafirs' are not His children and not worthy of living on the earth. Why do you think the whole world should pray in a specified manner else they will go to hell irrespective of what good they have done to the humanity? Why do you think there is only one road to reach the abode of the creator- father?"

'*Pani*; Water.' He gasped licking his lips. I was not sure if it was part of his theatrics or a genuine need. The men gave him a glass of water. He drank in one go and put the glass on ground with a thug.

"And now you have committed *Kufr*; blasphemy, by drinking water in one go. Your beards are also overgrown and.........."- I tried to say something further but he cut me short.

'Peshab: Urine.' He expressed his urge to go to urination. Men tried to take him. I stopped.

"Now after this you will ask for food and then for commode. Are you carrying them with you." I despised remembering his words at New Theed.

"No. I am not. Peshab. Peshab. Peshab." He repeated pressing his urgency.

"Why are you not carrying your urinal and commode? When you can carry so much of muck in your brain why can't you carry your commode on your head?" I asked.

Men shouted at him- "no, no no. *Ye kya kiya tumne;* what have you done?"

He had urinated on his pyjama. I was puzzled whether this was part of his theatrics or was it imagined fear about his future in the hands of an army officer whom he had humiliated, ill-treated, cheated and abused in most inhuman way. Was he dreading the worst in the hands of those who wielded extra-ordinary powers: the army men, with regard to life and liberty of the suspects and whose even misadventurs are, at times, beyond scrutiny and probe?

"And yes. Are you carrying your Coffin, Qafan and Kabr?" I asked him, recounting his dialogue spoken during our first encounter.

'*Pani, Pani, Pani*'- he squirmed; sincerely or as part of his drama, couldn't have been said for sure since none of us had even touched him.

'You should have carried your '*Pani;* water', nay everything you may need including Coffin, Qafan and Kabr. You would never know when death will strike and you may need these things. So what will you do, who will arrange for your Coffin, Qafan and Kabr?

"Sir, *mujhe maaf kar deejiye. Mere bachche yateem ho jayenge;* (Sir forgive me. My children will become orphan)." He pleaded.

"Why are you pleading? I will not even touch you; a burden on humanity. I wish you a long life to die in bits and pieces so that you keep on asking for water. Even if you think I am a Kafir I trust Him and his judgement and leave it to Him to decide your fate." I signalled my men to move out and told the sentry to take charge.

"But remember." I said while leaving;

"There are a few things which only others can do for you; the first and last cloth on everyone's body is put on by others, the first and last bath given to all is by others, the first and last movement of every person is on others shoulders. No one carries everything one needs or may need any time, you silly; its Qafan, Coffin, Kabr, bathroom or even water. It is how 'the Creator' has willed." I signalled all men to leave him where he was and move out.

It was lunch time and all officers were moving towards mess. The detention cell was on the way to the officers' mess. The adjutants asked looking at three of us:

"So how was the interrogation?"

"He urinated and was about to shit." One of the soldiers spoke up, finding the pause too long since I did not speak.

"So you `sorted him out' (actually he was meaning 'tortured') properly? Good." He smiled looking at me.

"No sir. I even did not touch him. Urination, I feel, was his theatrics." I clarified.

"What? But I had told you he is a hard nut, a never ending source of hate and vitriolic propaganda; an ISI agent in the garb of religious teacher. Only young officers like you can "break" him by experimenting with innovative techniques of interrogation." He smiled.

"He is the same Maulvi who had slipped out of cordon in New Theed. He is the same whose photograph you had given me at New Theed but the photograph was without beards." I disclosed. His face blushed, his breath became heavier.

And I felt I had taken the best revenge by forgiving him and had handed over back his fate in to the hands of specialized interrogators with additional inputs.

Now he was heading to reap the crop he had been sowing for long—I was sure.

****

Qayamat par farishtey ne poochha pak-bajon se:
"Gunah kyon na kiya, kya khuda karim nahi?"
Aur phir hanskar bola -'Kafiraan?'

On the judgement day the angel asked the puritans:
"Why did you not commit sins, do you think God is not merciful?"
And then pronounced laughingly "Non-believers?"

****

Chapter 10

The Protesting Women

22 November 93: Nava Kadal

"What are you doing? It is not gentlemanly and does not fit in to the dignity of an army officer; least in yours, who keeps on preaching us about treating all women with dignity." My senior: by a few years in service, Captain Shaant Singh; Company Commander of another Company was holding my cane. Realizing it amounted to questioning the wisdom and judgement of a fellow officer in the circumstances, which he was not fully aware, he took me in his arms, affectionately, to make it look friendly and unoffending and pushed me back, leaving the woman behind; all alone. I was not ready now, after reasoning with her respectfully in an effort to convince her to behave, to forgive her deliberate act of assault and abuse on me, my country and my men; the soldiers. The hurt was not personal now; it was direct insult of the 'state' and state's authority which I was very much representing. Deliberate and repeated insult of our country and army men was not acceptable.

My men thought I was showing undue and undeserved respect to abusive women, who were not only insulting and abusing but physically assaulting the military men, taking advantage of our leniency. My men thought we could and should not respect a group of traitors only because they were women. The women were assaulting those soldiers who wielded extra ordinary powers and hence the women were mistaking soldiers' decency as their weakness. It was nothing but testing our patience. More than me, my men were agitated. "Respect for women does not mean accepting humiliation from them." One of my JCO complained on my patience; which was stretching, as he perceived, beyond acceptable limits. On the other hand the women were also proving me consistently wrong by being obstinate and abusive; denting my effort to assure my soldiers that soon things would be better. One among these women, the leader, was instigating the crowd to assault and abuse by shouting offensive slogans.

Captain Shaant Singh would have also done what I was doing, to my guess, a bit earlier than I did, had he gone through the rowdiness of the women a few minutes back. But still I left the woman where she was, only to show respect to my senior.

The shocking aggression of women folk in Nava Kadal area; among oldest and thickly populated localities of Srinagar city, was bewildering. I was not able to fathom why they had become so aggressive without any provocation until I received the news of arrest of top commanders of JKLF from their hide outs. Cordon and search was a routine matter and detaining suspects'was part of it. It was no provocation for anyone to be so aggressive.

It was a cloudy, snowy and extremely cold day of November 1993. Contrary to operations in village, it was more difficult to carry out operations in the urban centres. Village is an independent unit, has its boundaries clearly marked, hassle free approach from all direction and most importantly; lesser possibility of outside interference. It's difficult for a trapped militant in the village cordon to escape, whereas in the cities it is very easy; wall to wall at times interconnected houses, no physical boundaries and tremendous chance of external interference.

We started cordoning the area soon after we reached the predefined spot of disembarkation as defined during briefing and identified by the experienced CHM on ground. I, as company commander, started deploying the stops or pickets of two or three men at important junctions of lanes and by lanes until I could tie up with the neighbouring company commanded by Captain Shaant Singh to ensure that the area was sealed and no one could come in or go out. Men started putting up stops in most vulnerable condition; there was nothing between them and likely fire from the unknown, invisible enemy.

But intelligently they devised and improvised some defence by putting hand carts, push-carts, some stones etc to create some barrier; psychological, if not real, to protect themselves from likely fire. Some of them suffered from "Pavlovian Conditioning" and were sure that placing an object in front of them, automatically brought protection irrespective of what the material was made of. I shouted at a newly 'crowned' Havaldar from a Naik, when I noticed he had placed left over of packing material of paper carton of a washing machine in front of him, and not placing his picket at a tactically viable place.

"*Sahib, Chahaa Dhya*": (sir have tea). said the Havaldar in Marathi extending his hand holding the tea cup and showing little concern what I just told him about deployment of stops in proper way.

"Sir, what protection in thickly populated area, you protect the front and flanks and they will throw grenade from the top if they want or dare to. Do not worry, sir boys are very strong willed, nobody will dare to play with us. We will tear them in pieces. Let them know, we are fearless and do not hide behind any 'protection.' He smiled displaying care free body language like a wrestler, which he was, holding his own glass tumbler of tea. A newly recruited sepoy had prepared the tea on kerosene stove which he had brought to the operation area along with the arms, ammunitions and other paraphernalia. The stove was still aflame, fiercely, possibly to keep the custodian warm who had never imagined cold of this magnitude in the hot and humid climate of Konkan Region of Maharashtra where he belonged to. The coldest places he knew or could have imagined in his state are Mahabaleshwar and Pune; temperature never falling below 10 degree Celsius.

"Look around and change position of your stop for better protection. Use your brain." I converted my scolding into an advice. A pungent smell of kerosene repulsed me from sipping the tea but again I upped it not to offend the men. An excess of sugar and milk powder globules, had suppressed the test of tea. Only sub-zero temperature outside had made it worthy of sipping.

As usual the intelligence section of the CO's staff team had reached the mosque and instructed the *Muezzin* or *Maulvi* to announce about the cordon besides announcement by own PA system at work.

"All men above 16 years and below 70 years; are directed to get congregated at the field of school building. All women and children to remain at home." He announced in Urdu and Kashmiri alternatively. He further announced:

"Anyone seriously ill can be at home but has to have prescription of the doctor ready to prove his justification for being at home. Anyone violating these instructions will be treated sternly. These are instructions from the army."

After placing the pickets, I quickly moved to the congregation since I was the one who was to manage the crowd. All men between the age of 16 and 70 started coming, as announced, and started gathering; mostly sitting on their squats; as the ground was slushy due to melted snow which had just fallen. It was too cold to allow any part of the body to come in contact with it. I had an overview of the crowd by running my sight over the congregation; fixing my eyes momentarily hither thither. Assorted head gears; caps of different design ranging from Afghani to local skull cap, pheren, and kangris were almost common to all. It was a big crowd of more than five hundred people.

By now it was going to be ten in the morning. The Sun was playing hide and seek with clouds, teasing all who expected some warmth from the Sun rays. The surroundings had deserted and depressing looks. In the winters most of the trees become leafless in the valley. The recent snow fall had brought severe cold to the city of Srinagar. All men at the congregation were hiding nay keeping their kangris inside their pheren so that the heat remains trapped within, keeping them warm.

All in the congregation must be cursing us today, though, we the army men, were certainly no better. We were putting on several layers of thick woollen clothing, two layers of socks; inner of thick cotton and outer of thick wool and then snow boots. We were having frequent tea; more to feel the warmth of the glass through our hands than to have the tea.

Difficult situations find their own solutions. After start of counter-insurgency operations in the valley, the children had become very important. Children were the only species permitted to come closer to the congregation where their grandfathers, fathers, elder brothers, uncles or just near dears and neighbours were sitting; thirsty, hungry and at times suppressing call of nature, feeling it demeaning to raise one fingers to seek permission from an army Jawan for urination and two for bigger call, like a primary school child. Children would bring tea, coffee, kahwa, milk, bread, meal and most desirable; the addictive indulgences like cigarette, hookah, etc. which were important to control the anxiety and fear arising out of thought that who would be 'spotted or identified' as suspect today.

But it used to be an ordeal for all the three; the congregated, the congregators and the waiters i.e. the children, who used to wait curiously to get permission from the military men to reach their beloved one to hand over the food articles or addictive indulgences. Invariably the food articles used to get cold, by the time they reached their destination. But the medicines were always hot; some for asthmatics, heart patients, cough, fever and what not. I cannot forget when a very cute child of 7-8 years had brought medicine for his elder brother who in young age had become patient of heart due to frequent "crack down"-as he called it, and subsequent fear of being detained and interrogated by the forces.

When I permitted him he still remained hesitant to move closer to his brother. On asking why he is not going ahead he had said - "Sir, *wo aapka jawan mujhe phir mat maarega?"* (Will your soldier not hit me, sir?) - fearing the Jawan standing close by oblivious of the gap between my permission and his obstruction. He was practical; a Jawan was more feared than an officer.

"Go give and come back fast. The Jawan will not trouble you." I had assured him. He ran towards his brother and with his run started my troubles. All the children waiting at the periphery started running towards their already identified targets thinking a blanket permission had been granted to all to hand over the food article, creating confusion in the mind of my men guarding the congregation to maintain order.

"Hold on." I shouted at them -"Food, etc. only after 'spotting' is over". Some stopped but some kept on moving towards their targets. I ordered my men to stop them forcibly. All the men, except one, acted fast and prevented the children from reaching the congregation. One Jawan who was sleeping while standing got lost as to what to do on my sudden order, which due to nap, he could not interpret and instead cocked his rifle to be ready to fire. This discomforted me, bemused my rest of the men and amused the congregation. Some hid their smile by lowering their head, rest in the congregation; smiled within, since laughing on the mistake of a soldier could invite trouble.

Intentionally, despite being sure that dozing off in the given circumstances is very natural and that no crime has been committed by the Jawan, I smiled at the JCO to whose platoon the Jawan belonged; just for fun and to gauge his reaction since he was very particular about discipline. The JCO had very poor opinion about people who used to sleep since he was suffering from insomnia, permanently, but never accepted the fact and thought it was a blessing from Temlai Mata; the Unit deity, to keep him awake, alert and vigilant in the environment of fight, fatigue and stress. The JCO got wild on the Jawan since he felt let down in front of me; his senior, due to dozing off of this Jawan:

'*Ghaal eek laat yaacha magah. Salaa jhoplas aahe;* give a kick up his backside. Bloody idiot is sleeping'- he ordered in Marathi to the closest Havaldar, ensuring no one in the congregation, hopefully me too, understood what he said. The Jawan hurt but unsure no one else other than men in uniform had understood his humiliation moved a bit far from the gaze of the JCO.

Suddenly, I saw two-three people in scuffle in the congregation. Several people got up; a few to separate the warring men and a few out of anxiety to know what was happening. A state of confusion prevailed for some moment. A lot of barbs or abuses or both were being exchanged, I guessed, but not sure: yep not sure, since could not understand; all in Kashmiri nay high pitched high speed Kashmiri with tremendous amount of finger raising, hand swinging, showing of eyes and body language. Such sights were not uncommon in the congregations.

There was a lot of anger against several entities including the erstwhile ruling dispensations of a dynastic clan, though others were not spared either. Almost all the politicians were considered stooge and puppets of either country; mostly of India but a few of Pakistan. General populace of Kashmir had, those days, a lot of contempt, hate, anger, and despise for politicos, whom they considered prime cause of the muddle. Majority of Kashmiris had bundles of abuses and scorn to throw on the Jija-Sala (brothers-in-law of Abdullahs and Ghulam Mohammad Shah. The Abdullah dynasty was most scorned those days) combination whose perceived corrupt practices and inept handlings, they considered, were the prime-cause of upsurge. Their anger on politicos was multiplied when they found that after application of AFSPA, all the prominent politicos had abandoned the valley and were 'holidaying' in Delhi, London, Paris, Rome, Geneva etc depending on how much wealth they had accumulated before disruption and disturbances.

I told men to calm them down and moved myself towards them to see what the matter was. With me moved my scouts, radio operator and a JCO. I was not in a hurry hence I moved deliberately slow, allowing men to command them to behave and maintain calm. It had no impact on our ops; more of a matter of amusement than that of anxiety for us. In such cases we were sure how to control the situation.

"What is the matter?" I asked directly and jointly to the fighters; one in his late thirties and other in early forties. All had sat down by now barring the fighters and two three more supporters each side.

"Sir he is abusing me." The man in thirties said in flawless Urdu; indicating to the other man, while pulling chain of his pheren up which had got opened due to scuffle. He had thick moustaches.

"He is a thief and supports a party of thieves who looted Kashmir from the day it got independence from the Dogras." Said the other man in forties with flowing beards and no moustache. He also spoke in chaste Urdu, it was better than the previous speaker; man with moustache and the antagonist. Apparently he looked more religious with his black spot on top middle of the forehead due to regular touch of ground while offering his prayer; indicating his unmissed daily Namaaz.

"Both of you sit down quietly. This is not a place for settling political scores. Fight and exchange abuses at your place; at your home when army is not around. We will not tolerate this nonsense." I told them sternly.

After enquiry, it came out that the man in forties was very frustrated, angry and worked up due to circumstances under which he had to sit on the ground in freezing temperature. He was blaming everyone, whomsoever he thought was responsible for the state of affairs, except the army; whom he either thought was not responsible or he, despite being sure, thought it imprudent to blame the obvious due to fear. I told him it was army who had called you in the congregation and that I was responsible to make you sit on the wet ground. But he was sure and insisted that it was not the army responsible for his woes. Substantially he was blaming, accusing and abusing a dynasty which had ruled the state for a considerable period after state's accession in the Indian Union, decorating them with soubriquets like thieves, looters, conspirators and (Indian) agents.

Nobody would have taken umbrage but he openly took names of some of men present, accusing them of being supporters of this party named National Conference. The accused men had tried to dissuade themselves from any affiliation but he heaped on them the 'guilt' of supporting the political outfit. This had angered a miniscule hibernating tribe who had publically switched and sworn their loyalty to the Jehadis, to look flowing with the stream of contemporary rage. Their objection was more to the effort to associate their name with the political outfit; which had become taboo and, less with the abuses to the outfit or them.

"Sir, those thieves, whom these co-brothers (with abusive

connotations to the sitting antagonists) supported, are siting cosily in London and Paris, in palatial houses purchased from the looted money; picnicking in Switzerland and Rome, leaving us hear in the open cold to sit on the wet ground in freezing temperature. Sir, they are responsible for your difficulties too else why should you be standing here in snow. Their corruption and loot is responsible for uprising, their rigging of election is the cause of anger. I will spit on their face, if they come back. These in-laws (with abusive connotations to the sitting antagonists) of those looters are responsible for our miseries and they too deserve spitting on their face." He aggressively moved towards the target; the man in thirties with moustaches.

"If they looted money given by India for development of Kashmir, you are looting money given by Pakistan for Jehad in Kashmir."-The man had not only fuelled but fanned the fire effortlessly by directly accusing him for supporting the Jehadis; the insurgents, militants or the terrorist in military parlance, in front of army men.

"You and your in-laws (with abusive connotations, indicating to a political dynasty of Srinagar), your co-brothers are a fraud. They are such a chameleon that now we can easily guess their location by the statements they give; in London and Paris they are internationalist, in Geneva pacifist, in New York pragmatist, in New Delhi nationalist, in Jammu regionalist and in Srinagar separatist. They are humanist in Vienna, secularist in New Delhi, Islamist in Islamabad, unionist in Muzaffarabad and Kashmirist in Srinagar. Like snakes, they have forked tongues; one for use in Delhi and other for use in Srinagar. Son of a primary school teacher from where has he accumulated so much of wealth? Where is he? Call him and show the mess his father, he himself, his in laws and his family have created for us Kashmiris." He was indicating to the slushed ground wet with melted snow where he was to sit. He cried red in rage. His light pink moustache-less face was turning dark red revealing intensity of his anger. Now he had many cohorts to support his view.

"Now you will also become rich, keep on harbouring them." The other man pricked by accusing his opponent of harbouring terrorist. He was getting isolated but not ready to relent.

*"Kahan hai wo kudich**. Bula usko. Uski maa jo kursi ke liye jinda beti ka namaaz-e-zanazaa padhti hai. Wo bahan jo khabind ko kursi pe bithane ke liye Kashmir me aag lagati hai. Kahan hai sare dramebaaz."* From Urdu to Kashmiri to Punjabi and even in English–he abused and accused choosing most appropriate words from all languages he knew. Due to anger he had lost tongue control literally; his saliva dripping from the sides and falling on the beards and then on the pheren. It was due to cold or anger- was difficult to guess.

"Enough is enough. If both of you do not sit down calmly within a minute by watch, I will order arrest of both of you and take to the interrogation centre so that you can disclose your 'information and knowledge' to the interrogators for better use." I warned them and told men to close in. A few in the congregation scolded both of them, despite siding and supporting the bearded man. They also knew taking them to interrogation centre was not a mere threat, though they knew it was not likely. One of them told me not to mind what the man had said because the poor man suffered from convulsions of anger. He was very touchy about Kashmir and kept on blaming all and sundry for the present circumstances, depending on who had been initiated for the blame in the discussion.

All sat down; including the 'warriors', still frowning in anger on each other. Their over flowing anger, in the form of murmur, irritated me beyond control and I lost my cool. I commanded in loud voice audible to all to keep quiet and told the 'warriors' that if they opened their mouth any more it won't be tolerated. We would not tolerate chaos in the name of politics or political discussion. This kind of drama was rare during congregation and was possible only in down town area.

My Company was carrying out cordon and search in several small groups like other Companies. But I was not there to supervise physically though I was in touch via wireless. The crowd control was most important in down town due to various reasons. Today it was at two places due to paucity of space and better crowd management. I was in charge of one; the bigger one. I decided to sit down for some time as I was feeling tired by standing for so long. I told my men to place a folding settee, close to the warring friends so that I could sit there, which my men always carried for the officers' use. I was feeling comfortable after long standing and walking. But it was not to last for long.

I heard some noise coming from far and tried to decode the assorted slogans in Kashmiri and Urdu, being shouted alternatively, and tried to locate the origin or source of the slogans. I was more amused than amazed to see menacingly forwarding crowd of women. I had heard about Dukhtaraan-e-Millat but had never come across any member or activity of theirs. I thought today I was meeting them. But there is no reason or provocation for any protest since we always carry out our operation in most professional manner; no undue trouble to innocent, no mercy to militants. Later I realised it; the slogan shouting had nothing to do with Dukhtaraan. The slogan shouting was spontaneous or sponsored–was difficult to conclude and had no practical value to our operation.

Slogans were becoming clear "'*Bharteeya kutto wapas jao;* Indian dogs go back', '*Begunahon ko chhod do*; release the innocents', 'Allah-O-Akbar', '*Hamein kya chaahiye-Azaadi, Azaadi, Azaadi;* what we want-Freedom, freedom, freedom'", alternately in Urdu and Kashmiri; probably translation of each other. As a precautionary measure I thought of informing the new development to the Commanding Officer but in vain. His wireless operator informed that he and his QRT were busy in some important special operation. My wireless operator suggested and sought permission whether he could put me through to the Adjutant; the staff officer of the CO controlling the operation.

I found the proposal appropriate and gave go ahead. After waiting for long the Adjutant came on the radio to hear what I had to tell. After giving him overview of the prospective situation I requested him to requisition a section of female constables from CRPF; the only force having female constabulary in the vicinity, nay in the country those days. He was sounding under stress and in hurry. My request was flatly refused due to lack of time and other hassles. He rather chastised me for behaving like breastfed-child and advised me to fend for myself. He sounded preoccupied and did not bother to address the real question of dealing the female crowd. He mocked me for looking for assistance of "female constable" despite having hundreds of best trained men under my command and having extra ordinary powers of arrest, detention and even kill under the AFSPA; which he said, does not exclude female.

It was very easy to deal with female crowd if I had no reservation about using force under my command. Even there was no legal hurdle. The AFSPA does not discriminate in male insurgent and female insurgent or male traitors and female traitors. My men were highly disciplined and respectful to local populace in general and females in particular. Not a single complaint, from any quarter during last two years,was testimony to their impeaccable conduct and behaviour. But I was averse to use them against female even if the female folk were so offensive and abusive. I thought of using my skill of communication, which I was very proud, to convince and pacify them by trying to understand the reason for their behaviour and address the grievances. I told my intentions to my men and told them not to use force even if provoked until I told them.

We were caught off guard when I tried to talk to them. They, without listening, started pelting stones, bunch of barbed wire along with assorted abusive slogans; mostly decodeable but not all. Distinctly, the crowd was led by an exceptionally fat and comparatively dark woman, by the parameters of light skinned Kashmiris. She was average height, had small roundel face and was over wearing green coloured Pheren. She had covered her head with a scarf.

The crowd was closing in aggressively. My JCO in charge came to me and advised to beat these "nagging women" back before they created more ruckuses or incited passion, but I could not respond since I was imaging the worse; if the crowd of men also joined them, the situation would be dangerous. There would be blood all over and army would get a bad name. There was little chance of any danger to any of my men; they were heavily armed with munitions. The area was covered by fire of light and medium machine guns. The thought was naïve but practical. A few times women had tried to snatch weapons from military men by closing in unsuspectingly and giving them the surprise. At times they had lobbed grenade among the soldiers and quietly moved away. If caught they accused the soldiers of molestation. Mostly it was on the instructions and instigation from terrorists, insurgents and militants. I looked at the congregation of men who were sitting quietly in groups mostly on the peripheries since main ground was low lying, wet and slushy.

I moved towards the ferocious female crowd with my radio operator and a few more Jawans, to talk to them. The slogans were extremely offensive, provocative and not in sync with the kind of opinion I had about people of Kashmir, particularly women folk. I always carried tremendous respect and empathy for women; even when I was made butt of joke to the level of ridicule from my peer group.

"Stop it. What is your problem?" I asked the crowd focusing on the leader.

"Why have you picked up our innocent and sick boys and taken them for interrogation?" She exhorted amid chaos and slogan shouting.

"If they are innocent, they will be left. No sick person

having sufficient proof of sickness is ever picked up." I tried to convince her not knowing who has been picked and by whom.

As a common practice, all sick and infirm were allowed to stay at home irrespective of their age, in addition to old men, women and children. But at times hard core militants feigned to be sick, put fake plaster on leg and hands to show they were unable to walk; infirm and sick to evade spotting or identification parade. It was known to all how Yasin Malik, the JKLF chief had deceived the security forces by feigning sick and insisting for hospitalization and then slipped away from the hospital in connivance with a few doctors and paramedic staff. The custodial force; CRPF was left red faced by the deception and had to do a lot of explaining to the nation. There were medicos who issued false and fake prescriptions freely, issued fake medical reports in advance or as and when needed to the militants; most of the time given in the possessions of the militants for use during cordon.

My thought process was disturbed by sound of fall of stones close to me. A Jawan was also hit. The JCO got agitated and complained to me. He requested me to come aside, away from the noise and then confided:

"Sir, you are my senior so please forgive me. But you are unduly sensitive about sentiments of these people whereas they are not. We are army men; we act for effect and not for show. Even, as you know sir, we do not fire in air but to incapacitate or kill to tell the world that we mean business. Our over tolerance is being construed by these bitches as weakness. Once during our operation near Dustgeer Sahib, women had created similar ruckus. Major Kishor was the Company Commander. He told us to sort them out. When our soldiers gave a few canes all ran away, leaving their slogans of Azaadi behind."

After making disgusting face to express his displeasure, he continued: "You think they are our fellow citizen of secular India but they think we are subjugating forces of Hindu empire. We think they are part of India, they think India starts after

Jammu, the southernmost part of their "country". We think they are women and should be treated with respect but they think we are beasts thirsty of their blood and do not deserve any respect. We think they should be treated with dignity but do they treat us with dignity; the dignity soldiers deserve? They are traitors; male or female, enemies of our country. They are calling us dogs forgetting in 1947 when Pakistanis came looting, raping murdering them; we, the men of Indian army, gave our life and blood to save their honour."

I tried to move away to talk to the abusive women but he followed me and continued:

"They are disgraceful and ungrateful people. India gives all the liberty and pampering, so much of money for their development, but they eat up and ask for more like discontented dogs. They talk of Islamic brotherhood and they wish to be part of Pakistan. They have forgotten so easily what Pakistan did in Bangladesh in 1971. As a young sepoy, I was part of the war and had seen it all. When millions of Bengali Muslim refugees entered Indian territory, breaking all border restriction and when it became impossible to take any more refugees, India decided to intervene to save again; the Bengali Muslims from Punjabi Muslims' atrocities. The way Bengali female folks, including Muslim women were raped, children killed and maimed, was unprecedented. You know, they know, the world knows. All is recorded in the history. But still these people have not learnt."

Feeling uncomfortable of his unending long lecture I cut him short:

"Saheb! That is why we should talk to them to change their opinion; their mind-set and make them understand the realities."

He wanted to continue his lecture but his effort of sermonising his boss was disrupted by another volley of missiles. Men were alert and held the crowd without use of

Medical assistance to troubled citizenry: Our Medical Officer examines a local elderly man for teeth ailment and cure in Srinagar.

A typical cordon and search assembly. The loss of productive man hour has been humongous: a tell-tale of lost opportunities and decades.

force. Now it was becoming extremely difficult. Fortunately, none was hurt.

"No, I will not allow use of force on women. Understand it very clearly. The CO has told very clearly in the briefing to officers and later to all in the 'fall in'. Do not try to use the last tool, as the first control measure. I will talk to them. All senior officers also emphasise use of force as last resort. You wait I will be able to disperse the crowd by convincing them. I am confident of my convincing skill and good command over language and most importantly my art of pep talk." The JCO looked disgusted and moved away without showing disrespect to me by pretending to have gone to give instruction to the men in the far corner.

Amid slogan shouting, I addressed them directly:

"You all are like our mother and sisters. We respect you a lot. We do not mean any undue harm to anyone. You also know we are not here on our sweet will but to perform specific duties assigned to us by the government."

"Shut up, you Indian dogs go back to India." One of them shouted from the crowd In Urdu, interrupting my lecturette. In the resultant din nothing else was heard. I was sentimentally hurt and angry. My JCO, as if knowing the end, was instructing the men to close in with their canes. It looked as if he will overrule me but it was not possible in the army; he knew it.

I continued:

"See, I have allowed your children to give food and medicines overruling the standing instructions of not allowing the same until spotting is over. I empathise with you and understand that you all are in very difficult situation. We do not want to trouble you; the general populace, but want to weed out the terrorist, the misguided militants."

No one was ready to listen. In-between I was interrupted by the call of the radio operator who told me that Adjutant wanted to talk to me. It was impossible to say or listen anything worthwhile in the hubbub. I moved away a bit to talk to the Adjutant. He informed me that they have caught area commander of JKLF with his cronies, three AK-47 rifles and a lot of subversive literature. He elaborated that they were feigning to be sick and hiding inside the quilts to look like patients. They had managed even false prescription for bed rest. They were hiding; four of them, in four different households as sick and infirm.

During cordon when soldiers caught the militants, women got together within minutes, as if already prepared for the eventuality and started slogan shouting, stone pelting, chest beating and likewise theatrics to put all kind of pressure on us, including psychological, to release them. Later after sustained and tough interrogation they dug out their weapons also. He further informed that the women were creating ruckus at their congregation so I should be careful at mine. I did not tell him, keeping in mind his snub last time; when I had asked for help, that what we were going through. Rather I assured him, not to worry and take care of his location, without showing any trace of complaint or grudge.

But, after this radio talk, my paradigm was changed about these women and reason for their slogan shouting. I told my JCO to tell them if they would not disperse within a minute we would choose our own means to disperse them. All civilians; the locals in the congregation, who were sitting a bit far were alerted and looked worried but they neither got up nor tried to intervene. The JCO announced in very commanding and authoritative voice venting his accumulated anger in to curtly worded order.

"You are given one minute to disappear. Go back to your homes."

"Tum kya karega. Hum log nahi jayenge jab tak hamare bachche nahi chodega; what you will do. We will not go until our children are released." Said the fat women instigating the crowd to throw whatever they had.

"The one minute is not over yet." The JCO told her contemptfully looking at me as if reminding me, "I had told you sir: the end of it all."

Thud, thud thud—fell near us the stones, pebbles, barbed wires and a few hot Kangris. It was aimed and it did not miss. The JCO, two jawan were hit but not much to the effect since winter had already forced them to cover almost entire body with thick layers of snow-proof and waterproof lining. I had already handed over the situation with clear order to the JCO, after trying and failing to reason with "respectable" women. Convincing the crowd was a difficult job which I had taken, dispersing them was much easier; to be handled by my JCOs. I stood behind; relaxed like a commander should be, only to give order to the ever obedient men to execute it with precision. When you overcome your sentiments or sensitivities you are relaxed. The JCO signalled men and led the baton charge. They did not corner any one, did not catch, just caned. All women got threatened and ran away: shouting, shrieking crying; leaving everything behind except their physical self. What was left was identified as Chappals, shoes, socks, scarfs, Kangris and of course the fat women.

Men ran towards her. I told them to leave it to me.

"You called us dogs. So the commander of the dogs is coming to you; I had lost my control due to her repetitive abuse, her insult thrown on us, her incitement to other women and finally; her audacity not leave the place despite requests and warnings nay light caning. I felt the JCO and Major Kishor were right in their assessment and I acted a bit late and too naively. I snatched a cane from the nearest Jawan and started thrashing her—one, two, three-------------"

Not four. My cane was caught from the behind.

"What are you doing? It is not gentlemanly and does not fit in to the dignity of an army officer; least you who keeps on preaching us about treating all women with dignity." My senior by a few years in service, Captain Shaant Singh; Company

Commander of another Company was holding my cane. He took me in his arms affectionately lest I felt offended. He was instructed by the Commanding Officer to come and assist me in controlling the crowd. He was sent when the Commanding Officer realised the gravity of the situation on the feedback of the Adjutant and on seeing the drama in his own location.

"She is a hired 'queen' in the game of chess who is still fighting to save the king; when the pawns have already ran away. She is worthy of pity and not punishment, unaware, that the 'king' has already been checkmated by us." He spoke in the language of chess baring all the truth in two sentences and indicating that such slogan shouting is instigated and organised by terrorist groups to divert the attention of the army when either some important militant is trapped or caught. The hapless women and children are invariably caught between proverbial "devil and the deep sea." If they did not do what they were told by the terrorist, they would be 'taught' lessons later.

"So, was the fighting among the men in the congregation also part of the drama?" I tried to analyse but could not conclude for sure anything.

I looked back. Captain Shaant Singh also looked back. The woman was standing alone: defeated; not by my canes and the pain it gave but merciful withdrawal imposed by Captain Shaant Singh and by the news of arrest of the 'king'.

She looked at me and then at Captain Shaant Singh. No tears, but fear and defeat in her eyes. Her abuse and assault was sponsored or spontaneous, had no value for me. I was deeply hurt. Yes deeply hurt; not only because I was abused and assaulted or because I had to order caning, but because my painful effort of treating the women with respect, was defeated; from within and without. I thought of over-shouting press and overbearing media to have been present there to tell me what else I could have done.

I could not forgive her for ensuring failure of a humane and civilised effort of a soldier to deal with his compatriots in compassionate way. A failure which had portrayed me as a 'naiveté' in front of my men, 'un-officer-like' in front of my colleague and a 'perpetrator' of 'excesses' on 'unarmed' women in the eyes of the world. It did not matter to me that the world was not present; no one was watching. The paradox of the situation and conflict of the conscience was enough for me to remain wounded for long.

Chapter 11

When Silence Cried

While the slogan *'Aie Zalimon, aie Kafiron, Kashmir hamara chhod do'* (O perpetrators, O infidels, leave our Kashmir.) echoed piercingly in my ears, I thrashed him mercilessly with the cane and my brain spontaneously re-coined the deafeningly echoing slogan. I shouted the re-coined slogan like a mad man singing on the highest scale of the octave;

'Aie Gaddaron, Aie Hattyaron, Kashmir hamara Chhod do.'

'Aie Gaddaron, Aie Hattyaron, Kashmir hamara Chhod do.'

'Aie Gaddaron, Aie Hattyaron, Kashmir hamara Chhod do.'

(O traitors, O murderers, leave our Kashmir.)

"Mai sab kuch chhod dunga, sir. Khuda ke liye aap mujhe chhod deejiye. Mai begunah hoon." He cried in chaste Urdu/Hindi.

It fuelled my anger like petrol on a receding fire.

"So, you bastard, you know Urdu and you know Hindi but pretend to knowing neither." I increased my receding force on the cane. My soldiers were stunned. The commander of the search party, a senior Subedar, was so shocked, perplexed and frightened that he came closer and he went away: undecided, with the dilemma of interfering or keeping off. He wanted to hold my cane but could not gather courage to come close enough to hold his senior commander's rage; flowing through the cane.

This was a day time operation in Habba Kadal, a locality named after a very beautiful, sensitive and melancholic poetess of sixteenth century Kashmir; Habba Khatoon. I was commanding a Company and we had started moving at about eight after early breakfast. It is a tough task for the army to move in this area with heavy, wide-bodied troops' carrier trucks. Redis; the hand carts, tongas; the horse cart, are seen moving all around: like omnipresent obstacle course in all other north Indian cities. They pose a challenge to fast moving mechanical transport. The responsibility to clear the traffic and ensure that the columns do not stop, was with Dandamen; a hybrid word coined by Hindi word Danda or cane and English word 'man' to give the danda wielding soldier an identity.

Sudden hue and cry forced me to come out of my analysis and look out of my jeep. I was on a narrow Kadal; a bridge. Nothing was moving except our military vehicles. Our Dandamen were finding their way for our columns, moving to cordon off down town area of Habba Kadal. Rest all were either like statues; ducking themselves along with their carriers, or running in panic to find a place to become a statue: at a safe distance from our Dandamen. The woman holding her one child in her left arm and two children walking holding her other hand, was about to fall in the river from the Kadal due to sudden push by a hand carter who could not give way in time to the Dandaman's military truck and got a Danda from the 'He-man.' In panic he pushed his cart aside hitting the poor woman and the children. The walking children screamed and the mother yelled at the carter but all became as quiet as statue after noticing the convoy. Nobody was bothered about anybody: not even for small children. The Darwinian theory of 'survival of the fittest' was at work.

The cordon was laid as per plan. The area had very few human beings seen moving around; creating suspicion of something fishy at first thought. I looked around and realised that in my Company's area of responsibility there were many vacant and abandoned houses of Pundits; uprooted from their deep roots of thousands of years. I was told this was among the areas where Pundits were in substantial number before their mass exodus in 1989-90, when they were forced to leave their big beautiful houses to live in shanties and torn stinking tents. All were not having palatial houses or big mansions. Many were just average and had small houses with sufficient covered space to protect them from vagaries of nature.

But yes all were proud to be in their 'own house' and in their 'own environment' that they called home: their ancestral home from the days of sprouting of civilization in the valley. In fact several thousand years back their forefathers were the one who entered the valley first and sowed seeds of civilization. Big or small, the houses were once their havens; protecting them from cold, heat, rain, storm, the Sun and from all mighty forces of the nature, proudly declaring: 'there is no place like home.' But neither palatial nor modest houses could protect them from vagaries of man: many men fighting the 'Jehad' and spilling blood of '*Kafirs*' to establish 'Kingdom of God; the Nizam-e-Mustfa'. By eliminating the '*Kafirs*', they wanted to convert Kashmir in to 'Dar-as-Salam', a 'place of peace': ironically.

I told my escorts and the radio operator to follow me while I had a round of the area. All my pickets were placed properly. Wherever it was needed I carried out minor adjustment. We were of the view that more than 'spotting' or identification parade 'search' was the operation to be emphasised in this area.

Before distributing area of responsibility for search, among my subordinate commanders, I decided to have a look myself.

Depressing it was going around. Many houses, big and small were empty; devoid of any human being but full of other beings including insects, bats and nocturnal animals. The cats particularly had gala time; eating, shitting all around, breeding and multiplying. Most of the houses were locked from the front, deceptively declaring to be 'secure' but had multiple entries from broken windows, broken rear doors, and at times; broken walls. In between were houses still 'alive' by hustle-bustle of its residents; almost all Muslim's houses. Many houses were big and grand. I got a fair idea of the locality's extend, lay out and nature.

I saw a temple, no actually a tin shed like enclosure used as temple adjacent to a boundary wall, was desecrated. The glass on the frame of the photo of Lord Krishna was broken into pieces and the photo pierced through with a rod. Idols of all other deities were scattered. I was aghast not because I was seeing something unexpected but because the then Home Minister had lied to the nation on the subject. I remembered the speech and reply given by the Home Minister S.B. Chavan in the Parliament a few days back that no temple was desecrated in Kashmir. Indicating to the desecration, I looked at my senior Subedar who himself was a Maratha from Maraathwada region of Maharashtra, from where the then Home Minister was elected for the Lok Sabha, and said:

"Look at this and remember the statement of the Union Home Minister, the Maratha leader originating from your district, a decedent of Chhatrapati Shivaji Maharaj; champion of Hindu pride. He has told the nation through the Parliament that no desecration of Hindu temples has taken place in the valley. Whereas every second locality we enter, we find the opposite."

The men looked indifferent but the JCO spoke up:

"Most of them are liar sir. Their truth is only vote. Secondly their entire information is second or third hand. They never come and see things on ground. They speak up whatever is fed to them by the babus at Delhi or the politicians from Srinagar. Had these politicians taken trouble of coming and seeing things on ground themselves in Kashmir and taken steps in time, the situation wouldn't have come to the edge where Pundits have to become refugee in their own country within 50 years of independence. And demand of independent country on religious grounds wouldn't have arrived once again."

A glance of the area had made me extremely sad within but I was not able to fathom exactly why. I came back, formed a few search groups, briefed them, emphasised on 'dos' and 'don'ts', and instructed them to carry out thorough search of each and every house. The Pundit houses were considered hideouts of the terrorist hence it was imperative to search them more cautiously and thoroughly. The chances of encounter were very high hence I decided to be in close vicinity to all the search parties and managed it by hopping from one search group to the other. I told them to first 'sweep' the entire area and all houses; occupied and vacant, then specifically search scattered vacant houses of Pundits, so that chances of sneaking of suspects from vacant to occupied houses and vice-versa were minimal or nil.

One strange thing I noticed while sweep-searching the area and individual houses: availability of books. Muslim houses, in most of the cases, were much bigger than the vacant Pundit houses and had everything except books. If at all there was one, it was Quran. The number of houses having books in Muslim households was much lower than even in vacant and abandoned pundit houses. However there were exceptions as well. On the contrary Pundit houses had everything or nothing but invariably had some books scattered or stacked. In some cases their almirah, lofts were full of books; mostly of syllabus of different classes and subjects but not exclusively. At places there were rare books on assorted subjects including religion and philosophy, including Quran and Bible.

Contrast was not limited to variety, quality and quantity of books but also diversity of script. In one modest abandoned Pundit house I could discover books and writing in five scripts; Roman (English), Persian/Urdu/Kashmiri (could not distinguish), Hindi (Devnagari), Sanskrit and one script I had never seen hence could not decode. It looked something between Gurumukhi and Tibetan; curves very close to Devnagari but shapes unrecognisable, alphabets unreadable. Later someone guessed and told me it would have been Sharda script; Kashmir's own, developed from Sanskirt several centuries back.

My love for books and earnestness to understand Hindus' exodus sucked me in the abandoned houses; from one house to the other and then next. The hop looked unending. I felt possessed. I stood and watched the houses from outside and from inside for several minutes when there was nothing worth watching, rather all depressing. I watched plates on dining tables with bowls and glasses; some toppled, some fallen some intact at the right place. I looked at dried obstinate food sticking to the plates; silently telling the owner of this house suddenly left without eating, when food was already served on the plate. I watched beds and bed sheets intact but covered with cat shit, mud, dust, etc. adorning it. I watched wall hanging, paintings and photos of Hindu deities on the wall; some still hanging as they were left, some sagging, some fallen. I watched calendars on the wall, silently telling the day and month of the year from when they had not been turned and touched; apparently declaring the date of exodus. I watched many letters scattered that were received from different parts of India, and at places, from different parts of the world. I watched a few letters written for various destinations but not posted. My world was changed I was sucked into someone else's world.

No one entered these houses from the front, including

us. There were many entries already created by unknown intruders; may be looters, may be neighbours, may be terrorists to hide, may be central police forces and army to search the houses out of suspicion, may be love birds to have secluded place for romance, may be children to play hide and seek, or may be all of them for their assorted purposes. In the frightened and frightening environment, where armed forces have all pervading presence, anyone wanting to have some private place, may find it here. After all no one's bed room had sufficient privacy. So how does it matter to anyone of above what pain, sorrow and devastation these empty houses symbolise? But mostly they were being used by terrorist for meetings, hide outs, hiding arms, ammunition and subversive literature. It looked as if dead bodies of the innocent were being used as shield by the killers, and the shroud of the killed; to hide behind to evade the advancing army.

While teams searched several houses, I got entangled in one; with strong reason. It was a modest house of three or four rooms but maximum number of books; as if belonged to some scholar or teacher having limitless lust and unquenched thirst for knowledge or to be precise for reading. The strong wooden rack was so stuffed that it looked it might give up any time. Some books had fallen off or ransacked; couldn't be said for sure. May be the owner himself might have scattered them to find and take along most loving one leaving the rest helplessly, if at all he had left.

I started glancing through them; Kalidas, Tagore, Vivekanand, Shakespeare, Premchand, Gorky, Bernard Shaw, Khalil Gibran, etc: endlessly amazing, writers from almost all the continents. I could recognise only those books which were in Hindi, English or Sanskrit or I had seen earlier. I wondered a young man who had spent so much of the time in rich library of Allahabad, even at times bunking his classes, had not heard some of the names of the books and its writers. Neither there was time nor possibility to go through any of the books. After glancing through the cover, name, writer, etc. I kept them all aside. I had more interesting things to read: scattered letters.

I could only read those written in the language I understood. When I tried to lift the first long letter in wavy hand writing in English, my conscience scolded me: "these are very intimate communication between two hearts in the weakest moments of their life, you dare not touch them." I pulled back; squeezed my forehead, kept the rifle aside, looked for a space to sit down. A broken chair assisted me. I sat and leaned back only to see a black board carved out on the wall; to write by chalk and erase it. So was it used as tutorials also; may be, or it was only to teach own children some maths and puzzles. The black board still had writing intact on the top of it:

"O Lord! Do not take away burden from my head, do not make it lighter. Instead, make my back bone stronger, so that I can bear it." —Rabindra Nath Tagore.

"What is wrong if I read these letters? I want to know what went in their mind before they left everything behind and ran away leaving their food in the plates served on the dining table. Or leaving their intimate letters, their books, their essential utensils and what not? What morality? It had been buried deep here all over; when their bedrooms were encroached and their daughters molested and raped, their innocent children killed in cold blood and families eliminated, for no rhyme or reason: except that they were Hindus. Then I am not going to harm someone by misusing these letters." I consoled my soul before picking up a few of them. I glanced through many. Some had references so private that I had no inkling what they meant: not of any use to me.

This one seems to have been written by a son to his father. OK I can see this not much of morality hassles. The father has written replies also but not posted.

** Nov 1989

'Dear Dad,

I have tried so long and so hard to get in touch with you through phone but could not. Has our line been disconnected? I felt so terrible when could not get through. All kind of thoughts are coming to my mind. Media reports are so disturbing, even though, I know, they are under reported. I am so sad. I am so worried about all of you, specifically for Radhika. She is tender. What might be going through her mind; my little sys? When I feel terrible I visit ISKCON temple. ISKCON temple, in Bangalore, some say, is biggest and grandest in Asia and my room is very close to it. It gives me some peace of mind. As requested in my last letter and insisted during telephonic talk last time, I request you again to leave that place, at least for time being and come to Bangalore. The climate here is moderate and better than Jammu and Delhi and all places of your interest do exist, even though a bit far. People like us do not need woollen here so you can pack very light; leaving all your woollen behind for use once you return. Radhika can continue her studies here. This place provides among the best educational intuitions. So what is your worry?

The custodians of Sri Ram Krishna and Swami Vivekanand's teachings; Ramkrishna Mission is among the places you would love to visit and be there. One day when I felt extremely disturbed I discussed with the Swamiji about everything relating to our crises. Surprisingly he repeated your words. Like children born from one mother are womb brothers and sisters and have equal right over the mother. Similarly all living beings born out of mother earth's womb are real brother and sister; they have equal right to live on this earth. Every living being on the earth comes from the same mother earth; feeds on her so all have equal right to exist including all animals. All beings have their own purpose of existence within the plan of the creator. He further spoke like you that those fighting in the name of religion and pretending to protect it are silly. A true religion does not need any protection. It naturally pervades human conscience and never leaves it.

To my amazement he quotes the same words of yours: "*Dharmo Rakshati Rakshitah;* Dharma protects those who protect it." He says one need not protect true religion rather a true religion will protect any one who 'wears' it not on the sleeves but in the soul; in thought, conduct and action. The only way to protect Dharma is by living the values it enshrines. True religion will protect all those who protect the humanity and human values. When he said all this, I remembered your words about Guru Teg Bahadurji, who did not protect it by fighting like savage with swords and arrows but by living the values. He defeated the perpetrator by defying agreeing that God's name as pronounced by him only is right and that other names of God are not names of god. He defeated by declaring that he believes in the same God as the perpetrator but not ready to pray exactly same way as the perpetrator wants. He defeated his perpetrator by defying bending to pray the way he wanted and declared that sincere prayer by a different gesture and posture would be answered with same grace by the most benevolent. He laughed at the perpetrator for his ignorance that God will accept the prayer only in one language.

Dad, I never realised what a great soul you are until I heard the same words of wisdom from a scholar and a saint acclaimed world over. I could never decode why you insisted to always remain 'human' even while dealing with beasts. Your advice was nothing more than 'impractical idealism' when you used to say never leave your values to counter hate and violence. I remembered your example that no animal can tame human beings but 'human' can'tame' all animals including the most savage, violent and powerful by being 'human'.

I respect your values and understand now how you practice them so honestly. However, without questioning your wisdom and your faith, I doubt any of your friends will come to your rescue. Not because I doubt sincerity of their assurance but truth all over the world has made it so apparent. When frenzy of fundamentalism arises, all liberal forces go in to hibernation and those active are sent to incarceration, if spared elimination. So practically they become non-existent and derive satisfaction by keeping quiet. So many selective killing have already taken place but has any one of your type of friend come to resist or even show passive disagreement with the perpetrators? Has any one of them even written a letter to the editors of those newspapers that are publishing threats and advertisements issued by the zealots and terrorists? Then how come you think they will come to your rescue? And if you are depending on your students, nothing is more self-denying than this. The problem with people like you is that they think it cannot happen with them.

Dad, I do not know whether this letter would reach you or not but if you get it please move out immediately to Jammu. From there I will take you to Bangalore. You do not allow me to visit the home, you do not allow me to come to Srinagar, you do not allow me to come and take you only because you fear they may harm me. But what if they harm you or mom or Radhika? Will there be any thing left for me to live for?

Please tell me over phone (if lines start working) or send me letter/telegram from where I have to take you out of that death well and beautiful hell. I have never defied you and am sure you will not force me to defy you where I have to land up suddenly, pack up or no pack up and move out with you all.

Yours

..........'

The father seemed to have deep differences in perception about ground realities and had no plan to shift from where he was;

**Dec 1989

'Dear.........

The very idea of leaving our home kills me. I can never imagine my existence out of this beautiful valley known as Kashmir, not even in other region of the state; Jammu or Ladakh. Why do you think God created such a high wall around it; Pir Panjal in south and west and Karakoram and Zanskar in the north and east? Because it is a protected land, it is a privileged land for scholars and knowledge seekers. I have not given name Sharad Desh; country of goddess of knowledge, it is from time immemorial named by outsiders. This land was made worth living by our forefathers several thousand years back who left banks of river Saraswati but carried Saraswati with them; the goddess of knowledge.

They were the first to nurture this valley. They were the first to vibrate this paradise on earth by giving meaningful phonetics; different from sounds of birds and animal, that the world calls language. They created their own phonetics, their own script, their own language, their own grammar, their own literature. While they indulged in these creations, the Creator Himself smiled thinking He has created creatures whose offsprings think they can replicate His creations. He did not disturb but protected us from the outside world to allow us to indulge in our endeavour.

When our forefathers blinded by power and independence started doing what absolute power and independence bring with it; mental myopia leading to commit atrocities, the Lord lifted his grace. Then they were attacked by outsiders; barbaric and savage. They went through hell. Their own people tormented them. They were reduced to miniscule. Many left the valley to avoid persecution and rest were forced to change their religion. But someone who went through all this and neither left the valley not abdicated his belief, was one who was our father, grandfather, great grandfather or someone in that line. And now you are asking me to do what our great forefathers did not do. Son! This is not for the first time we are being persecuted. There is a long continual history of our persecution.

Our forefathers abandoned all power, all authority, all wealth, and all worldly possessions to preserve only the culture and knowledge that their forefathers had created. They went through all humiliation, all torture, and all dispossessions only to live for the values they inherited from their ancestors. And my son! Now you are asking me to leave everything and come to unknown place. Do you have there the smell of this air, fertility of this land, purity of the water streams, our Sumyar temple, Kheer Bhawani, our Vitasta; the Jhelum? With whom do you expect me share the joy of Navreh? When I go out I see crying children clinging to their mothers speaking and nagging in babbled Kashmiri. Can any language replace the joy of that sound? How do you expect me to live without listening to that joy day and night? Where will I be able to listen the sweetest sound of Kashmiri: it sounds as sweet whether spoken by a Muslim or a Hindu.

My son! Do not worry about our safety. I have spoken to my neighbours and friends and asked them whether they want me to live or leave, whether they want to see me alive or dead. I asked them whether our blood, bone and chromosomes have changed from the moment they stopped going to temples and instead chose to go to mosque. I asked them whether our creator has become different when they chose to pray differently. They all felt very ashamed and all of them have said in one voice:

"We will not allow you to leave. If you leave we will also leave this place."

They assured me in our locality madness will not be allowed to take over sanity. My son I know them, not all but many of them are sincere and truthful. I saw our blood flowing in their veins and their bones supporting my structure. All this is a temporary phase, it will be over soon. People are not bad, only circumstances are. Most people are not evil, circumstances make them. We have common forefathers and no amount of denial will wipe that out.

I have suggested you not to come, not because I fear something going wrong here, but on the way; from Jammu to Srinagar, from airport to Habba Kadal. Son! You are right, Swamiji is right, Man can never protect God; only God can protect human beings. They are fools who pretend to protect existence of God in their prayer halls.

May God protect you there and us here. I have decided to stay and see whether it is man who runs the world or it is He, whether it is men who protect the God or it is God who protects the men.

With Blessing

........'

Second incomplete and un-posted letter of a later date was in my hand. I wondered these are letters or essays on un-precipitated human emotions flowing over the brim.

** Jan1990

'Dear....

I could not post the previous letter and thought of writing one more and posting both together. It is not because of any problem. Do not conclude anything negative. Nobody had stopped me. It was my own choice due to my double mindedness about your proposal. There are selective killing taking place but no one is able to understand the criteria of issuance and execution of death warrants. Everyone looks puzzled. I had spoken to my neighbours and friends and asked them what the aim of all this murder and violence is. Many said the boys are frustrated due to unemployment, a few said they want 'Azadi'; others were of the view that it is because of neglect of the state. Corruption restricting the percolation of benefits to the lowest level of the people was another reason, they opined.

I had called them for tea after *Namaaz* of *Magrib* in the evening. Despite whatever is happening, I am not afraid to ask what I want to and open up my mind. They had no answer when I asked them whether killing of Pundits will wipe out all the evils you perceive, or are Pundits exclusively responsible for the evils? How many Pundit Chief Ministers have ruled the state that they ate up all the developmental funds? I asked them if it is 'Independence' why the slogans of Nizam-e-Mustafa, why talk of 'Islamic Republic of Kashmir' and not 'Secular Democratic Republic of Kashmir'. Why the slogans of 'Kashmir without male Pundits but with their female folk.'

I reminded them that the first person to suggest that Kashmir be 'Independent' after end of British paramountcy, was Ram Chandra Kak; a Pundit. So why target us? Why talk of Islamic Revolution in Iran and not freedom struggle of India against the British rule. Some of them were extremely uncomfortable. Janab........ said that they were not spoke persons of the Jehadis that they should answer on their behalf and that they are equally puzzled. When they heard sloganeering outside, they left in huff. For the first time I noticed they were irritated on my questions. They did not answer and left without sipping the tea. I was aghast. I wanted to confront the sloganeers but your mom and sister closed all the doors and windows and tried to confine me in the bed room but I reached the balcony and they followed me.

The sky reverberated:

"Hame kya chahiye;

Nizam-e-Mustafa, Nizam-e-Mustafa, Nizam-e-Mustafa."

(What we want: rule of Allah, rule of Allah, rule of Allah.)

"Yahan kya chalega,

Nizam-e- Mustafa, Nizam-e- Mustafa, Nizam-e- Mustafa"

(What will prevail here: rule of Allah, rule of Allah, rule of Allah.)

"Kashir banawon Pakistaan, Batav varaie, Batneiv saan":

We will convert Kashmir into Pakistaan, with Pundit women, without Pundit men.

"Islam hamara maqsad hai, Quran hamara dastur hai, jehad hamara Rasta hai."

(Islam is our aim, Quran is our guide, and Jehad is our path.)

"Aie Zalimon, aie Kafiron, Kashmir Hamara chhod do."

(O perpetrators, O infidels (Hindus), leave our Kashmir.)

I shouted –

"Have you ever read Quran properly you fools? You are indulging in blasphemy of teachings without understanding them. Do you understand what religion is? Who is a Kafir? Me?; who believes in the omnipresence of God, who has been faithful to His existence or you who believe He is blind and does not exist to see your senseless killing of His innocent children. You mad men you have our blood, bone and chromosomes and I have yours. Stop this madness else the same Allah will put you in the hell."

They could have never heard me due to their own shouting. Frightened, your mom and Radhika dragged me away from the edge of the balcony. They think, of late I have gone mad; shouting on everyone and everything……'

The letter was left incomplete. I wondered he never got a chance to proceed further or did not find it worthy of writing anything in the letter or, the need of writing further had altogether vanished. Or else….he …was……. May be yes, may be no.

"Sir, we have found these posters and banners hidden here." A soldier of my search team was indicating to a bundle hidden between a rotting carpet and a heavy steel box on the floor.

All was in Urdu or Kashmiri in Persian type script that rendered me as good as illiterate. But yes some posters were so revealing created only by pictorial depiction; without or with minimal words.

A person with braid and topknot (*Choti*) on his head and a sacred thread across his shoulder on naked torso and only a dhoti below the waist (symbolising a Hindu in general and a Pundit in particular) was being hit by a heavy hammer on his head by a bearded man (symbolising a Muslim) wearing Islamic flag (crescent moon with star on black/green back ground), in the first picture. The second picture in the same poster showed the Pundit becoming flat on ground like a *Papad* with a crying-frightened face and many bearded men ridiculing and laughing at him, while many people with vermillion hiding behind a wall (symbolising rest of India or Hindus) watching with disbelief but not coming out.

The bundle had several posters of assorted content on waterproof paper, flags of JKLF on fabric, extremely offensive caricatures depicted and slogan written on the posters in Urdu/Kashmiri written in Urdu/Persian typescript. Today the soldier, who could read Urdu/Kashmiri and could translate it, was with some other search party. I ordered my scouts to locate him and get him here to reveal the concealed hatred and read out the posters.

I got up from the broken shrieking chair to have a look inside rest of the house. Until now I was entangled in books, black board and the letters. On a wall was fixed a Swastika crafted very artistically by driving the nails in a pattern on the surface of a square-smooth policed wood and then yarns weaved over the nails back and forth anchoring them end to end. In the same style there was another creation; symbol of "OM" written in Sanskrit. It had fallen off and was muddied, several times kicked around by assorted visitors; looters, hiders, searchers, lovers and who not. It looked so artistic, so beautiful and so pure, but perpetually prosecuted. I lifted it. Wanted to re-fix but it fell. I kept it on the rack. I entered the bed room. I looked around. The house looked ransacked. After all, it's more than two years no body stayed here. I began hearing cries, shrieks, scenes of hiding running appearing and disappearing. I began hearing cries for help and sound of gun shots. I tried to remove my sight from the ransacked bedroom and looked on the wall. Something in Hindi/ Sanskrit was written on paper in bold pen and pasted on the wall. No, no it was patch work on canvas; faded, torn, semi-readable. Yep only I could read it, only I. Because only I knew what it constituted and what was its meaning:

'Janani Janmabhumishcha swargadapi gariyasi'

"Mother and motherland are greater than the heaven."

"The owner looked quite audacious. He could still declare all that." I thought.

I tried to close in below the bed. It was dark but something moved silhouetted. It exited from other end and ran out of the house. I shouted to men- "catch him". All reacted spontaneously but could not catch him at the exit. I ran behind him; full force, but empty handed, without my rifle. I had left my rifle beside the shrieking chair. A few men also ran behind me. One of them shouted 'sir you duck I am firing'. I shouted "no, no, no. No firing, I will catch him". He tried to take out something from his jacket but in the process got entangled in a bush and fell flat. The object rolled out; intact, a grenade. All men panicked and shouted to me to go flat. But I did not. I had not seen it, I didn't know about it. Thank God the safety pin was not removed or could not be removed. I caught him. A few soldiers had reached by now. We lifted him and dragged him closer to the house. We brought him close to the shrieking chair.

To gain my breath, my composure, I sat on the chair. But instead of composure I felt overpowered by anger nay; inferno of anger. I was feeling possessed. I had lost my senses. I was losing my uniform. I was losing my clothes. I was feeling suffocated. Breathlessness was killing me. I had lost myself some where there. Soldiers slapped and kicked him. For a few moments I could not decide what to do. I was over powered by anger. The cries of silence around encroached and intruded house were unbearably loud. I had gone two years back. I was hearing the slogans over the loud speakers from the pulpit of mosques, from the sloganeers on the streets and from the surrounding areas:

Aie Zalimon, aie Kafiron, Kashmir hamara chhod do.

'Hame kya chahiye;

Nizam-e-Mustafa, Nizam-e-Mustafa, Nizam-e-Mustafa.

"Yahan kya chalega,

Nizam-e- Mustafa, Nizam-e- Mustafa, Nizam-e- Mustafa."

Kashir banawon Pakistaan, Batav varaie, Batneiv saan."

"Islam hamara maqsad hai, Quran hamara dastur hai, jehad hamara Rasta hai."

I ran out to breathe, some men followed me. I dragged the grenade thrower out in the open. He was in his early twenties. I was bare hand; my rifle was near the shrieking chair. Another search party bumped in me. They had brought more subversive literature from another Pundit house. I looked at my watch it was going to eleven in the forenoon. Spreading the posters, banners and seized material I asked him in Hindi/Urdu:

Can you read these?

`Kihin.'

'Do you understand Hindi/Urdu/English?'

'Kihin.'

'OK, I will teach you all the above today. Come with me'.

I was possessed and felt outragious, I snatched a long hardened bamboo cane from the closest Jawan and started beating him as if he was an animal. He cried:

'Rahem, Rahem, Rahem. Mei chui begunah. Ya Khuda bachav. Moz-oo, Moz-ooo bachav….'

While the slogan *'Aie Zalimon, aie Kafiron, Kashmir hamara chhod do'* (O perpetrators, O infidels, leave our Kashmir) echoed piercingly in my ears, I thrashed him mercilessly with the cane and my brain spontaneously re-coined the deafeningly echoing slogan. I shouted the re-coined slogan like a mad man singing on the highest scale of the octave:

'Aie Gaddaron, Aie Hattyaron, Kashmir hamara Chhod do.'

'Aie Gaddaron, Aie Hattyaron, Kashmir hamara Chhod do.'

'Aie Gaddaron, Aie Hattyaron, Kashmir hamara Chhod do.'

(O traitors, O murderers leave our Kashmir).

'Mai sab kuchh chhod dunga, sir. Khuda ke liye aap mujhe chhod deejiye'- 'I will leave everything sir; if you leave me.' He cried in chaste Urdu/Hindi.

It fuelled my anger like petrol on a receding fire.

"So, you bastard, You know Urdu and you know Hindi but pretend to knowing neither." I increased my receding force on the cane. My soldiers were stunned. The commander of the search party, a senior Subedar, was so shocked, perplexed and frightened that he came closer and he went away: undecided, with the dilemma of interfering or keeping off. He wanted to hold my cane but could not gather courage to come close enough to hold his senior commander's rage; flowing through the cane.

"Sir, please sir. He may die. You were never like this. What has happened to you? Sir please… for God's sake….sir. Sir, they are traitors, our killers but leave him. We will deal separately." He tried to close in, whereas soldiers spontaneously began drifting away. The sole police constable, accompanying the search party, hid behind my men with his dated action bolt rifle.

The baton broke. All had sigh of relief. I breathed like a tiger who had missed his prey.

The JCO shouted at the soldiers in Marathi; *'Laukar, Saheban chya sathi pani gheun ye;* Hurry up, get water for the officer'.

"I am alright. Do not worry Saheb. Where is my rifle?" I asked as if nothing has happened, leaving the 'grenade thrower on ground.

He blocked my way to my move back to the same house where I had left my rifle.

"No sir, please no." He pleaded.

"I am not mad." Please get aside.

"No sir. That house seems to have been possessed by ghosts. You were changed sitting there. Now please do not get inside again. The men have already brought your weapon."

My assistant got me a glass of water, his hands trembling and so the tray he was holding.

The JCO shouted at all of them particularly my assistant for not taking care of my needs. He pronounced a few expletives in Marathi scolding them. He was angry that men had tea twice but did not offer me even once, as if not having tea was reason of my madness. He had no idea about real reason. Not his fault. After all he was a simple soldier and not a psychoanalyst. The assistant told the JCO meekly that he had brought tea twice to me but I was so engrossed that I even did not respond to his offer.

Another search party informed over wireless that they had hauled a big bundle of military uniform and a packet of explosive hidden in the bed box of an abandoned house. The Commanding Officer was informed and he visited our location and the house from where it was recovered. He saw everything and congratulated me and men of my Company for the haul. He eventually came to know about the beating of the youth who was seething in pain.

He took me aside and gave short lecture about having control over myself particularly as an officer. He appreciated the extremely difficult situations under which we were fighting the sponsored insurgency but cautioned not to throw out the baby with the bath water. I could not ask him whether a grenade thrower needs to be treated like an innocent civilian. He took the youth with him to the congregation for further interrogation.

Our search of all houses continued; occupied and vacant. I went back to the same house to tell my soldiers to wind up everything subversive they had discovered from desolated houses. While men sorted out the JKLF flags, offensive posters, explosives, anti-national literature, anti-Hindu propaganda material, I glanced through a few more books. I noticed a book mark, fallen off the book. It was a Sanskrit Shlok cut from some print and pasted on the hard board, for use as book mark. It instantly soothed my body, mind and soul. It displaced all my negative thoughts. These two lines looked representing the essence of our cultural ethos, our eternal values and greatest teachings of our Rishis that everyone on the earth is our family: *'Vasudhaiv Kutumbakam'*.

I told men to re-fix the *'OM'* on the wall so well that it does not fall easily. But what about the message on the book mark? Its print and size is so small. It deserves to be read by the whole world. It blesses all human beings to be happy, healthy and achieve salvation. It proclaimed in Sanskrit:

"Sarve bhavantu sukhinah, sarve santu niramayaah.

Sarve Bhadraani pashyantu, maakashchid-dukh-bhagbhavet"

"May all be happy, may all be healthy; free from physical, mental or psychological disease.

May all achieve salvation and none may have any pain or sorrow."

We moved on to do what we were ordered to do by the nation through the will of the Parliament; military operation. We moved on to destroy the enemies of our motherland and narrow minded fanatics who have misconception that they protect the God and not vice-versa.

I looked at the book mark and wished it could be placed high in the sky for all to read, understand and know that we wish every child of the God, every 'being' on the earth; happiness, good health and salvation. We believe all 'beings' born on the mother earth are our brothers and sisters, irrespective of how they look, how they pray and what they believe in; including the perpetrators and the fanatics.

****

Prishtha par aane na paaye, haashiye par rah gaye;
Daudkar kante, gulabon ki bhi kahani kah gaye.
Kya pataa gathbandh kaisa, lahar ka patwaar se;
Naav mein baithe rahe sab, sirf maajhi bah gaye. -Unknown.

"Not allowed to stay in the centre, they were thrown on the margins of the page;
The thorns claimed deligacy of roses, and told the world their story of the age.
Collusion; between waves and the rudder, so mysterious so confound:
All sat safely in the boat, only sailors drowned."

****

Chapter 12

The Prized Possession

August 1992: Down town Srinagar

Finally, the old gentleman came walking to the spot where we were waiting for him. He came out of his house which was four or five buildings away from the place where we were waiting for him. We were sitting in a three storeyed house with the old lady, the owner, who was more desperately waiting for him and his help than we. She was continuously sobbing. When I met the old gentleman, I was impressed by his elegant appearance. All was white indicating purity, at least in appearance: spotless white Kurta and Pyjama in contrast to the traditional pheren, white hair, white eye brows and milk white skin with layers of wrinkles.

He was putting on stylish golden framed glasses and was

supporting his lean and thin old body frame on a beautifully curved walnut wood walking stick with intricate design. To match his white Kurta and very loose pyjama (something like Lucknowy pyjama) he was wearing off white leather sandal. No trace of teeth in the mouth. It seemed, he forgot or intentionally did not put on his "complete set of dentures". He was experiencing difficulty in talking; partly due to breathlessness and partly due to absence of denture which supported the tongue to pronounce correctly. I felt a bit awkward that I insisted to call him instead of going myself to his house. I guess he was more than thrice my age.

As army officers operating under the Armed Forces Special Power Act, in a'disturbed' area, we were extremely powerful and elite lot vis-à-vis life and liberty of the civilians. Every one under ' disturbed area' wanted, mostly against their wishes, to keep even a sepoy in good humour. Somewhere this extreme authority over civilians, as local perceived, had disrobed many military men; particularly lower and younger lot among them, of desirable decencies. A few thought it was due to their nature of job. "We are not here to garner vote and support but to carry our surgical military operation to catch or kill the traitors." One of our seniors was heard occasionally saying to men.

"We are here by process of selection to do a professional job and not by process of election that we indulge in popular gimmicks. We are not politicians and our sole criteria of action are national interest and sole criteria of speech are truth; not diplomacy and niceties," were usual rhetoric of our adjutant to shrug off any charge of ill treatment.

However, I had my own ways of dealing with civilians. And this elderly gentleman, due to various factors including his past position, was different. The sobbing woman, who had sought this gentleman's help, had informed before hand that he was a retired judge of Jammu and Kashmir High Court. He looked like an old angel, at least by his appearance and bearing. His body language was so open and friendly that when he came closer, he smiled like a toothless baby and stretched his right hand forward towards me for handshake; I spontaneously gave him the respect he deserved.

"Good afternoon sir, how are you?" Instinctively came greeting from me and I stretched my right hand to shake hand with him, holding my AK-47 in the left hand pointing down.

He shook hand very warmly and immediately clamped my hand by both his hands, his stick included and replied- "good afternoon officer, I am fine, thanks".

"I am sorry to trouble you sir, but in the interest of the old lady and on her reference I had to." I said.

"Oh, it's alright. You have not troubled me we are troubling you". He said in modulated tone leaving me intrigued to uncover its meaning. Was it a genuine statement or a taunt, I could not guess.

The old lady gestured all of us to sit down in her drawing room. The judge moved in and fell on the central couch to control his breathlessness.

The toothless smile on his face had openness and innocence of a child and spread its charm. Now she had stopped sobbing and taken out her spectacles to wipe the tears. The gentleman spoke to this lady of almost his age; maybe she was a bit younger in age but surely above seventy with a lot many wrinkles on her face. He spoke a few sentences in Kashmiri to the old lady which I could only guess but could not clearly understand. He asked short questions and got long explanatory answers. I guessed she was explaining the same thing in Kashmiri which she had told me in chaste Urdu. She was sufficiently educated to communicate in Urdu and she used a few 'heavy'sounding words from Persian; not clearly comprehensible to me. I was convinced by her explanation but I had a different issue.

My soldiers, under the command of a Junior Commissioned Officer or JCO, had recovered a soft bag containing precious stones and bundle of currency notes amounting to several lakh. The wealth was kept so casually in the wood stack on the open top floor that anyone could suspect it to be either not her or kept without her knowledge. The men suspected that the 'booty' was part of extortion or collection by the militants for Jehad and the old woman knowingly or unknowingly was being used as a conduit for its safe upkeep. Else why would she keep it in the wood stack instead of his safe or locker? The logic looked so apt that I also could not find any reason to differ. Her vague and incoherent explanation only compounded and complicated the matter. But she insisted the money was her, given by her late husband for Haj. I had reached the spot, leaving all other work, to sort out the issue.

I had to hand over the valuables and the cash, after satisfying myself that it was genuinely her. It was prudent to hand over the valuables in front of some witness to be clear off any charge of impropriety at later stage. We had locality elder who was part of search party and witness to what all happened, but it was neither sufficient nor the local gentleman could give convincing support. We needed a few more witnesses with 'identity' in the society and unquestionable credentials. In fact the locality elder and the women had suggested this gentleman's name: a retired judge of the high court, a neighbour and family friend.

Testimony of the judge was sufficient for me to hand over the valuables to the lady. We were waiting for her son to reach the spot; his house, back from the congregation, to proceed further. When we recovered this bag of treasure, more than three lakh rupees in cash and gem stones of un-assessed value, I had informed the Commanding Officer over wireless. The CO was at the stadium; the site of congregation. I had explained him everything and requested him to find out the person by telling him the name, as told by the lady; which I do not remember now. I had requested the Commanding Officer to trace him from the congregation and send him under 'escort' to his home. The Commanding Officer had already ordered the soldiers to identify him and send him to me. Let me give him an assumed name; Ashraf.

"How much time will it take for Ashraf to arrive? Has he been informed?" The judge inquired. "He is on the way but still it will take time because they are coming on foot." I told him.

"Who they, Only Ashraf is coming?" the judge asked suspiciously.

"He is escorted by our men for obvious reasons." I informed.

"That's good, else if roaming alone in a cordon he may be caught as a suspect on the way." he said, revealing practical fears and the realities on ground, based on his experience.

"He will surely be caught since the area is under cordon and nobody is allowed to roam free. He may be even harassed and questioned on the way if soldiers do not accompany him." I added.

To avoid undue difference of opinion on the point which was a non-issue, I thought of doing business and asked him his version of this "discovered treasure" being with the lady.

"Sir, the lady has told me about this cash and gem stones but can you tell as to why this huge amount of cash and valuable was hidden in the wood stack instead of being kept securely in safe or locker." I changed the topic and tried to extract the information of my interest and use.

"Three lakh something cash and assorted gem stones of unknown value." I informed gesturing my men to bring in everything recovered to show to the judge and continued:

"This is what we have found in the heap of dried fire wood on top of the house securely wrapped in a small cloth bag. The old lady claims it has been given to her by her late husband."

"Is this all?" he asked to the lady in Urdu instead of Kashmiri, apparently with intention; so that we also understand what was going on between them.

"*Haan (yes).*" She said nodding in affirmation.

"kuchh kam to nahi hai dekh lo, baad me mat kahna; Look and be sure nothing is deficient, do not blame or allege later," asked my JCOs emphatically to clear off any charges of stealing, extortion or misappropriation in the latter stage.

"Nahi. Sab poora hai. Aap log bahut achhe hain." She said in emotionally choked voice, again wiping the stream of tears gushing out of her eyes.

"I will tell you everything about this lady, the money and their problem but can you tell me how you found it and what is your apprehension?" he spoke with authority and confidence of a judge, though retired, and questioned me before answering.

"You see, my men were carrying out house to house search and this particular search party was headed by a JCO who is sitting next to me. There was no one in this house except this lady. My search party has one person from the locality, whom you see sitting with us and I am sure you know him." I stopped my narration to confirm if he knew the local gentlemen accompanying our search party.

"Yes, yes, I know him, he is a teacher and a nice gentleman." he elaborated.

I continued-"My men searched all the houses very meticulously, so was this one also; for any kind of arms, ammunition, explosives, objectionable material including anti-national and communally sensitive propaganda material. However, the prime targets are suspected militant hiding inside the houses; of their own, neighbours' or somebody else's'. At times they are in well concealed hide outs which are extremely difficult to discover and..."

"Did you find any in this locality so far?" He interrupted.

"No, not during this cordon and search today, at least until now, else this area has high concentration of such elements." I emphasised and I continued noticing him maintaining silence with blank look towards me.

"…. At times they hide themselves in haystack, layers of quilts and blankets, firewood stack, etc. So after reaching the house soldiers went up on the top of the house and started searching the firewood stack. During search of entire house the lady remained indifferent and non-chalant attitude even when they went up."

"So the cash and the gems were found inside the firewood stack." The judge interrupted my narration to cut the story short or out of curiosity, was not clear.

"Yes, cash and the gem stones were kept wrapped in a cloth bag, inside an unlocked wooden chest, which fell out when men started removing the stack layer by layer. What puzzled us was her casual approach towards the cash and articles hidden in the stack and lack of plausible explanation from her about so much cash and gems kept there. Initially we thought it is not hers since she did not show any sign of uneasiness and we concluded that it is stolen or extorted booty of militants who hid it at this house of an innocent old lady, so that either it is not detected or, if detected, it is not blamed on them." I explained.

"When did she claim that it is her wealth?" The judge asked me.

"Only when I reached here after getting report over radio from my soldiers that she claimed. It seems she was waiting for an officer to arrive, to tell her story and not to anyone else, about the money. However, she could not tell me convincingly, why she had kept it so casually and insecurely. Moreover choice of place also created a lot of suspicion in our mind; instead of keeping in box, suitcase, or locker she had kept it in the haystack."

"What did she tell you about this money?" The judge wanted to know.

I continued-"She says it is the cash her husband had given her, before his death, for her Haj pilgrimage. The gem stones are residual pieces of unsold stones after closure of shop of gems and jewellery which her husband was having in the main market of the city at one point of time. I want a confirmation from you about this version before handing over the cash and articles to her."

"What is your doubt?" The judge enquired.

"My apprehension is that this amount has been 'hidden' by militants for 'subversive activities' and it is part of 'extortion/ collection' they have been indulging from the beginning. Further my apprehension is that the woman, probably under duress, is acting as conduit to give 'temporary protection' to the illegitimate wealth; recovered as cash and articles by us, which, I apprehend, belongs to the militants; the Jehadis."

He took a deep breath and prepared himself for long narration shifting his walking stick from between his two legs to aside and positioning his one leg over the other; cross legged and began, "Captain it is antithesis of your conclusion, unfortunately."

He said, while fitting his dentures which his daughter-in-law had brought from his home, when she had noticed that he had forgotten it. She knew he would find it difficult to talk properly without them. He further changed his position and tilted to face me better and prepared himself to deliver long discourse by making himself more comfortable on chair in the drawing room of the lady who by now, had regained her composure after arrival of the judge.

"Her husband was a respected goldsmith of this area who carried on the family business of several generations until he died two years back. From 1988 onwards the business was bad due to frequent closure of the city; the market, the business and almost all aspects of life, except strife. Frequent visits by Jehadis for financial assistance or extortion, whatever you choose to call, proved to be the proverbial 'Scabies in leprosy'.

One fine day he came to my house in the afternoon, which was unusual, as he used to be at his shop. After usual customary greeting I asked him why he had not gone to the shop or whether he was unwell or whether visitors had decreased." The judge disclosed and continued the elaborate reply he had received from the goldsmith:

"No, in fact, visitors have increased during these days only their profile has changed. Instead of visitors coming with currency notes, gold or silver to buy and sell, now I receive visitors with Kalashnikov, who neither buy nor sell but snatch."

The judge continued to elaborate the reply of the goldsmith friend who was his neighbour:

"He had stopped to clear his throat and wipe flow of spontaneous tears. I had never seen him in such a pitiable situation. Before I could think of saying something he had continued"-

"Substantial amount of my business and profit was not from gold but gems, precious stones and pearl. A large number of my clients were Pundits, who have since fled. The Muslims have also decreased visiting our shop out of the fear that the Mujahids will come to know that the visitor has 'purchasing power' and he will become a target."

"But who are they?" The judge had interrupted the goldsmith, feeling puzzled.

"*Pataa kya chhui*; know not, such people have never been seen by me in the area. They seem to be outsiders some even non-Kashmiris." He had confided.

"Pakistani Afghani." The judge had tried to guess to ease his friend's dilemma.

"Seems to be, they cover their faces making it so difficult even to guess." He had said with disgust and despair and continued.

"Even if you identify what can you do?" The judge told that the goldsmith had said.

"What can I do to help you? Even I feel completely irrelevant. I have resigned from the Red Cross Society of India and told Punditji that I cannot work even for the Society in the environment prevailing now. Punditji is among few prominent Pundits who have decided not to leave the valley, let what may come. I appreciate his courage and determination. I have lost most of my intellectual friends, since they left for known destinations but uncertain future; south of Jammu." The judge revealed his reply given to his goldsmith friend.

"I had stopped suddenly, realizing, instead of advising and assisting my goldsmith friend, I was also posing my problem and reversing the direction of my dialogue." The judge had elaborated about his talk with the goldsmith.

"What you intend to do." The judge had asked the goldsmith friend.

"I am not replenishing any of my stocks. I will kill my business and shop slowly and allow them to disappear like melting snow on the ridges by May-June. Whatever end proceeds, I will invest in garment shop in Delhi or Calcutta; which my son is looking for, and both of us; me and my wife plan to go for Haj, Inshallah." The judge revealed and continued.

"He looked finished. I found myself in a position where neither affirmation nor negation of his ideas was a good idea. So I raised my both hands up, looked in the sky gesturing to say-all God's wish."

I interrupted the judge in his description of his dialogue with the jeweller.

"So could he go for Haj?"

"God was kinder than he thought of Him." The judge continued about the jeweller.

"He picked him up from Srinagar without detour to Mecca. He died of heart attack two years back in June after seeing the fast melting of snow on the ridges, and of course slow melting and vanishing of his business from the valley to down the river in plains."

"So is his son doing well in garment business in Calcutta or Delhi." I interrupted.

"Doing well is not known but he is doing business in Calcutta."

He straightened himself in the chair as if had decided to end the conversation. "But this cash of three lakh and precious stones are left over of the slow melting and draining of his ancestral business. The lady keeps crying very often since then. It brought destructions of all kind to her; loss of ancestral business, prestige, honour, stability, security and most painful; death of her 'Khabind'(husband). It has thrown her son away 2000 kms; less for business but more for being away from troubles."

He continued-"I convinced her to go for Haj this year itself before something bad happens. She has kept the money, given by her late husband, for her Haj pilgrimage." The judge elaborated.

"But why she hid it in the firewood stack." I asked more out of curiosity than suspicion.

"*RAM RAM SAHIB, YA MANASA LA ME GHEUN AALO*; Salutations sir, I have brought that man." Suddenly Commander of a small contingent of my soldiers who were escorting Ashraf, had barged in with Ashraf, interrupting my engaging and analytical dialogue with the judge, even judge could not begin his sentence.

"Jai Hind sir."

Ashraf greeted me with the words which were rare to hear from a Kashmiri, but more I was surprised with this gesture.

He was more like a Marwari than Kashmiri. A man in his late thirties, he leaned forward in his greeting gestures, bending from waist with folded hand. He was tall slim with moustache, in a Salwar suit, without pheren as overall. He looked happy and confident.

"Jai Hind, come Ashraf, we are waiting for you only. Count your cash, count and check the precious stones and give me a report; if all is well."

I returned his greetings while giving the most important instruction from my side and gestured him to sit down.

"Sir, I am so grateful to you. Each and everything is intact, I have nothing to complain. Your men are honest and you are -----."

He was so moved that he could not complete the sentence. His eyes became moist and his throat obscure.

"I think everyone and any one would have done the same." I broke the silence.

"No sir, one can expect such integrity only from the army. Had it been ****, probably I wouldn't have got it back and most likely, would have been arrested; irrespective of my convincing explanation. I am afraid; even judge Saheb's defence wouldn't have worked." He revealed his perception and fear, naming a police organization. I told him not to make perceptions about any organization based on some incidents and not generalise behaviour or conduct of a few people to apply it on all for good or bad.

"Sir, do you know what the value of these gem stones is?" He looked up to me to make me understand what we have returned to him.

"We are neither goldsmith like you nor we are concerned about its value. What we are concerned is that irrespective of value it was yours and it has been returned to you. I think I need not bother about its value but I would surely like to get educated. What are these stones or gems? Can you identify them and introduce me?" I asked seeing different colours of the gems.

"This blood red is Ruby, this blue one is Sapphire, this yellowish is Topaz and this green one Emerald and this ...."

"Diamond." I interrupted since this was only one which I could recognize.

"And it has cumulative value of more than ten lakh." He resumed his identification with pride and emotion and continues:

"So you are returning more than thirteen lakh worth of my wealth."

I was really awed by his disclosure. It was a huge amount, at least, at that point of time.

To be on safe side and as per directions of the Commanding Officer, I told him to give an undertaking that he had received his valuables accurately and intact from us. The judge also countersigned. What an irony, I thought. The man, who used to examine the witnesses, is a witness today.

But before the judge could sign and we could hand over, there was unusual dilemma on the way. The radio operator informed me to hold the transfer. Someone suspected to be militant and picked up from identification parade was claiming that he had hid some amount of cash and precious gems in a house in the same locality which he had 'collected' for Jehad. I was in deeper dilemma since I was convinced that the amount genuinely belonged to the claimant old woman. "But if the suspect is able to give accurate description and provides sufficient proof of his claim what would happen to the prestige and credibility of the judge?" I was concerned. Many thoughts came to my mind. If the 'booty' belonged to the Jehadis what role the woman was playing? Was she trying to protect the militants and anti-national elements?

The suspected claimant was brought to the spot under a large posse of troops. He accurately indicated the house. The woman looked unnerved and the judge aghast. They could not see the face of the claimant as it was covered to conceal his identity. The posse of soldiers asked him to identify the place where he had hid the booty. The suspect identified wrong place and to cover up, asserted that the house owners might have moved it away. The women cried inconsolably as if the tragedy of loss of her ancestral business and death of her husband was not enough to face the ignominy of association with the Mujahids.

But contrary to the woman and her son Ashraf, the suspect could neither tell the exact amount nor quantity and type of gems. Based on the feedback and recommendation from me, he was taken back for further interrogation to uncover the truth. I had to hold the transfer until things were clear. During thorough interrogation, the suspect broke down and disclosed that he was trying to buy time to save himself from the torture of interrogation so he threw this point. He had heard troops talking about some cash and gems being recovered. He further begged that he was innocent and did not know about anything; about any Mujahid or money. The writing on the wall was clear. The bag was handed over to Ashraf.

"So now I am leaving." I said.

"No sir." Ashraf pleaded, "please don't leave me in death trap."

"Death trap? How?" I wondered.

"If the Mujahideen (militants) came to know about this wealth, either my mother will not be able to go for Haj or I will not be there to receive her."

"So." I wondered what more he wanted from me.

"So you have to order the bank manager who is in the congregation to open the bank and allow me to open the locker and further you have to provide escort up to bank for safe deposit of all this." He said confidently as if he was sure that he had a right or authority to order me.

"So you are ordering me." I commented, in lighter vein, on his audacious request.

"No sir, there is no other option. Nobody listens to anybody now a days in Kashmir. The bank manager will not listen to me or any one else. In Kashmir there are only two entities that can never be ignored by any one; army and Mujahideen; the military and the militants. So you have to help me."

I was perplexed since it was a very complicated issue. Army men have never gone to do such 'personal and individual welfare' ever; it was like stretching too far. I was getting uncomfortable since I had, against my choice, got embroiled in a non-operational matter and not able to supervise and co-ordinate my Company operation.

By prevailing parameters of good work in the army, I felt, I was 'wasting time and resources'. The parameters were not how much goodwill one has generated or how among civilians you have been able to change the perception or how you have rendered help in the time of crises but "catch" and "kill"; catch or seize of arms, ammunitions and militants or the "kill". I knew, on these parameters, I was not a "very successful" Commander; if not out rightly a "failure." At times I was teased, though in lighter vein, as "friend" of the locals; who, for many in security establishments, were synonymous of militants. It all was because of my soft corner for them.

I could not have taken such a big decision of sending military men with Ashraf to secure his personal wealth. So I was option-less, except to talk to the Commanding Officer over wireless. He was away at the congregation. I convinced him about providing the escort and instructing the banker out of turn. But in completely contrast to my gut feeling he agreed after a light remark.

"So the friendship is flourishing." He had taunted followed

by break of laughter. But contrary to my fear he continued showing his generosity and humane side.

"OK, send all of them in army vehicle to this location and I will organize the rest." I was so relieved. I told one of my JCOs to take Ashraf in a military vehicle along with three soldiers and meet the Commanding Officer at the congregation.

"Why don't you come to my home and have a cup of tea/Kahwah until your men come back from the bank with Ashraf?" the judge changed the direction of thought and talk.

"I don't mind." I said since I was eager to talk to him on the prevailing chaos in the valley.

He led me to his house along with my integral followers; one wireless operator and two escorts. The house was old but grand. His daughter in law opened the door; the only human being inside the house. We sat down in his drawing room which was simple and modest than I had imagined about a retired High Court judge's house. Both of us got so engrossed on Kashmir issue that neither could he ask anything about me nor I about him.

I thought of asking the obvious: "Sir, what do you have to say about state of affairs in Kashmir."

He took a deep breath, adjusted his spectacle and started:

"It is a very complicated issue now. It is politics, religion, history and even geography all mixed up, nay; messed up. It is politics of one-upmanship reaching to brink manship from all sides. The men in the helms of affairs of Kashmir have always handled it with shrewdness of extended intelligence; befitting to their interest, but with shrunken wisdom. It is a result of personal ambition of individuals and a victim of international politics in all possible meanings."

"Sir, you have confused me more than you have clarified. I am afraid I am more confused and lost now than before asking the question." I wanted to hear more.

"See, one thing is very clear in the minds of majority; Independence or status quo but no Pakistan. The land of Rishis and Sufis; Kashmir, is much closer to 'Indian secularism than Pak theocracy. You know, I know, the layman knows that they are the one who have pushed us where we are, Pakistanis have made several attempts to grab Kashmir but failed every time; mostly due to military might of India but not exclusively due to it. The Kashmiris also have ensured failure of Pakistani attempt every time. And I am sure this attempt will not have different fate. But this time there is a difference; the leadership has its 'centre out'. The leadership this time has been hijacked." He wiped his face while placing the empty tea cup on the peg table close to his couch.

"Sir, it is mystifying to hear similar things from majority of people from the valley but then why this armed uprising." I poked him to understand how he looked at it.

"You see the main cause of anger is a perception; genuine or generated in the minds of people about corruption: committed or allowed to be committed by the ruling dispensation in Jammu and Kashmir. People also perceive the two ruling dynasties at Delhi and Srinagar as mutually supportive of each other and not allowing new entities to sprout and challenge them. Nothing concrete has been done to dispel this perception; genuine or generated, and this is the root cause of the inner dynamics of the problem. Rest all, including Pakistani abetting, is on the fringe."

"Similar things I keep on listening from many people. However many go beyond it and say that they have been deceived by "India" since promise of plebiscite was never fulfilled." I added.

"It is true. Pt. Nehru had promised that wish of people of Kashmir would be supreme and final decision would be taken after plebiscite but it was not done." He supported the popular view.

"But how can he fulfil until Pakistan withdraws the troops

from occupied (POK) areas, as mandated in the UN resolution." I asked most obvious question.

"That is true that is why I said all have dealt Kashmir with extended shrewdness but shrunken wisdom. Legally and practically Pakistan has more share of blame than India." He said.

"But can all this be a cause of starting armed struggle and Jehad? What it has to do with Jehad as everyone has full religious freedom under Indian constitution."

The judge kept quiet.

We never realized when we had finished our tea. The talk was very captivating and interesting. He described how he was nominated to be part of the committee which was tasked to translate the constitution in to Kashmiri. His daughter-in-law became very nostalgic about the past glory when he was a judge. Ashraf entered the house with my men.

"So mission complete?" I asked all of them collectively.

"Yes sir, and I will never forget your help." Ashraf grabbed the opportunity to thank us.

"So now we would like to leave. Kindly allow me to leave sir." I extended my courtesy to the judge and got up.

"Oh sure. It was such an ordeal for you." He said smilingly.

I shook hands with the judge and Ashraf. I looked at his mother; she was in tears, now she sobbed.

"Moz, why are you crying now, when everything is OK? We have gone out of way to secure your personal wealth and gift of your husband." I said in a puzzled tone.

"Crying is my destiny. Crying is our destiny. Crying is Kashmir's and Kashmiri's destiny.

We cry when we are sad, we cry when we are happy, we cry when we are normal we cry, cry and cry."

"But why?" I interrupted.

"Because Kashmir has fallen on evil's eyes, on Satan eyes; it will never be the same. Our happiness has shrunk but reasons for our happiness have grown manifold." She continued

"Nowadays, we feel happy when we get our own wealth back, we are happy when our son comes back intact from crack down, we are happy if we get uninterrupted sleep, we are happy if we are able to drink water and are able to have tea at the time of our choice. We are happy if we can have food on time; our own food. We are happy if we are allowed to enter in our own house, we are happy when we don't hear blasts and firings, we are happy if we get medicine of our prescription even on higher price. We are happy for the reasons which otherwise may be a reason to be sad."

"All will be OK soon. Now you would be going for Haj. Please pray for the Salamati; safety of Kashmir, its people and for safety of all those who are true well-wishers of the Kashmiris. After all, you have got your 'priced possession' back."

"Young men like you are our prized possession and not currency and gem stones." She had fired a deadly salvo which stunned me.

She said placing both her hand on my soldier, standing face to face. She was short in height, I realised, hardly reaching up to my chest. She was putting on thick framed glasses with thick lenses clasped within them. I felt my "catch" was far superior today, in comparison to catching the militants or seizing arms or ammunition.

I felt rewarded.

"And do not forget to pray for me there during Haj. I would come to know, if you do not pray for me."

I said while wishing her a happy pilgrimage and poked words intentionally. Sometimes, I remember of my childhood, teasing a motherly woman brings immeasurable pleasure.

She smiled for the first time.

I felt she; the old woman more than my mother's age with several wrinkles on her face, wanted to hug me but something; unknown to me, more than the flowing tears, forced her to abort at the last moment. Instead she wiped her tears, turned to her son, hugged him and cried; as if the emotions were the same but direction was changed.

Ashraf smiled with immense gratitude, the judge looked on and we moved away.

Chapter 13

Toy on LOC

15-27 Oct 1998

After almost three years' peace tenure at Amritsar, in the month of Oct 1997, our battalion once again moved to Jammu and Kashmir. But this time we had to replace a deployed battalion who had completed their two years' tenure on the LOC at Uri. I, as Rear Detachment Commander, was assigned the responsibility of handing over everything at Amritsar and then move to Uri. After completing the assigned task, I joined my battalion at Uri three months later in mid-January 1998. After a few days' stay at the battalion headquarters at Uri town, I was told to visit entire deployment of our battalion on the LOC, so that in case of need I could command the troops on any axis.

After long tour of almost fifteen days, and a few days stay

at various locations, I could understand the deployment of all four Companies. Finally, after end of the tour, I was ordered to stay put at Delta Company Headquarter, familiarize myself well and then take over the command of the Company, since the incumbent had to proceed on leave. It was the most important location of our deployment due to various factors, including regular flag meeting with Pakistani army and passing of NH1A from this axis.

I had come to the Alert post, which was Company Headquarter of Delta Company, for the first time and was being introduced and familiarized with the surroundings. The outgoing officer had briefed me about the area, the people, the dos and don'ts, besides details of deployment of our own and Pakistani forces. In course of introduction, he had called Khalid also from the neighboring village. He wanted to introduce me with Khalid, a very interesting and mysterious person; who was going to be pivotal character of our stay at the LOC. In almond coloured Salwar-Kameez and Afghani cap, Khalid looked weak, sick and pale. Although he was in his early thirties, he looked as in late thirties. He was frail-framed thick-bearded man with forward bent body, stained teeth, long sharp nose and salt and pepper hairs; typical bonny and skinny Pahari Muslim man.

He was breathless when reached my post and had complained of suffering from asthma, attributing the cause to hookah and cigarette. I guessed it was not only smoking but physical and mental stress he had gone through and still was going through that had made him look older than his age, though, to some extent, he himself was responsible for it. But mostly it was a fait accompli wherein he was treated as a toy between two armies or rather nations, fighting proxy war. He reiterated to me what he had told to my predecessors in this location, though no one believed him, that he was forcibly taken to '*Paar*; the other side' (POK/Pakistan). The officer of the handing over battalion opined it was unclear whether he was taken across by Pakistani agents or had gone voluntarily to become a Mujahid, but later he was converted in to a spy,

The author near LOC during second tenure (1997-1999); in the far background touching sky line is seen snow clad ridge (Peer Kanthi) under Pakistani occupation.

was an open secret. "And this was the hard undeniable truth." He had emphasized.

Khalid himself had disclosed that he was trained to become a Mujahid and trained to fight for the *Deen*; the religion, to eliminate the infidels from Kashmir and 'free' Kashmir from the clutches of *Kafirs*. But noticing his potential for covert operation; his quiet nature, high intelligence and shrewdness, his innocent composure, vicinity of his home to the LOC, his potential to come and go across so easily etc, the trainers decided to use him as spy. He insisted while talking to me that he never wanted to become Mujahid but he was helpless. He was just 23-24 years old when in 1989-90 he was forcibly taken away by the agents for training in POK. His mother had cried for months and his pregnant wife had suffered convulsion and seizures that had resulted into miscarriage of his first child.

He had claimed that he wanted to come back but without weapon, whereas he was forced to carry a sack of Kalashnikov and leave it at a specified place. He was told to leave it and somebody else was to pick it up from there. The success of first operation made him star in the eyes of the handlers but brought perpetual misery to him. Then onwards he was called through 'messengers' to go across frequently and bring arms, ammunition and explosives this side of the LOC for use by Mujahids. His good understanding of geography, topography, terrain and his knowledge about deployment of the army this side of LOC was used to the fullest; from sending subversive material to taking potshot on army positions this side. His knowledge about deployment this side was used to lay Pakistani guns other side to drop artillery shells accurately on Indian positions. Gradually his role was forcefully expanded and he was used to carry out bomb blasts and IED blasts this side of the LOC.

He carried on this task until one day caught by the Indian soldiers while coming back to his home after delivering the consignment to the agents. He was noticed in the thick bushes very close to the LOC, where even soldiers rarely ventured. He would have not been caught but to the wild bear who chased him forcing him to run helter-skelter. This hide-and-seek resulted in to noticeable unusual movement in the bushes. The soldiers surrounded the area and encircled the cause of stir in the undergrowth. The soldiers claimed they had caught him after long chase inside 10-12 feet high grass along the Nala, which is imaginary LOC, in the coniferous forest. However he claimed he intentionally ran towards Indian military post since he was fed up of being used as a carrier and wanted to get rid of it.

He was a man rightly under tremendous suspicion but did not disclose anything as instructed by his masters or so concluded the army men who interrogated him. Even if he wanted to defy his masters and accept his involvement in subversion, he would have been in tight corner since it would have pushed him into category of terrorists. He initially tried to befool army men by feigning to be insane and by giving several contradictory and confusing statements, but nothing worked. He was not let off the hook even when he had defecated in his pajama. Soldiers thought it was his trick to befool them, whereas he claimed he could not hold it due to fear and pain. He was interrogated and tortured but he did not reveal as to what he did and what the secrets of his past were. He kept on pleading innocence and helplessness. Finally, not being able to extract confessions or anything substantial, army thought of using the stick from the other end.

"We know more than one way to skin the cat." Said the Commanding Officer of the previous Unit to his officers who were then deployed in the same area and who had caught him for the first time. Then they decided to use Khalid like holding the cane from the other end. Khalid was assisted financially, assured of security, his family given a few privileges and protection. Khalid was brain washed, nurtured, groomed and convinced, but not trained since he already was, to do the same for 'India' that he was doing for Pakistan till yesterday:

spying. Now he was darling of both sides; India and Pakistan. Then over a period of time he disclosed everything as to what he really did the other side. Now his hurdles were nil. He used to cross border at will, of course after due discussion and permission from both the sides; but without one side knowing about the connivance of the other side and living in utopia that he was exclusively working for their side only.

It was impossible to know what and how much he had revealed to the other side. Slowly he moved to the gravity, to his rightful place where most of the people in this category fall: the point of no return. He was like a table tennis ball, LOC being the 'net.' Then the players started their game. Gradually he was not in his control, and later in no one's control; neither this side nor that side. From a 'human being' to an 'object', and in between; a freedom fighter, a recruit, a Mujahid, a terrorist, a carrier, a spy, etc: his journey was interesting and his end mysterious and mystifying. When my Unit took over from the previous Unit; who had caught Khalid, we were briefed about him in great detail. We were told how important the man was since he could get accurate information about deployment of Pakistani forces, their strength, the details of weapons, details of officers etc. Khalid had no problems of staying other side.

He had a few relatives other side of the LOC hence he stayed as long as he wanted. He could go even to Muzaffarabad as he had obtained or was provided POK identity cards. Pakistani agents had assisted him in getting all necessary documents to prove he was a resident of '*Azad Kashmir* (POK)'. They were also extracting information about Indian positions this side of the LOC. This game carried on until both the sides realized; sooner or later, that he had become a double edged weapon.

He had met me second time on my call when the CO was very upset due to sequential blasts in our area. He had instructed me to call Khalid and warn him not to indulge in anti-national activities else he would face extreme difficulty, though there was nothing apparent to suggest his involvement in the blast. The CO was convinced that it was Khalid only, who was lynchpin of the subversive activities and had cited specific intelligence reports indicating his involvement. When Khalid reached my room he started swearing by Allah unstopped, despite being breathless.

His appearance and mannerism had created instant empathy for him in my heart; he was looking more ill than during the previous visit and tried to portray his innocence more logically than last time. He had also brought a few kilograms of odd shape-sized, sick looking apples as 'presents' which were produce of the apple tree in his own small orchard near his house. On my advice to take the apples back for his family, he claimed that it were his family members who had insisted that he brought apples for me: "how can he go empty handed to meet someone?" He had said to have been asked by his wife. It was against rich Kashmiri culture; hence the apples. On my advice that he should not involve in anti-national activities he had cried and had sworn by the Almighty to prove his innocence. He had cursed his place of birth for his ills while revealing his dilemma: "No one believes me. The Pakistanis have also sent the same message through their agents. Now where should I go?" I had accepted his 'presents' and had sent some presents, including toffies, from my side to his family, particularly for the two small children he had. Overwhelmed by my gesture, he had requested me to visit his place for lunch.

After some time both sides started baying for his blood and the darling of yesterday became 'devil' of today. To save his dear life he appeared and disappeared from his home, lying to his family members that he had urgently been called by the army; leaving it unclear whether army of this side or that side. At least our side was very worried and thought of arresting him and prosecuting him for spying. Some thought of just eliminating him without trial since he was and is a 'terrorist.' Pakistanis also ran behind his blood. They felt more cheated since they thought Khalid had betrayed the very people who nurtured him, assisted him financially and allowed him to meet his relatives that side of the LOC. The Pakistanis felt he had committed grave sin by deceiving fellow Muslims and had betrayed 'the faithful and the religion'.

Time passed on. As per operational requirements, at times, I moved out of Alert post to some other location on the LOC. Occasionally, I proceeded on leave as well and rejoined. On 15 October 1998 I came back from leave and reached Uri. While having lunch with the Commanding Officer in the officer's mess, I was briefed by him about the latest development on LOC. After completing formalities of asking about my family, parents, etc. he disclosed that I have to go to 'Delta' Company HQ at "Alert" post and relieve the incumbent Company Commander; Major Kishor, who had to urgently proceed to his home town due to some family exigencies.

The CO confided to me that he would have preferred to keep Major Kishor at Alert post until two important events were over but domestic exigencies at his home were not permitting his stay any longer. Further he had opined that he felt I would be able to manage everything with equal ease due to my maturity and extensive exposure to that area of the LOC. Then he had disclosed the two events which were going to take place within a fortnight; 'flag meeting' on 17 Oct and 'Black Day' protest by separatist element on 26 October. Like in the past, the separatists had planned to mark 26 Oct as 'Black Day', as token of their disapproval of accession of the state in India that day in 1947.

The CO had revealed that anti-India elements based in POK, with the covert help of Pakistani army and rangers, were likely to create serious trouble by organizing 'Black Day' on 26 Oct. They had declared to Pak media, extensively reported in Indian media also, that they would cross the LOC to show disapproval of "accession" of Jammu and Kashmir in India. They were likely to create scene at several places near the LOC but our area being closest to Muzaffarabad and falling on the National Highway 1A, was likely to have more crowd. The call had been given by Hizbul Mujahidin, JKLF, etc. and consent by Huriyat Conference; an umbrella organization of separatist groups this side of the LOC. He had also told me to keep an eye on Khalid. In fact he was of the opinion that Khalid had become dangerous for us and our nation.

He had advised me to move immediately after lunch so that, preferably, I should reach the "Alert" post today itself, take over command from the incumbent, take briefing and spend night together for familiarization and a sense of continuity.

I started in a military gypsy with one military Nissan vehicles each ahead and behind mine, as protection. As the convoy moved I started appreciating the beauty of the nature. It's so serene, green, and ever fresh; an art of phenomenal proportion, which man will never be able to copy or replicate despite having might of scientific inventions. Deodar, cypress, pine and a few other varieties of coniferous trees: swinging silently. At places reside orchards of apple, interrupted by sporadically planted trees of walnut and almond: as if commas and hyphens placed by human beings on the continual poetry of nature having no full-stop. To my right is flowing river Jhelum; the Vitasta, as mentioned in ancient Sanskrit literature, leaving behind all the town of our side of Kashmir. Golden rays of descending Sun, falling from the south-west on the river bed and reflecting in the eyes, create perfect illusions of molten gold flowing down streams and entering into the Pakistan Occupied Kashmir (POK).

After reaching the base post, I spokeover phone to the incumbent officer at 'Alert' post; Major Kishor, about weather up there. He informed that weather was alright and I could start the climb straightaway. We started our climb on a snake-curved road, negotiating frightening bents; the vehicles mostly in first/second gear. The road was nothing but a cut out of mountain slopes: plain enough only for one vehicle to move on, and at places wide enough for two vehicles to crisscross. Projected rocks, boulders and rocky patches create a scare for a first timer. Despite being familiar and having moved several times, I was still frightened thinking- "if the tires slip or the driver loses even a bit of control?"

Finally, I reached the base of the 'Alert' post; the disembarkation point, from where I had to walk on foot since this was the last point of motorable road. Passing through several sentry posts, trenches, ups and downs I reached the Company HQ, which was a cluster of huts. One among them was residence-cum-office of the Company Commander. The present incumbent-cum-prospective predecessor was standing to welcome me at the gate of the complex. I saluted him and shook hand. He hugged and welcomed me with warmth. Everyone was so happy. In this close world any new comer brings new energy and happiness. So was I.

Hardly had we entered the complex than it started pouring. The bright sun and cloudless sky half an hour back were deceptions to allow me to come in but not allow my comrade to go down. It was pretty cold and dark by now. The Sun had already set. We sat near Bukhari; the room heating devices ran on kerosene oil. During tea snacks, dinner, etc. Major Kishor briefed me about overall situation and scenario in the area. It was fifteenth of Oct and I had neat ten days to familiarize and settle before "Black Day" buzz of 26 Oct. He briefed me about two important events; 26 Oct as 'Black Day' and before that flag meeting with Pakistani army on 17 Oct. I had not much of botheration about either since neither was new to me. This was going to be my second 'Black Day' anniversary and I had already attended numerous flag meetings with Pakistani army in the same location.

On 17 Oct, before proceeding for flag meeting, I wanted to meet Khalid. I sent across a patrol early in the morning to his place, with a message for him to come and meet me at Alert post. But the patrol party came back empty handed: Khalid was not at home. He had left early in the morning to "meet army"- as told by his wife. I was intrigued. I never called him and he never visited me during last two days; from the time I came to Alert post. It was puzzling but I thought of leaving the issue for time being since I had to prepare for the flag meeting. Other officers, constituting part of the delegation, had already arrived. As per procedure, we placed white flag one hour before actual start of the flag meeting, at designated place, to indicate that we were ready to proceed for the flag meeting. Time for raising the flag was the same: 0900 h IST and/or 0830 h PST. Almost simultaneously Pakistanis also raised their flag, indicating they also had the information and were ready for the meet. Everything went smoothly and as per procedure until we reached the venue.

The military flag meetings are never like meetings of diplomats or political leaders. But that day it was in very hostile environment. The Pakistanis, it looked, had come prepared with some hidden agenda and spoke all kind of irrelevant things. They pushed their JCO to start with very irritating and agitating question:

"Why do you not allow Muslims in your country to recite *Namaaz*?"

We were so aghast on falsehood, stupidity and irrelevance of question that for some time we could not gather how to respond or all other did not respond thinking it's my prerogative. The question was outrageous for us as we all knew it was as baseless as irrelevant. I said it is complete misconception. In India, we have complete religious freedom for all including Muslims; who have special status with regard to their religion, personal laws and education.

"No sir, it is only for propaganda. In reality you do not allow Muslims any freedom." The Pakistani JCO again asserted.

"In fact minorities including Hindus have no rights in your country. In our country we have Muslim in all positions including the President, Cabinet Ministers, Chief Ministers, Chief Justices, Service chiefs, in police, in bureaucracy and where not. We have much bigger number of Muslims in our country than your entire population. What do you have? Did anyone from minority community have ever reached any position of prominence in your country? Theocratic and sectarians should not lecture secular people about minority rights."

But I was interrupted by one of their officers;

"Yes, yes we are aware you all have a couple of Muslim show boys and show pieces to fool the world that you are secular and care about minorities."

"I suggest you also keep a few Shias, Ahmedias and Muhajirs as show boys, at least to save yourself from being branded as naked racist, sectarians and zealots. The world would have a better view of you. But we know you can't tolerate even show pieces from your own religious group who are not Sunnis, leave apart any Hindu or Christian."

I snubbed him and tried to bring all back to agenda and not discussions out of the mandate.

"And we are not here to discuss constitution or decide policies. Let us talk within our limited agenda and move off. We are not here to discuss religion, society or politics." I asserted.

But now one of the officers had a different point to irritate:

"If you push that 'goose' again to our side, we will kill him and bury him on the LOC." I could not understand his indication very clearly but guessed he was referring to Khalid, who actually was their own creation.

"What childish and irrelevant things you all are talking. It's appalling. However, I also warn you, that if you do not stop exporting terror, you will see another 1971." I upped the pitch indicating to the terrorist they have been pushing to our side and continued:

"Please, there is no end to rhetoric and we are not here to talk out of turn. We have no powers vested in us to discuss all this so let us confine to the agenda."

"Do not live in fool's paradise. It is not 1971, it is 1998. I am clearly telling now if Khaliq is caught this time by us (me), we will not return during flag meetings, we will kill him and bury him on the LOC." He spoke in warning tone before discussing the agenda points.

"You create and nurture Taliban, Mujahids, militants and terrorists. Most of the ills around us are your illegitimate children. Now when they have started destroying you, you want to blame someone else. What you do with them or they do with you is none of our business." I again tried to put an end to irrelevant talk without any sign to show that I have any clue of Khaliq/Khalid.

Then one captain rank officer from amongst them, putting on a name tab written only 'Khan' stared at Captain Husain and said with a crooked smile:

"Why do you fake your identity?"

"What do you mean by that?" Captain Husain blushed.

"You are not a Muslim but putting on Muslim name?" "Khan" pricked.

"Do you know more about me than I myself? We do not fake but genuinely think differently. I am first am Indian that too by choice; yep we chose to stay in India. Being a Muslim is by chance since I was born in a Muslim family. So being Indian is by choice and being Muslim is by chance. Any problem do you have?" Captain Husain cut him short standing erect in an aggressive posture. Some where he had felt hurt.

"I doubt a true Muslim would ever put on a vermillion on his forehead and fight against another Muslim." "Khan" nudged.

"You may be having a lot many doubts but we have none. The world has seen Pakistani Muslims killing Bangladeshi Muslims, Punjabi Muslims killing and burning Muhajir Muslims, Afghani Muslims killing Afghani Muslims and Iraqi

Muslims killing Iranian Muslims and vice-versa." Captain Husain retorted and continued:

"By the way fifteen days back when you, the Pakistani Muslims had fired without any provocation on people this side of LOC, only Muslims were killed; yep innocent civilian Indian Muslims. To bring you all to your senses we had retaliated. Resultantly one of your posts was blown off by a rocket and, I guess, a few of your men killed. You know, it was me who had fired that rocket personally; an Indian Muslim to kill Pakistani Muslims." He revealed a truth 'in rapid fire speed' going overboard which was not needed. I never wanted and never expected him to be so emotional and rash. But he went over board to prove his point in Lukhnowi style, where he belonged to. I signaled him to keep the limits and tried to abort any further out of topic argument.

But the Pakistani officer reacted as any soldier should have. Things looked becoming ugly. It looked they were going to exchange blows. I told their head of the delegation; a Major, to prevail over his delegates to maintain some decorum in their conduct and talk. Better sense prevailed; the Pakistani Major 'Ashfaq' who was heading the delegation prevailed over his officers and told them to keep quiet. He told 'Khan' to go behind and other ranks to get on the job of repairing the hot line which was passing through the LOC and which was one of the reasons to convene the flag meeting. He, like an officer and a gentleman, said sorry for his men starting the talk in aggressive manner and out of agenda. No one could say for sure whether it was genuine or as per pre-plan. We both were meeting second or third time; rest all the members of our and their delegation were first timers. As a matter of reciprocation, I also regretted remarks and acrimonies thrown from our side.

After that, all went well until we left the place. Immediately after end of the flag meeting, the Pakistani delegates started moving back to their locations and we started towards our location; the Company HQ at 'Alert' post. As per understanding at the level of DGMOs which had consent of the Governments, both the sides were to keep the white flag up for next one hour of end of the flag meeting. One hour's cushion time was kept to ensure that all members of the delegation, comprising of army personnel of both the sides, should reach their respective locations safely.

But hardly after ten minutes of end of flag meeting, the Pakistani army had started firing long burst of automatic weapons on us. We had not been able to enter even the forested area to have some cover and were in the exposed patch along river Jhelum and had to reach alert post; a few hundred feet up and inwards. The white flags; symbolizing generally 'peace' and specifically, in the context, - 'ceasefire', were still up, at least our side.The Pakistanis had, in violation of the instructions from DGMO, removed their flag immediately after end of the flag meeting. They were exploiting the advantage they had of reaching to the safety; to their posts sooner than us.

Whereas, we had to walk longer to reach to our post; exposing ourselves to the visibility and vulnerability of Pakistan army's line of fire. This was most unsoldierly and most immoral act I had ever heard or seen of Pakistani army in this sector of deployment. In the earlier flag meetings they had been behaving and conducting in appropriate manner; saluting each other as per ranks, shaking hands, exchanging and sharing food articles, sharing tea/coffee, etc. with us besides exchanging pleasantries and jokes. But never had they fired on the delegation. Most importantly, unlike today, never in the past they had racked up controversial issues and deviated from the set agenda.

Except mortars they had opened up all war weapons their infantry had in the vicinity; LMG, MMG, HMG and what not. It was clear they wanted to kill all of us; four officers and almost double the number of other ranks who were accompanying us. None of the officers (we) had any weapon on them, not even personal small arms, as during flag meeting weapons were not carried by officers of either side. Although other ranks carried AK-47 rifles, carbine, pistol etc, they were of little use: no Pakistani target was within the range.

So was the case with Pakistanis. But they opened up fire from their permanent locations; the deployments near the LOC. We were in complete exposed position whereas they were firing from concrete bunkers. I, as head of the delegation, was the most worried; I was responsible for safety and security of all, at least morally. I told them to touch ground and take cover behind the trees. I myself stood behind a Deodar tree. Bullets flew all around us, many penetrating deeply the very treetrunks we had taken cover behind. I was more worried to imagine how my entire deployment was going to react than thought of us getting hit or killed. I doubted if at all our posts are going to react. For them the flag meeting was still on.

There was no means I could have used to lodge my complaint or protest on such treacherous and immoral act with just departed Pakistani delegation. I had no means even to communicate with my post commanders, who were spread over several kilometers on the LOC. We had carried radio sets just for extreme emergencies, which had now popped up unexpectedly. But we were not in a position to use, as we were at the bottom of the valley and there was no signal due to thick forestation and deep depression. One line order given by me to the senior most Havaldar at Alert post, before leaving the Company headquarter, saved our life and the day for us:

"In my absence take your own decision assuming you are in war zone and you are the Commander. If necessary, pass appropriate instructions to other posts as well, on my behalf".

To our luck the Maratha Havaldar proved a great Commander. Our deployments were in advantageous position because we had superior weapons. There was an anti-aircraft gun with us in a ground firing role besides every thing else the Pakistanis had; LMG, MMG HMG, etc. The anti-aircraft gun proved a game changer in silencing the enemy. There was heavy exchange of fire for more than half an hour from various positions in the frontage of more than four kilometers. When our soldiers let loose hell on the Pakistanis, they diverted their fire from us to our firing posts. Hence we were saved. The Pakistanis stopped firing on us only when they were battered by our men; got more than what they had given us. For some time it looked like a full-fledged battle but soon they were silenced only by superior brute force and more aggression. The depressed ground was also our saviour.

We came out unscathed but all shaken; more due to treachery than fear. Everyone in the delegation was seething in anger and thinking of taking revenge by blasting the enemy off after reaching the Company HQ. We also became extremely apprehensive that if this was the trust level we could never have a flag meeting in future. Amid intermittent exchange of fire, after an hour's walk through unconventional route, we could manage to climb up closer to our side, then to our nearest post and finally, under the cover of thick coniferous forest and its undergrowth; to our Company HQ at 'Alert' post. Immediately I gave the report to higher headquarter about unprecedented incident of firing on the delegation gone for flag meeting. The CO was also shocked and assured that the report would be sent to the Pakistani DGMO through proper channel to lodge our protest. We also removed our white flags at scheduled time:1200 h IST or 1130 h PST.

By now it was noon. We all had lunch at Alert post. We could not stop ourselves from discussing about probable reasons for today's incident and our survival from the jaws of the sure death. Some were of the opinion that the arguments and scathing replies by Captain Husain were cause of their anger, and subsequent firing. Since Pakistanis could not win the arguments, they tried to display their frustration by treacherously firing on unsuspecting returning unarmed delegation. However the Engineer officer thought that they are perfidious people and did not need reason for their rogue behavior. The Signal officer opined whenever a Muslim officer attended the flag meeting from Indian side, Pakistanis' hearts burned and concluded that Captain Husain's presence made them go wild.

While recounting the turn of events Captain Husain had different opinion. He thought they had done everything as per preplanning; else why the Pakistani JCO should open up with an idiotic question like why Indians stop Muslim from reciting *Namaaz* when whole world, including Pakistanis, knows Muslims have full rights vis-à-vis their religious freedom in India. "Further why should they prick about I faking my true identity; they know there are hundreds of Muslim officers in Indian Army and several thousand Muslims in other ranks." Capt Hussain opined. The discussion moved towards recounting everything that had happened during that day's flag meeting with the Pakistanis.

But who is this Khaliq? I have not heard or seen any person of this name. So was it a bluff or there is some person with one name this side and another that side? Is it Khalid of this side who becomes Khaliq that side? I contemplated. Once the delegates left for their respective locations, I began analyzing the whole issue of Khaliq/Khalid. It was constantly in my mind that the CO had also suggested to keep an eye on the activities of Khalid. In fact there were two important points of briefing of the CO when I had joined from leave on 15 Oct: the flag meeting and the 'Black Day.' The flag meeting was over today and 'Black Day' was a week ahead.

So, has Khalid gone across to POK? Was the CO right in suspecting his role during the Black Day? Was his disappearance from his home today morning only a chance or was it to go across? Was the firing on our delegation today after flag meeting a covering fire to get Khalid in POK? Will he be used as guide to infiltrate on night of 26 Oct? But mystery of unprecedented firing on the delegates' gone for flag meeting, and disappearance of Khalid the same day in the early morning, was bothering me beyond any reconciliation. My anxiety was multiplying due to 'Black Day' events on 26 October.

I started visting the forward locations, when tension of flag meeting got over on 17 Oct, to oversee the preparation for the 'Black Day'. One day while on my way to the neighbouring Company I was passing through the village. One of my escorts indicated to a lady in her early thirties and told me that she was wife of Khalid. Seeing her shifting the bundles of paddy hay-stack in presence of her two sons, I asked her as to what she was doing. She disclosed smilingly with a bit of shyness;

"The clay toy children used to play got broken two days back. Now they are crying and troubling me to search for the same. I am trying bluffing them by pretending to be searching in the hay-stack (for the non-existent toy)." I smiled back and moved on neither of us knowing it would have far reaching meaning in her life.

Time passed on and the D-Day arrived. Massive preparation had taken place to tackle any eventuality despite knowing this was just a posturing by Pakistan incited elements and not a serious attempt. But army is different. It does not take anything lightly. Detractors within the army, call it; 'Zerome' or zero error syndrome. The CO wanted me to move to the forward post from where NH1A was passing through and be there on D-day instead of my usual place of stay; the Company HQ at Alert. I moved to the forward most post, which was closest to NH 1A on the D-Day. This post was almost at eye-ball-contact distance from Pakistani post but venturing out was impossible except when one was ready to count it his last day on the earth.

On the due date almost entire stretch was heavily guarded; covered by fire and some additional temporary obstacles. We had augmented deployment on NH 1A passing through the LOC; from Srinagar to Muzaffarabad. I had sent out patrol parties along the line of control with instruction to stay put until midnight. The patrol parties were told to carry dry survival ration and look out for any bid of crossing or infiltration.

Everything went well. There was no attempt from them to cross the LOC. Pakistan army could not have allowed them to even reach close to the LOC. But if 'Jehadi or Azadi brigade' could have reached the LOC and tried to cross, we had our arrangement in place to deal with it effectively. There was no firing and no attempt to cross the LOC, at least not visible to our side. It was a quiet affair as far as our side was concerned. After the sunset I had sigh of relief; now it's safe to move back to my location. I gave detailed report from the forward location and after due permission moved back to Alert post. The move was full of adventure. Walking through thick coniferous forest supplemented by dense under growth was an experience, nostalgic enough never to forget. The strange sounds of unrecognizable insect and animals converted it into a memorable event of my life.

After having good warm water bath, I sat with a sense of satisfaction and fulfilment. While I had dinner, I watched news on Indian channels with poor quality audio-visuals. Wavering weak signals forced me to keep on changing among very limited channels just to see something on the screen. When saturated, I turned to POK and Pakistani channels for some entertainment and novelty. The drama; scene of gathering of people from 'POK' near LOC, was repeatedly being shown on Pakistani/ POK channels. Leaders were shown with deliberation on the screen, spewing venom against India, shouting in high pitch Urdu repeatedly vouching to free Indian Kashmir from the clutches of the occupying forces of 'Kafirs' and bring both the Kashmir together under Nizam-e-Mustafa; under the rule of Allah. I had to pass time till mid night; until the patrol on LOC came back safely. So I watched whatever was served on TV from either side of the LOC.

At about 30 minutes past mid night the Company Havaldar Major (CHM) came to report that the patrol party from the LOC had come back as ordered by me. I told him to bring in all of them. I spoke to them and took debriefing about the overall scenario. They reported that all was well and no unusual activity had been noticed anywhere. I told them to break off and instructed the CHM to pass order to all the posts to remain alert and report if there was any unusual activity during rest of the night. I went to sleep.

In the morning the CHM came to give me routine morning report. He reported everything normal except post "X" which have reported hearing two–three burst of AK-47 somewhere in/near the Nala, which virtually is the LOC. They claimed they had heard muffled cries also though for a very short duration. In anticipation that someone might be trying to sneak through the thickly forested area, our troops also fired in the general direction of the suspected activity. Firing from permanent Pakistani positions was quite common but any firing close to LOC was very rare. I asked him as to how he assessed the incident to which he replied that no one dared to come close to the LOC unless he wanted to die. It seemed some Pakistani post might have fired which our men mistook for firing in the Nala, probably due to echo in the mountains. "The muffled cry seems to be their hallucination, which is not uncommon among men on duty due to various factors, including fear of unknown and superstition." The CHM concluded.

I did not contest him but was not convinced. The words spoken by Captain "Khan" of Pakistani army during flag meeting and his reference to some Khaliq echoed in my ears. Further I was suspecting Khaliq to be actually Khalid since in Pakistanis' indications had strands of similarity. Then Khalid had been missing for long from his home. "If he is not this side, he has to be the other side." I thought. All movements of locals towards mainland are recorded by army through its check posts. No such movement had been reported. I told the CHM to send a patrol party after breakfast to the suspected area and try to find out.

The patrol party almost confirmed my suspicion. There were dragging marks of blood, some old clothes etc, observed through binocular by the patrol party, of course from far. No one dared from either side to go closer to the LOC. A few yards toward the Pakistan side looked a newly created grave.

They suspected it was Khalid who was killed by the Pakistanis and buried almost on the LOC. They suspected either he was hiding in the bushes for long and Pakistanis knew it or he had gone the other side and was returning back this side. Despite heavy deployment, at places the actual LOC remained out of covering range of fire and beyond the observation of soldiers, since most of the places it had 'dead' areas due to depression, undergrowth, thick forestation and uneven terrain.

I remembered high pitched drama on the TV the previous night. I remembered promise of leaders of POK/Pakistan on TV the previous night to fight for the cause of Kashmiri Muslims till their last breath, I remembered words of Major 'Khan', I remembered duel of Captain Husain with Captain Khan during flag meeting. Then finally something struck me like lighting. The words Khalid's wife had uttered so innocently with a carefree smile while explaining me why she was searching for a toy which she knew was already broken and did not exist:

"The clay toy children used to play got broken two days back. Now they are crying and troubling me to search and find the same. So I am trying bluffing them by pretending to be searching in the hay-stack (for the non-existent toy)."

A few days later Khalid's wife sent across a close relative to meet me and find out when Khalid would be back. I was in dilemma. What to tell him. At the first place we had never called him. Where he went, where he was, what he did, etc was only a matter of guess. Was he alive or dead was also a matter of guess only. I could not have told him the LOC grave. What a predicament. I consoled him:

"I had never called him. Where he went only he knows. Like in the past, I guess, he will come back, someday. You all wait."

Everyone is fooling someone and everyone is being fooled by someone; innocently or intelligently, obviously or obliviously, helplessly or happily, shrewdly or susceptibly: And worldly games are going on both sides of the LOC.

Chapter 14

Gift of Shroud

November 1998: Chakra village near LOC in Uri, Baramulla

Whenever, I looked into the colourful Kashmiri-silk wall-hanging pegged on the wall of my drawing room, invariably, I remembered the sunny, shiny and eventful day of November 1998. The floral design and the patterns brought back the memory of the momentous night that had followed. I was Company Commander of 'Delta' Company deployed on the LOC in Uri sector. Area under my Command included 5-6 kilometre long stretch of National Highway 1A that, ultimately, entered into POK from India.

Those days the road, for a distance of almost four km; two km each side of the LOC, was non-existent. It was destroyed deliberately due to security reasons or was damaged naturally due to negligence, was only a matter of guess. Later, as part of confidence building measures initiated by Vajpayee government, it was repaired and prepared for plying buses of '*Aman Ki Asha*.' Both sides of the road were divided by a gorge that virtually was the imaginary LOC. To connect the road now a bridge, named 'Aman Setu' or 'Peace Bridge', has been constructed.

The silk wall-hanging was gifted to me by a teacher from Chakra village. After persistent pursuance by him, I had agreed and gone to his home to have lunch. The teacher, very affectionately and respectfully, had given me the wall-hanging as souvenir; a memory, when I was leaving his home. On my refusal he had cajoled me to accept it since, he insisted, in their custom giving a gift of cloth is considered respectful and auspicious. The piece of cloth was so beautiful and artistically woven that I had looked at it for long to discover several patterns and designs when I had opened it for the first time at the base post same day. Precisely, however, not the souvenir but its comparison with white shroud covering the two dead bodies was the real reminder. Following night, in another incident, similar words were spoken for the 'gift of shroud' as for the 'gift of wall-hanging'. The words spoken while giving both the 'gifts' were so similar that the wall-hanging had become reminder of the 'Gift of Shroud.'

My JCO in-charge of base post; the last deployment on the motorable road on NH1A, had been insisting on me to accept the invitation of the teacher from a nearby village named Chakra. The gentleman inviting me for lunch was a local school teacher, living 8-10 kilometres inner side, in the penultimate hamlet from the LOC. The village sat on a small picturesque hill top, on the left bank of river Jhelum; as it flows towards POK. Two- three km down from the base post, Jhelum enters into the POK after crossing the gorge that signifies the imaginary LOC.

A dilapidated 'hanging bridge' of Dogra period meant for light vehicles, existed on the gorge. My JCO had been insisting that I accepted the teacher's invitation since he was a nice, educated gentleman with patriotic feelings and fervours. He was shy of approaching me directly. Hence pursuing my subordinate officer, a Subedar who was commanding the base post within my area of responsibility, to convince me and convey his invitation for lunch at his place. Every time, in the past, I had got out of the situation by promising that I would think over it and let him know.

Today again my JCO, while giving routine report over phone, reminded me about the teacher's invitation. He further informed that in case I could not go to the teacher's place the teacher was ready to visit my location at 'Alert post' near the LOC, if I permitted. I held the hand set of the military field telephone and pondered over to 'kill' this long pending issue forever. I asked him to talk to the teacher and find out why he wanted to meet me, or rather why he was requesting me to visit his place; a request which was very unusual and rare. People living within 20 km of LOC or near LOC did come to meet the army officers concerning their various problems; since the area had special status and civil agencies had limited access, but no one insisted so much to visit his place for lunch or dinner. There are reasons we avoid visiting any one's place in Kashmir or near LOC. I was more concerned about him and his family. He might be requesting me to visit his place for any other reason but his adversaries might brand him '*Mukhbir*': an informer and put him in trouble for no rhyme or reason.

The JCO elaborated:

"Sir, I had asked him everything you could have asked. In fact I enquired much more than, probably, you could have. I informed him our officers do not visit places of local residents even on invitation other than relating to operations. However, he claimed to know all that since, as he insisted, he has been staying in this village from his birth. Many units came and went. He has special respect for you and wants to invite you for lunch at his place. He wants you to be with his family and his children. He also wants his children to meet you and discuss their future plan of studies."

After a small pause, making sure that I was listening, he continued:

"He thinks you will surely inspire his children. Both his sons also expect your advice and guidance on their higher studies, out of Kashmir, in various cities of India which provide better educational facilities. He has come to know about your interest in reading, writing etc by the books and newspapers that we keep on sending up for you. He regularly passes through our post while coming and going to his school. One day he enquired as who reads so many newspapers and books. When we informed about you, he expressed his desire to meet you. He regularly was enquiring about you and your interest."

I was discovering perceptions people had about me. I did not know whether I was fit to give any advice on educational matters but to reciprocate his respect, his sentiments and to look unpretentious, I accepted the invitation with multiple purposes in mind. I would not only fulfil his long pending request but might visit my nearby posts, familiarise with the area, interact with the villagers as a good will gesture, might get some important information, etc. I pondered over and told the JCO to convey that I would visit his house any day this week but on a short notice. So he should spell out what all days he was available.

"OK sir, I will tie up everything as you have spelt out." The JCO said with a sense of fulfilment.

In contrast to the central part of the valley, the areas close to the LOC are calmer, less troubling and less infested with Anti National Elements or ANEs or militants or terrorists; all of which have become synonymous in general use, at least in military parlance, despite their dictionary meaning being different in literal sense. The areas near the LOC are internally calmer because of several factors like; different composition of ethnicity, sparse and scattered population, proximity with the troops and permanent deployment of the army, etc.

The mountainous regions on the periphery of the valley are inhabited by, mostly; Bakarwals, Gujjars, Paharis, Daris who have, comparatively, care free and down-to-earth life style. Among them, those close to the LOC are substantially dependent on the army for their livelihood. They work in close co-ordination with the army as semi-skilled workers; mason, carpenter, electrician and labourer. Many of them work as regular porters also since access of mechanical transport is limited only to fair weather conditions. Ethnic Kashmiris, in these areas, are lesser in number but socially and educationally more advance than others. The teacher was among most advanced and educated in the village and was an ethnic Kashmiri.

People residing near LOC in Uri sector are, as I perceived them to be, mostly; friendly, loyal, supportive and trustworthy. But terrorism and deception are not completely absent or, to assume so, would be naive on part of a military man. So I took time to analyse and plan my visit accordingly; to take all due precautions and have trust in my host. That is why I told him to visit his place at short notice any day convenient to him.

Due to one or two trips of visitors of varied arena every day, I always remained busy. Over and above operationally and administratively being important, there were several reasons for my location becoming the most visited place in the entire sector. Besides having motorable road up to the Company headquarters on its axis, it had National Highway 1A; the only road connecting Srinagar with Muzaffarabad. The important road, joining the two capitals of now divided Jammu and Kashmir, passed through the area under my command. Easy access, picturesque surrounding, all-weather motorable road, enchanting beauty astride the road all along river Jhelum; coming from Srinagar up to the last point in Indian side, and presence of big hydro-electric project in the close vicinity on river Jhelum, were other reasons for frequent visit by privileged visitors.

But the biggest attraction was a peep into Chakothi, the first township of POK, clearly visible by naked eyes from our Company headquarter location. Our location dominated the area in close vicinity and gave an overview, in clear weather, up to twenty-twenty five kilometres deep into POK. One can see contiguous small valleys, then lateral layers of mountains up to Nanga Parbat. Many visitors having interest in history and religion tried to locate, the Sharda Peeth; grand ancient temple of Devi Sharda (Saraswati; the goddess of knowledge) in Neelam valley of the POK. The visitors included Indian and foreign media men, NGO on social and environmental studies with prior permission from the competent authority, dignitaries of a few select countries, and of course families of military men; mostly army officers' who were the most privileged.

I chose Thursday since it looked free to me; no visitors. No message from Uri; our battalion headquarter, 20-25 km from my location. It was going to be nine in the morning. I told my JCO that at about twelve in the noon I would be visiting the teacher's place. Further I instructed him to take a patrol to the village to inform him and ensure dominance of the area before I visited it. I had to come down inner side from my Company headquarters which was on the height and in the forward location, overlooking POK whereas the village was deeper inside, at least 8-10 km from the LOC. I came by vehicle up to the base post and from there started climbing on foot on another axis to reach the village. A ten minutes' walk, with the scouts and escorts; taken from the base post, I was there on the boundaries of the village. The scouts and escorts were already earmarked and left behind to accompany me by the base post Commander who had since proceeded to the village with patrol.

The teacher and the JCO were standing to receive me at the outskirts of the village. I was meeting the teacher for the first time. He was in late thirties; at least ten-twelve years older to me, tall, slim, fair and had a long sharp nose; a common feature of Kashmiris, Hindu or Muslim. He was putting on a sky blue coloured Salwar-suit and a cream colour pheren; an integral part of Kashmiri attire. He was looking fresh and extremely cheerful and welcomed me with warmth and courtesy. We walked together to his home where his wife also greeted us with warmth, showing customary gestures and impressive hospitality. His children, the two sons were not at home. They had gone to school/college at Baramulla more than 60 km from this location. Half of his desire would remain unfulfilled since his children won't be able to meet me due to constraint of choice of time of my visit.

There were very few in the village those could afford the 'luxury' of sending their children to school or college at Baramulla. Majority of the children in the area did not study beyond tenth standard; up to the class available at Uri, if at all they started their education. Surprisingly, most of the youth were literate in this area taking the literacy rate above national average but they still worked as porters, carpenters and semi-skilled labourers. It was more due to terrain, distances and lack of facilities than lack of desire to grow. Many of them were self-employed as artisans.

The house was modest but well kept. The surrounding beauty of nature seen through several windows was charming. From azure sky above to clean waters of Jhelum at the bottom on the surface of the earth was visible from here. The CGI sheet roof tops of other houses were shining due to fall and reflection of sun light from them. The families of conifers swinging close and far covering the peaks and slopes of the mountain were hypnotizing. I was lost in the charming beauty of nature seen from the windows and then suddenly realised I was sitting in the company of my host in his house.

"You have done very good thing by continuing your children's education even if they have to commute to and from Baramulla every day. Education is emancipation. At all cost you should continue it for your children."

I started the conversation to break the ice of inertia of initiation.

"Sir, you are intuitive. In fact I was so eager to meet you and discuss with you about further and higher education of my children.' He clutched my one hand from both his hands and continued-

"Before lunch would you like to have some Kahwa, noonchai; salty tea or sweet tea?" He wanted to be clear since Kashmiris, unlike people from the plains, mostly take salty tea instead of sweet one and special brew; Kahwa or kawa.

"No nothing. I will have lunch and then proceed back. You know I have to reach back to the "Alert post" before dusk. Now as the snowfall is likely to resume, the Pakistanis are in hurry to push the newly trained terrorists this side before passes are closed. To push them this side they resort to firing to keep our soldiers engaged and pre-occupied so that the sneaking for their recruits becomes easier." I told him as a matter of fact.

"Sir, I know it all. I have been living in this area since the time I saw the first light on the earth. I am born and brought up in this environment. For last nine-ten years it is to push the 'Jehadis' but otherwise also firing was always there, when there was no open support of Pakistan for such thing as waging religious war; 'Jehad' or fight for freedom; 'Azaadi'. Every summer; from May to Oct our life goes on the edge of knife. You all; the military men have proper bunkers, concrete shelters and most importantly, matching arms and ammunition to retaliate and pay them in the same coin. What we have to protect ourselves from shelling?' Nothing. These self-styled and self-proclaimed friends of Kashmiris and 'saviours of Islam'; the Pakistanis are true enemies of Kashmiris and Muslims. In the name of

Muslim brotherhood they kill us; the Muslims. Who dies when they shell the LOC? Almost all Muslims? And who dies when the Indian army retaliates and shells the other side of LOC? Again Muslims. 95% population both side of LOC is Muslim. So who dies either ways? Muslims. What nonsense they try to talk to the world and to us in the name of religion and in the name of Muslim brotherhood." He sounded frustrated, disgusted and agitated.

I tried scanning my brain to find some response to comment or add and in the meantime tried to judge the meaning of his statement. But it was a bit late for me. He continued:

"Sir, see there. The hole in the roof is result of damage caused by Pakistani mortar bomb. We were just saved due to the grace of God; The Pakistanis had killed us from their side." He continued:

"That is why sir, I wanted your advice to send my children away from this poisonous environment. Pakistan has become big factory producing 'Jehadis'. It is desperately looking for 'raw material' from neighbours. The cheapest supplier; Afghanistan is slowly drying up. Now cheapest, best and most easily available is in the eastern neighbourhood; Kashmir. The price to pay in lieu is cheap: fanning frenzy of a false freedom and deceitful propaganda of 'victimhood'. What would we gain additionally, which is not available now to us, after getting their kind of 'freedom?"

"Their concept of freedom is to run a puppet government headed by a Pakistani, under military dictators; like in Pakistan Occupied Kashmir. A country which has been ruled by dictators for more than half duration of its whole existence, talks about democracy and freedom. A country which murders, maims, mutilates and rapes its own citizens because they have different features and they speak different language; being Muslims had no meaning. What they did in East Pakistan, now Bangladesh, is unforgivable. That has shaken the very foundation of creation of nations based on religious homogeneity."

"You are right. But I do not hear such words very often. In fact you are among very few who speaks so." My JCO added breaking his apt attention of a 'captive audience.' I nodded. The teacher ignored my JCO's comment and continued in an agitated temperament:

"So it is importing innocent boys by conviction or coercion and converting them in to "Jehadis"; the fundamentalist and then sending them back to be killed by the Indian forces. Both ways it is Kashmir and the Kashmiris who are suffering and dying. Kashmir was never like this. Pundits and Muslims always lived in peace, shared food, and celebrated together all the festivals. There were never "Hindu-Muslim riots" like in many parts of India or like Sunni-Shia riots in Pakistan. Kashmir was land of Rishis and Sufis. It was land of scholars and artisans. But all that has changed now."

"I agree. Religion cannot be sole uniting factor." I supported his views.

"Most of educated and intellectual Kashmiris are against whatever is happening. Pakistan is misguiding those who do not understand the design. If being Muslim was guaranty of binding as one nation, there would have been only one country of Muslims. But there are so many; fighting among themselves. Why Iran and Iraq fought, why Pakistan and Bangladesh fought, why Shias and Sunnis are fighting, why Afghanis are fighting and killing each other; in most barbaric way, ready to suck each other's blood?" He spoke convincingly and flawlessly as if reading from a written script.

"What advice you are expecting from me and have thought me worthy of rendering, to a teacher; who himself is supposed to be an educational counsellor to all including his children?"

I wanted to change the topic which was too much discussed in the valley, and about which I felt saturated hearing for last seven years; from first tenure in the valley in the counter -insurgency operation to this second one on the LOC.

He laughed and then began:

"Yes; sir kindly tell me which city would be best for my children's higher education keeping my limited budget in mind and can you also tell them what profession they should pursue? Here most of the people, at least in this area, do not know anything beyond Jammu even I have very limited exposure south of Jammu."

"As far as choice of subjects or pursuance of a professional study is concerned, I feel, the individual choice, his interest and his potential matter the most. Hence it should be decided by the individual. However, I will surely tell you about Indian cities and professional courses available there, whatever I know. Best thing I can do is to purchase and bring a "Career Counsellor" when next time I am coming back from leave." I told him keeping things in brief.

"The food is ready." His wife told him in Kashmiri, which he forwarded to me in Urdu.

"Where is the wash basin?" I wanted to wash my hands.

"Sir, it is considered discourteous to send the guest to wash basin in our tradition. You can wash your hand in this." He indicated to a wide mouthed tub brought by his wife near me. He picked up soap in one hand and a jug filled with warm water in another and towel to be offered for drying my hands on his shoulders.

"I am not used to this kind of courtesy and I do not feel comfortable troubling my host for avoidable things." I told him as I was feeling a bit embarrassed by his extreme servile behaviour.

"I am also not used to troubling my guest." He displayed his wit stretching his courtesy a bit too far.

He poured lukewarm water over my hands and after I washed it he dried my hands by the towel in his hand without handing over it to me. I was embarrassed, though, I felt elevated and impressed by his hospitality. While having food we discussed further about his children's education. I told him about various options in various cities of our country in detail over the lunch. The food was very delicious, pure veg, keeping my eating habits in mind.

"But why you want them to necessarily go far away when options are available at both the cities of Srinagar and Jammu. It is more so when the environment has improved drastically in the valley vis-à-vis militancy and military operations." I asked my doubt which was not allowing me to get convinced of his intention or his apprehension.

"Sir, you please allow me to differ. The environment has not changed. The youth are still going the other side; freely or forcibly, and coming back with guns. The covert agents of ISI are still in huge numbers busy with their propaganda. The overt Salafi Maulvis in the name of religion are pouring venom in the delicate brains of teenagers by misinterpreting teaching of Islam. The disappearances are still taking place. From the time local police has been given prominence in operation, things have changed for worse. I am always afraid something bad may happen to my children while coming and going every day to Baramulla. So I want them to be away from the entire valley, nay the state of J & K'- he disclosed his worst fear while serving me rice and Rajmah.

"The police have to be given prominence since not primarily but exclusively law and order is their responsibility. Army had come in to picture in extraordinary circumstances. Now since there is elected government in the helm of affairs, they would like to keep the police in the forefront and the army at the back and rightly so. Army never wants to be engaged in the operations involving own citizens. As far as disappearances are concerned, mostly it is, propaganda of separatists, as I look at it. These apparent 'disappearances' are due to boys going or being taken across and not 'disappearance'. You should not be afraid since your children are not going to be part of all this." I tried to assure him while closing the plate.

"Sir, you know one day my younger son asked me whether it is true that Muslims are not allowed to offer prayer in India; he meant minus Kashmir. I was shocked to hear the question since I know that we have complete liberty of religious practices; here, there and everywhere in our country. When I asked him who told him about this, he told me that he heard it on radio "Azaad Kashmir" and some of his friends were also telling him. Sir I want to keep him away from this acerbic and adulterated environment."

"But why do you allow him to listen to `Radio Azaad Kashmir?'- I interrupted him since I felt a bit puzzled."

"No sir, I do not allow but the quality of reception is so good that they tend to hear 'Azaad Kashmir Radio (POK)' instead of 'Radio Kashmir or All India Radio', which sounds as if it is coming from Honolulu"- he mocked the regional and national broadcast. I did not contest since he was right.

Finding me quiet he continued:

"Sir, I want to keep them away from another reason also. I am afraid someone may falsely implicate my children; the neighbour, the classmates or the police, not for genuine reasons but for vested interest or just out of jealousy."

He continued and ended emphasizing:

"It is still dangerous."

"You must surely send your children out for better education but not due to this or that fear. The environment is changed. Sooner or later the militancy and terrorism will be eliminated. Then you have to have faith in God. He is the one who ensures safety and security of His children."

I tried to end the talk and gestured to my JCO to be ready to move while emphasizing:

"All would be well."

"Your words are very encouraging sir. We feel safe here on

His mercy and on the good will of officers like you." He said while holding my hand.

"Thank you very much for really delicious food and your memorable hospitality. It was great pleasure being with you. Do let me know if we can help you." - and then I thanked the lady specially turning towards her.

"I never knew you are such a great cook and cook pure veg dishes so deliciously. I wish you were my neighbour so that I and my wife would have learnt the art of Rajmah cooking from you." I tried to please her since the Rajmah preparation was really unique. I continued:

"Do let me know in case we can help you any way'.

"Sir, we will be grateful if you instruct your officers at the bridge to allow our vehicles to come this side; a bit closer to our house. It will save my children from long walk and also save an hour's time every day." She revealed her request.

I asked the JCO if there was any problem in conceding their demand. The JCO informed me they already were allowing all the vehicles up to the village for everyone. Only during night they imposed restrictions on movement. The JCO assured now they would not face any problem in future.

"Insha Allah we are grateful for your support. It was His wish that you visited our place. We feel honoured by your visit." She returned the courtesy.

While giving me send off, the teacher and his wife gave me a colourful silk wall-hanging. I resisted but they persisted on the ground that it was their souvenir; a small memory.

"Sir, we do not send off our guests without gifts. Most auspicious is gift of cloth." The teacher had emphatically said while pressing the piece into my hand which my JCO took over from me.

Later, the above words of the teacher became iconic proving to be paradoxical due to unrelated but coincidental circumstances, and the wall-hanging became one of the longest memories in my life due an incident which had to happen tonight.

By the time, I reached base post it was 3.00 pm. As soon as I left his house, I was in different grid. I was worried if there was any urgent call from the Commanding Officer or the Adjutant or from any of the forward posts. I wanted to reach the base post at the earliest. Wireless operation was restricted in this area other than emergencies due to possibility of interception. The precaution and resultant actions were the same both side of the LOC. In the mean-time I told my JCO in charge of the area to extend all possible help to the villagers and allow their vehicles as close as possible to their residences.

At base post I was informed that there was call from both; the Adjutant and the Commanding Officer. They wanted to talk to me immediately for some urgent matter. I told the JCO to arrange chair and table on the bank of the Jhelum, outside the post's small building built in beautiful Kashmiri style. I sat watching flow of water in the Jhelum; flowing towards LOC and them entering in to Pakistan Occupied Kashmir, just two three km from here. I told the signal man to get the telephone close to my chair and table. The JCO sat with me.

Until telephone line was brought up to my chair, I discussed with my JCO, over a cup of tea, various issues at the post and in the surrounding area. I told the signal man to first put me through to the Adjutant. First I spoke to the Adjutant to know what the matter was. The Adjutant informed that there would be five people who would be visiting my 'Alert post' next day. Since arrangements were specifically to be made for female visitors, he revealed in advance that there would be two male two female and one Sardar. When I reminded him to clarify the gender of the fifth person, he broke in to laughter realising his innocent, unintentional mistake. He was a gold mine of such 'innocent' slippage. Actually the Sikh gentleman was an acclaimed journalist coming along with four American broadcasters. The gender of visitors was necessary to spell out because, if there were female visitors, we had to carry out some modifications within the existing toilet to make it worthy of use by them.

When I called up the Commanding Officer he had a very different matter to reveal. He told me that the matter was important and I must confine it to the minimum men and exclusively to the concerned soldiers only. Then he explained:

"Tonight between 0200 h to 0400 h one police lorry will enter our area. The permission has been granted by our higher headquarters to allow them up to the last motorable post on NH 1A, on the request of very senior police officers. Hence they should be allowed unchecked free access up to our base post. There are likely to be five or six policemen including two inspectors/sub inspectors. Tell our JCOs at all the check post; at both the bridges, to check identity of every policeman thoroughly but not the lorry. At base post tell the JCO to co-operate and coordinate and at the same time keep a watch on their activities." I confirmed that everything was clear except their mission and reason for secrecy from us. He said:

"How does it matter to us? Once it has been cleared from higher headquarters, we need not think much. They might have already thought more than us? The police need to be assisted in all spheres so that they can take over the state of affairs as early as possible. We have been told to allow their vehicles, we will do that. Our policy in such matters is `don't ask don't tell'. You should only ensure that none of them stays or strays; so many should go back alive as many had come alive."

It had raised my anxiety but I did not ask further questions. I looked at the watch it was going to be five in the evening. I called my JCO in charge of the base post and briefed him about the police vehicle, its permission, entry up to his post, dos and don'ts. He also looked puzzled but it was not something new. In the past also such requests had come from the police and we had granted permission, though very few and far between.

I told the JCO to alert my driver and the escort group to be ready for move to the Company headquarter up at 'Alert post'. After some time the JCO informed that the group was ready to move but the weather up at the post was very bad. It was raining and the semi-metalled fair weather road had become slippery; not worthy of plying vehicle. Further the road opening party; a group of troops deployed to secure the road from any disturbance, had to be moved back due to early last light, lightening and rain. He requested me to take a decision in the given circumstances and simultaneously suggested to postpone the move till tomorrow. I decided to postpone the move and stayed put at the base post for the night. He sought my permission to wind up the ROP and after my nod, ordered all to go back to their respective locations. The ROP was moved back from where it had come; the alert post and the base post. Now the movement could only be planned tomorrow morning depending on the weather condition.

"Sir, whatever happens it happens for good." The JCO said and continued:

"You can go tomorrow with the American journalists from here itself. It will give them more time with you to understand things from the beginning. Further your presence will save me the stress of co-ordinating secret movement of the police men."

"No Saheb, I will rest. It is your post so you will do your duty. I have already briefed you and will brief the two post commanders either over phone or I will go personally depending on my mood and weather conditions, a few minutes from now. Who cares what the hell the policemen do. I may come or may not come out depending on my mood. However, please tell my Sahayak to wake me up when they reach our first bridge. If I feel like I will else, I know you can handle it; nothing great. It will take 30 more minutes for them to reach our place from the first bridge and by then I will be ready." I clarified in a tone of giving instructions.

"OK sir. I am getting the guest room prepared for your stay and in the meantime sending soup for you."

I roamed around with my escorts and thought of checking the motorability of the road beyond our base post towards the LOC; towards POK. It was not existing even 50 metres. The road had just vanished in the river. Roads in mountains need constant repair else they will just disappear. Here it may have not been repaired or may have been destroyed; effort fully by our own predecessors, due to security reasons. The LOC is just two kilometres from here, and first Pakistani post with heavy deployment on the other side; hardly two and a half kilometre. Although there were our posts with heavy deployment on the way to prevent any misadventures by Pakistanis, destroying the road was the best thing; extremely difficult proposition for the enemy to overcome in short span of time that too in mountainous terrain. Similar things Pakistanis had also done to their side, as our intelligence sources told us.

I looked around. It was so charming. The sun was setting; the western vista was turning copper from cobalt looking as if a big send-off was being given by redressing the sun in the same attire of cupric colour in which he lovingly had entered in the world from the eastern horizon. Like the sun, the feathered friends of all clan were returning to their 'havens' for night shelter. The villagers on the hill tops were also closing their day's activity to hide themselves inside there cosy homes. The mothers in the villages at the hill top were putting extra layers of woollen on already thick covering of their children. The surroundings; lush green, pleasantly cold air, pollution free environment deceived me to wish to live here forever. I saw three waterfalls, coming from three directions and merging themselves lovingly in Jhelum; as if ending their existence out of over joy of meeting their ultimate destination. The scene of endless families of cedar, fern, fir, pine and trees of similar genre bejewelling the unending mountainous crown, known as the Himalayas of the mother earth, was mesmerising.

It had become pretty cold outside. I went inside the 'guest room' which was warmed up by lighting a Bukhari and had become comfortable and cosy. I briefed the JCO in-charge of this post, about the Commanding Officer's instructions and the movement of the police personnel. I told him I would brief the two post commanders over phone, whose posts were on the way, to grant permission to the vehicle and he might co-ordinate the movements to assist the policemen, whatever assistance they wanted. The JCO left and I had good warm water bath which was a luxury at "Alert post". Here good quality water was aplenty due to proximity of the Jhelum.

After having dinner I went to sleep. I had walked a lot today so as soon as I lay down, I slept. I had kept the door closed but unbolted for unrestricted entry of my Sahayak to wake me up in the morning.

"Ram Ram Sahib." I was greeted and woken up by my Sahayak. I understood it was the time; the lorry had reached the first bridge and he had come to wake me up. While my eyes closed and still under the wrap of thick blanket, I asked him what the time was. He told me it was 03.00 am. I told him to lit the kerosene lamp and keep in the bathroom to which he replied in one go:

"Sir, the lamp is lit here. I will light petro-max if you need in the room and keep the lamp in the bathroom. There is no electricity. I have kept half bucket warm water in the bathroom. I have brought tea in the thermos. Should I pour in the cup or you would like to have it later. You need something more sir?"

I was never demanding but men never gave me any chance to demand. Most of the things were already there. They knew my personal habits, my needs at different times of the day. No one looks after their officers better than soldiers of Indian army, I thought. There were pickets around the base post and men on duty, as sentries, were always awake and alert.

"'I don't need anything else but you wait so that in case of need I can call you. There is no need to light the Bukhari or petro-max."

"The police have crossed the first bridge and Saheb (the

JCO) is waiting for you out side. Should I tell him that you are coming?"

'I will come but won't interact. I will come only to see what is happening. Tell Saheb he will remain the Commander and interact with those people to coordinate everything. I may come a bit late." I told him while getting out of my bed to get ready.

I came out of my room. The JCO along with two more men greeted me with customary salute, as usual; ready in proper combat uniform, their personal automatic weapons on them. I had also put on combat dress and slung my AK-47; not to look different. The police lorry came. The policemen had requested the post commander at the first bridge to give two army soldiers from the first bridge to guide them to the base post. May be they were scared of, in the night, something going wrong in heavily deployed area controlled by the army and Pakistani posts being not far. The two army soldiers escorting from the first bridge, introduced the police men to the JCO commanding the base post. It was quite dark and until one came very close it was difficult to recognise. As a practice undue lighting is prohibited in these areas; the Pakistani posts are hardly two km away; near village on the hill tops, the other side.

The Inspector; with beard, which is very common practice in Kashmir police due to religious reasons, shook hand with the JCO, exchanged customary salutes and greetings with 'Jai Hind' instead of 'Ram Ram' which was within our regiment. There was another inspector, no sub-inspector, I could see. Four more policemen got down from the rear portion of the lorry after jumping over the tail board. All in uniform and with personal weapons; not all AKs some carrying old outdated rifles. The inspector took the JCO in a corner to discuss further course of action in confidence. The JCO took him closer to the river bank.

They inspected the area which was hardly 40-50 meters from the place of parking of the lorry. The rivers having gradually sloping banks in mountains, particularly in this area are rare. The Jhelum has very steep banks; almost at 80-90 degree angle from the water bed, and looks like canal of plains. Two odd feet of misjudgement may slip one in the river. The inspector came back to the lorry after inspection and discussion with the JCO. I watched but could not hear the privy talk. The inspector instructed his four constables in Kashmiri.

It was pitch-dark. Wherever necessary they were using small torches. The sound of violently gushing water on rocky bed of the river was frightening. The sky was clear. Innumerable stars were shining and looked brighter in absence of the moon. The fireflies in the bushes were twinkling, disappearing and reappearing all around; near and far. Due to untimely motion and commotion, a pair of unidentified bird flew overhead from eastern to western peak across the river, making strange sound. We were in deep small bowl and above on the ridges were villages with scattered houses; all in deep sleep. Disturbed by the untimely activity, the dogs started barking in the close by villages. The jackals howled in packs alongside other nocturnal animals in far flung jungles.

The policemen opened the tailgate, unloaded from the lorry first object and then second; placed both on ground neatly covered in white virgin clothes. They mostly spoke in Kashmiri among themselves. I went closer but still a bit far from the crowd.

"Dead body?" Spontaneously murmured one of my Jawan.

The four policemen lifted the first one. The sub inspector led then in the light of his torch, the inspector and rest looked on. But all moved closer to the river bank, spontaneously. The fearsome sound of gushing water was becoming more intense as if roaring 'keep off'.

'Splash'- went the first one and then the second; after sometime.

The dogs started barking more ferociously. The quiescent birds in their havens on the ridges got disturbed. Many of odd sounds. Together, it sounded, questions. In the Himalayan region mountains, the glaciers, the rivers, the una, the animals, the birds, the sky and nen, the relations, the environment and the

agility was all over so tangible.

ne police men started speaking in Urdu among themselves nd with the soldiers indicating they were feeling extremely relieved. When under stress one tends to speak in the mother tongue and when care free, in 'other tongue' abandoning the 'mother tongue.'

The inspector and his men kept on looking at the violently flowing water of the river, off course in dark without any possibility to follow anything. The inspector lit his torch to focus on the thrown object and then suddenly shouted in flawless Urdu, as if crying:

"You killed my brother only because he was putting on uniform, because he was serving his government, because he was loyal to his country. You killed innocents, because they did not agree to your agenda of separation, violence and murder, because they disagree with your interpretation of the faith. Now go, from where you had come. We have given you a companion too, a friend who harboured and nurtured you, for your journey to your country. Go tell your bosses, if they send more, all would be returned from the same path as they had come: the infiltration route. They would be sent across the LOC, without visa and passport but, with virgin white clothes wrapped around their body."

"We Kashmiris don't send off our guests without gift of new clothes."

The last sentence hit me like lightening. I remembered my host saying the same word a few hour back; in completely different circumstances. What a contrast; he gave me the gift

of cloth so lovingly whereas this one so scornfully. Th
colourful and adornable, this one so frightful; no one
to wear.

They got together; the JCO, the Jawans and the policen
discussing all that was happening. The JCO had alrea
arranged tea for them. One Jawan brought a big thermos an
a number of cups in a big tray. Before it was poured in to cups
from thermos and distributed, I thought to leave. Military men also do not allow anyone to go without due hospitality, at least a cup of hot tea; after 'send-off' of the 'guests'.

There was nothing to 'ask and tell' for me. It was so apparent. I moved back to my room. I thought of my discussion with my host, his apprehensions; "it is still dangerous" and my assumptions and hope; "all would be well". In the light of the lamp I suddenly saw the colourful gift; the wall-hanging. It was looking pale white as if lost its lustre. Or my eyes were deceiving me?

Is it colourful? - I asked to myself. Yes and no, it was looking pale white and colourful, alternately. It had many shades; like Kashmir and its affairs. Between black and white I saw many colours; much more than in the spectrum of the rainbow: some extremely bright some extremely dull, some recognizable some unrecognizable, some familiar some strange and new. All messy and all clear, at the same time; depending where one was focusing. I stared at it; the gift of cloth. It was so puzzling, so mystifying; like epistemological discourses of the Rishis and love poetry of the Sufis.

And I discovered many new 'colours' and 'designs' in it. It was so maddening. I did what all of our leaders and predecessors had done from Delhi to Srinagar and all over. I closed it, folded it, hid below my pillow and went to sleep; buying some time until the (new) Sun rose.

Glossary

Adjutant. A Commissioned Officer, invariably of the rank of Capt/Major, who acts as administrative staff officer to the Commanding Officer.

AFSPA. Armed Forces Special Power Act 1956 is an Act passed by Parliament of India that empowers Armed Forces of India (primarily the Army) to arrest and search without judicial warrant, encounter and kill terrorists and armed-insurgents/secessionists/with sufficient immunity. The Act protects all members of the Armed Forces from judicial scrutiny and prosecution unless special sanction is given by the Central Government. The Act is imposed in areas affected by internal armed rebellion/insurgency/terrorism/militancy. This act provides the armed forces with an enabling environment to carry out their duties. However, in the areas where the Act is in operation, it faces stiff resistance and is called by many 'draconian'. All fundamental rights guaranteed in the Constitution of India, practically, get suspended in its area of operation.

Ambush. A surprise attack on opponent by soldiers/militants while waiting in concealed position.

Battalion Headquarters. It denotes that location where the CO and his staff are located and from where most, if not all, of the important functions of a Battalion are commanded/ coordinated.

Brigade Commander. An officer of the rank of Brigadier who commands a Brigade. Brigade is a major tactical military formation that typically consists of three to six battalions plus supporting elements. Its strength may range from 4000-6000.

Captain. Commissioned Officer in Indian Army that is below the rank of Major and above the rank of Lieutenant.

Colonel (Col). Commissioned Officer in Indian Army that is below the rank of Brigadier and above the rank of a Lieutenant Colonel.

Company. A company or column is an army sub-unit typically consisting of 120-150 soldiers (including officer/JCOs) and usually commanded by a Captain or Major.

Company Commander. A Company Commander is the officer commanding (officer in-charge of) a Company and generally of the rank of Captain or Major.

Company Havaldar Major (CHM). Senior most Non-Commissioned Officer at a Company level in Indian Army who assists the Company Commander in various operations and administration of the Company.

Commanding Officer. CO is an army officer commanding a Unit or Battalion. He invariably is of the rank of Colonel.

Cordon. An area encircled by soldiers to prevent any egress or ingress.

DGMO. Director General of Military Operations, a Lieutenant General rank officer controlling all military operations and reporting to Chief of the Army Staff. He is stationed at Army Headquarters, New Delhi. Or in respect of other countries, to their respective military Headquarters.

Division. A formation typically consisting of 10,000 to 15,000 troops and three to four brigades.

Field Condition. Over all condition in an area where military operations are in progress. In field conditions, invariably, families are not allowed to stay with military personnel.

IEDs. Improvised Explosive Device or IED is a homemade bomb constructed and deployed in ways other than in conventional military action.

ISI. Inter-Services Intelligence is the premier Intelligence Agency of Pakistan.

JCO. Junior Commissioned Officer is a term describing a group of military ranks who receive Commission from the President through promotion from ranks/cadre. JCOs are above NCOs and below Commissioned Officers. JCOs are above Havaldar/Sergeant and below Lieutenant.

Jonga. It is a Nissan designed vehicle used by Indian Army (now phased out).

Kalashnikov. Any of a series of Soviet-invented assault rifles especially AK-47 (Avtomat Kalashnikova-47) and AK-56. The word originates from the name of the inventor; armament engineer and Russian General: Mikhail Kalashnikov.

LOC. Line of Control is a 740 km long imaginary line (now substantial part barricaded by India on its side) between India and Pakistan where forces remained positioned after 1947 war on Kashmir and subsequent unilateral cease-fire by India.

Magazines. A holder or device on a gun for cartridges to be fed into the gun-chamber.

Mess Havaldar. A Non-Commissioned Officer who is in-charge of routine functioning of Army institutes/mess.

MMG. Medium Machine Gun or MMG, usually refers to a

belt fed automatic firearm capable of firing 600-800 rounds per minute effectively up to a range of 2000 mtrs. With telescopic device the range can be substantially enhanced.

Naik. Naik is a Non-Commissioned Officer in Indian Army, equivalent to Corporal; below a Sergeant/Havaldar and above Sepoy/Private.

NCO. Non-Commissioned Officers consist of Havaldar/ Sergeant and Naik/Corporal who are promoted from the ranks as a Subordinate Officer and often regarded as the backbone of any army.

Officers Mess. An institution for exclusive use of officers for dining, lodging and entertainment

Military Operation. Military action of various types during war and/or peace

Pickets. A soldier or detachment of soldiers deployed to warn/ stop an enemy advance.

Platoon Commander. An officer in command of a platoon. This person is usually a Junior Commissioned Officer.

POK. Pakistan Occupied Kashmir is the part of Jammu and Kashmir State under illegitimate control of Pakistan since October 22, 1947.

QRT. Quick Reaction Team is a small reserved team of motivated and suitably equipped men usually 20-30 in strength that is capable of rapid response to developing situations.

Quarter Guard. The quarter guard is the main point of security arrangements for the army camp/garrison.

Recce. Abbreviated form of Reconnaissance. Military action/ survey to gain vital information about enemy position, terrain and over all surroundings

Sahayak. A soldier assigned to Commissioned Officers as buddy and assistant.

Sepoy. The lowest enlisted combatant rank in Indian army. Also called "Jawan".

Signalman. A person whose occupation/duty is to provide communication to the fighting forces.

SLR. Self-Loading Rifle is rifle of 1970 vintage capable of automatic loading and firing single shots.

Small Arms. Personal arms carried by military men which can be fired by individuals. Like revolvers, pistols, rifles, carbines, and sub-machine guns.

Subedar. A Junior Commissioned Officer rank in Indian Army that is below the rank of Subedar Major and above Naib Subedar. Platoon Commanders in Infantry battalions.

UMG. Universal Machine Gun (not part of Indian Army's arsenal) similar to MMG.

Vanguard. The soldiers or the body of soldiers, who are at the front or head of an advancing formation of troops.

Index